The Colonial Chronicles; The Establishment of the Thirteen
Original Colonies

Part One

Foundations

1590 - 1617

By

Robin St. Taw

Copyright Page

First Printing

Some characters in this novel are fictitious because this is a work of historical fiction. Actual historical characters in this book are real, and appear in the narrative in the proper chronology of time. All characters mesh and blend to move the historical narrative. Any resemblance to real persons, living or dead, is expressly coincidental.

For Stephen

Courage, determination, and perseverance personified

The Colonial Chronicles

Part 1, Chapter One

The comforting sounds provided by the warming crackling fire in the giant heart did little to settle the disturbed spirits of Governor John White as he sat in audience with Queen Elizabeth I and Sir Walter Raleigh.

The currently silent trio sat at a large table, attended by numerous attendants and servants. Some stoked the fire, heaving great logs onto the great fire to maintain warmth in the cavernous room. Several diligent scribes sat at the table's distant end, awaiting the next portion of the discussion to write it into the queen's notebooks.

The queen's initial troubling gaze had settled resoundingly upon John White for several pensive moments before she gently, slowly rotated the same stare to Sir Walter Raleigh, where it rested a few moments, as if to gather support and a foundation upon which to address Governor White. Presently, the queen returned her quizzical glare back to White, who subtly shifted in his high-back chair. The fire crackled externally. White figured the queen was doing the same internally. Their eyes met.

"You did say, "gone," did you not, Governor White?" Queen Elizabeth shifted slightly. "I wish to be absolutely sure you said, "gone."" The queen looked to the far end of the table where her scribes were writing furiously. She waited for White's response. He was already nodding affirmatively.

"Yes, Your Highness, I did say gone. The entire population of Roanoke Colony was gone, and with no trace, Highness." White sighed deeply. "This is the most perplexing aspect of this entire

7

explanation, I daresay. I have no better explanation to offer, Your Highness. Of course, I was delayed in my return to Roanoke by three years-time to offer my services to the Crown in the war against Spain in the Armada." White looked fleetingly to Raleigh, who had financed the expedition.

"We only landed nine weeks ago. It was as if -except for the presence of residence structures and Fort Raleigh- no one had ever been there." White actually laughed, the sort of laugh that emanates more from shock than amusement.

"Fires appeared to have been discontinued for some time. There were no signs of struggle, no dead about." Governor White looked upon the Queen.

"Our only clues were carvings in the barks of two trees. One reading, 'Croatoan', and the partial carving reading, 'Croat' in the other tree bark.

"None of us could -can- fathom what could possibly have happened. All was well when I departed to return to England for fresh supplies." Again, White looked across the wide table to Raleigh for support, fully aware the man opposite him was the queen's favorite among all unknown favorites. He remained her most trusted advisor, and one of her most important military officers. White felt as though he needed Raleigh's support, even though rumors about the pair were quiet, yet rampant. For his part, Sir Walter merely shrugged his shoulders, sitting back in his chair, turning to Queen Elizabeth, whom had knighted him six years earlier, in 1585.

"Majesty, there are any number of postulations one could take on this highly speculative and highly unordinary situation." The Queen considered him.

"Do tell, Raleigh."

"Lack of food or provisions may have forced the residents to move-on with survivors. It is also known that natives inhabit the area south of the colony. Not all are friendly to outside settlers." Raleigh made an additional consideration.

"They may also have decided to return to England on one of Lord Kilan's vessels, but they, as we sadly are aware, were all lost in a great ocean storm." White sat forward.

"It may have been the same storm that forced us to evacuate Roanoke before a further investigation," White added supportively. Early explorers knew of hurricane storms, and feared them greatly, evading them at every opportunity. The Queen directed wine to be poured as she addressed her officers. She appeared to relax, sitting back upon her cathedra, but her audience was unprepared for her rebuke.

"In 1497, John Cabot sailed to Nova Scotia and Newfoundland and, in return, rendered to my godfather, King Henry VII, a title to all the lands of North America, and the power to control them and colonize them as seen fit for the Crown. Why, then, nearly a century later, with better ships, and a better understanding of our new lands, do you continue to prevail in only problems associated with establishing colonies in the New World?" Queen Elizabeth regarded her officers as she considered a new interrogatory.

"Is It a question of finance? We believe I have been quite supportive in funding all expeditions, as has Sir Raleigh, in this specific instance."

"No, Highness, the financing of expeditions has been, and remains, steadfast and highly generous." Her Highness seemed truly perturbed.

"Then, what is it, Governor?"

"Perhaps," White responded speculatively. "The problem might be a question of timing." The Queen regarded Raleigh as White drank wine.

"I shall listen to *reason* in regard to the continued problems in establishing English colonization," the Queen stated. Governor White shifted in his chair.

"Our ships cannot hold enough provisions and people necessary to initiate a new colony in such a short time span before the very harsh winter conditions of North America beset the newly arrived folk. Long-term plans for meats and produce require a season or two before success." The Queen looked from White to Raleigh and back, shrugging.

"Then build larger ships, Mr. White. Take more than one at a time, and depart at the best time of the sailing season. I cannot envision why this should be a problem that I should attempt to correct. We are neither the sailing captain, nor the assigned governor of a colony." The Queen turned to Raleigh, who had cleared his throat.

"Highness, Sir Humphrey Gilbert departed only seven years ago, and early in the year, and with five ships." White intervened.

"And he, Highness, and all three hundred men, and all five ships were lost at sea," he said firmly, yet politely, in efforts to assuage the Queen, who obviously was not yet satisfied. Raleigh spoke again.

"Highness, the point is that Sir Gilbert did leave early in the year, and with multiple vessels, much to England's -and your-great loss of English seamen and citizens, and vital sea-worthy vessels. Governor White may have a point about timing." The Queen nodded thoughtfully, as Raleigh abruptly added insurance to the conversation.

"Highness, we shall surely continue studying opportunities." Queen Elizabeth stood, causing the men to rise and wait. Walking to stand before the roaring fire, the Queen stared into its bright orange-yellow depths. She commended them to sit as she spoke.

"This fire's depth could be as deep as the oceans we traverse regularly. I want answers. We sank the entire Spanish Armada, but we cannot seem to start a simple colony in North America!" Her stare was direct, bordering on true anger. She turned back to the fire.

"Spain already holds a vast area of the North American continent, but, at the same time, Spain's power in Europe is waning. To me, that only foretells that the Spanish king will focus greater force, supplies, and investment to enlarge North American holdings with increased colonization." The Queen turned to her two officers.

"The Armada win enriched our vaults supremely with vast amounts of gold and silver. We shall not rest until this kingdom completely suppresses Spanish influence and hegemony in the American New World." She crossed back to the table to her cathedra. The men stood. She sat. They sat.

"The singular path to that domination is through successful colonization on North American land granted to *me*, not Spain."

A servant entered the room, approached the table, curtsying, waiting to be addressed. The Queen nodded at her.

"Your Highness, the Earl of Essex, Robert Devereux, awaits your audience as directed. What shall I tell him, Highness?" The Queen's mood changed suddenly. She became even more direct than she was in this instant conversation.

"Devereux," she said plainly to her two officers. "The force that cannot be contained." No one laughed, moved. They didn't even turn to look at the young girl awaiting the Queen's response.

"I shall see him in ten minutes time, Abigail. Thank you, dearest. You may inform the Earl for me. Thank you."

The girl, about ten, curtsied again, and retreated, replying, "as you wish, Highness," smiling at the young page attending the door of the meeting room. The door closed.

"We become more cross with the Second Earl of Essex with each passing day," the Queen stated firmly before turning to Sir Walter.

"Raleigh, is the ship fitting coming along for our naval forces against Spain? Since we cannot seem to establish a simple colony, perhaps we may defeat Spain through continued, diligent, naval warfare." The Queen cast White a dubious glance before turning back to her most trusted favorite, whose demeanor lightened, glad to be retreating from the negative aspects of colonization. Raleigh had personally funded the Roanoke venture greatly. He understood his financial losses, yet White's inexplicable report of a lost colony weighed greatly upon the Crown's ear, and not in White's favor, at least at this juncture.

12

"My son!" he shouted, realizing he had frightened everyone in the room, including the infant. He succored the babe, looking to Alice.

"Our son, Wife. He's yours and mine together." Alice extended her arms to take-back her infant. With a hug, Bradford returned the babe to his mother, the force that had brought him into the world in South Yorkshire. Bradford was excited.

"We shall celebrate with a special dinner, we shall, Wife!' he gushed. Meanwhile, the midwife and her assistant finished cleaning the room, promising the placenta to be burned.

"Husband," Alice inquired. "What shall we name him?" Without a moment's hesitation, Bradford replied.

"We will name him William!" he exclaimed proudly.

"So be it," Alice confirmed, looking upon their son. "He shall be named William. Hello, William Bradford."

Bradford moved to prepare a special dinner. He would kill a prized chicken for his wife to roast.

*****

Charles Edmunds sat astride a chair in his St. Alban's home in London, speaking with a group of gentlemen, like himself, all members of Parliament. Puritans all, their political power and their demands for reform in the Church of England, had been all but surgically hamstrung by Queen Elizabeth I. Presently, Edmunds was addressing his guests in his well-appointed drawing room.

"She cares not one iota about reform or religious freedom," he bemoaned to the agreeable assembled, enjoying a sherry before dinner. "When it comes to persecution, the queen is as dastardly as her half-sister, Mary, when she held the throne. We were all Catholics when all this began. Then, enter Henry VIII and his break with Rome.

"We were Protestant after that. Like it or not. Edward VII was only a regent king until his untimely death at fifteen years, rest his soul all the same. Mary ascended and we were Catholic once more."

"Catholic or dead," one gentleman stated firmly. All agreed, and Edmunds continued with a laugh.

"On that score, I am not quite sure which is the truly worst fate." The men laughed, sipped their sherries.

"Quite right, you are, Mr. Edmunds. Other than death, exile was the only other option. It was Catholic or self-exile if one could afford it and wished to live. There was no middle-ground to be found in any quarter."

"Here, here, Mr. Humbert," another added to the energetic discussion. "Presently, the religion has changed, yet the complete lack of moderation on the queens' parts -Mary or Elizabeth- has not. We remain under the scourge of religious intolerance." Another gentleman, younger than most gathered in the room, stood.

"I say, the queen's been on the throne -what- going on thirty years. How long will she live a reign so ruthlessly?" A heavy-set gentleman scoffed.

another time. Today, our business is war," The Queen said, retaking her cathedra.

"I detest war and its necessity, but there are times when one must employ oneself in the mantle of state security and international agreements." Elizabeth turned to her closest advisor.

"Lord Burghley, begin," she commanded, sitting back as wine was poured around the table. With the parchment unrolled and held tightly in Lord Burghley's hands, the big man started reading the Treaty of Greenwich, agreements made six years earlier, in 1585. Those agreements delineated the aid of the Dutch in their declared independence from all forms of Spanish control. Burghley looked to those assembled.

"The peace communications I have been secretly sending to Alessandro Farnese, Third Earl of Parma, have all failed. We are truly disappointed." Burghley, like the Queen, detested war and its unneeded waste of land, life, and destruction of important national resources, particularly finances. War demanded great sums of royal treasury finances. As he continued reading, the group drew-up plans to send ground troops to the Low Countries to aid William the Silent, Prince of Orange, and the Dutch people.

*****

Three days earlier, former Governor John White sailed from the western English City of Bristol, returning, in retirement, to his estate home in the southeast town of Tramore, in Waterford, Ireland. Following many years of service to Her Majesty, Queen Elizabeth I, White looked forward to retirement with his wife at their idyllic, Irish, Tramore estate. Included in the couple's belongings was a sizable, additional, land grant to

29

their estate, a gift for loyal service granted in thanks by the Queen of England.

*****

Life does not render happiness to all at all times. While Devereux, Raleigh, and Burghley laid plans for war against Spain, including their personal roles in said war, and, as John White and his wife sailed to Ireland across the sun-laden Sir George's Channel, William Bradford, the yeoman farmer and father to his sixteen-month-old son, William, suddenly fell dead while working on the family's farm, having no opportunity to say goodbye, let alone consider retirement.

William's brothers arrived at his simple home to inform Alice of the sad and terrible news.

*****

Two weeks after Devereux and Raleigh were assigned roles in the war against Spain in the Netherlands to aid King Henry IV of France, Queen Elizabeth I presided over the knighting of Ferdinando Georges, who would now be addressed as Sir Ferdinando Georges.

Soon after his official knighting, Sir Ferdinando was assigned to join forces with French King Henry IV against the Spanish.

*****

On 7 May 1591, in the town of Alford, Lincolnshire, in the east central section of England, the Reverend Francis Maybury, having Puritan leanings, prayed piteous thanks to God as his new daughter, named Anne Marbury, was baptized into God's holy family at the local church in Alford.

*****

Time is often said to assist at differing rates for different people. While the good times seem fleeting, the bad lingers. Yet, time passes at the same rate for all, though rewards do differ substantially for those chosen by fate or luck to win more in life.

Eight months following a highly successful military campaign against the Spanish Army, Sir Walter Raleigh returned to England in 1592. Upon his report to the Queen, he was granted land in Sherborn, Dorset, in western England as a gift from the Queen. Ready to settle after many years of travel, war, and continued service to the Crown, Raleigh and his wife, Elizabeth Throckmorton, welcomed the news of the new birth of a second child. Their first son, Damerei, died at five months of age the previous year, in 1591. Throckmorton, known as Bess, had been a gentlewoman of the Queen's privy chamber, or lady-in-waiting before secretly marrying Raleigh, eleven years older than she.

Raleigh, disliked by many for his haughty pride, brashness, and bent to free-spending, accepted the royal gift, stating he planned to erect a castle on the land, calling it Sherborne. As in the ways of successful men, Raleigh had enemies who, in calculating the sum of their disdain for him, bided their time in contemptuous silence, hoping that, with time, Elizabeth's reign would end, and opportunity to enact Raleigh's downfall would be revealed.

*****

That same year, 1592, in Scherpenzeel, Netherlands, bitter battles for Dutch independence continued. Life for all peoples must evolve in times of war and peace. During one of the

31

intermittent periods of quiet, the Reverend Balthazar Johannes Stuyvesant and his wife, Margaretha Hardenstein, welcomed their new son into the world, naming him Peter. At the same time the Stuyvesant's welcomed their son, the Gorton Family in the north-central city of Manchester, England, also welcomed their son, naming him Samuel.

*****

Robert Devereux, Second Earl of Essex, was used to having his own way. Rich, young, and brash, he coveted the position for which Robert Cecil, son of Lord Burghley, was being groomed to command. Devereux desired to be as close to the center of political control as possible, but his hubris refused to yield to his royal cousin's absolute royal will.

To achieve his goal of becoming her closest advisor over Cecil, Devereux set-upon involving himself in mastering foreign affairs in hopes of displacing the younger Cecil, who was about fifteen years older than himself. Devereux had recently turned twenty-five. The self-confident Earl was determined to infuse himself into the center-most position of international affairs as the Queen's chief advisor.

*****

In October, 1593, Raleigh and his wife welcomed their second son, naming him Walter. The news was shared with the news that Raleigh would spearhead an expedition to El Dorado, or the city of Manoa, rumored to be laden with gold.

Queen Elizabeth believed that the current war with Spain in support of the Dutch reduced Spanish attention on their South American resources. Raleigh explained the best navigation routes, sailing times, and the number of man and ships required for locating and capturing Spanish gold.

*****

That same year, Robert Devereux was named to the Queen's privy council, a small, tight-knit group of close advisors all privy to the most articulate ideas, plans, and functioning of any monarch's rule. Each man's input was seriously considered, discussed amid counter-proposals, and recorded for final review by the Queen, who made the final decision.

Devereux was quickly achieving his political goals. Astutely aware that Robert Cecil remained the primary candidate for the position the Earl sought, he sharpened his awareness of English foreign affairs.

*****

John White, former Governor of Roanoke, having retired some three years earlier after decades of service to the Queen, was sitting before a window at his Ireland estate as his wife prepared tea, the late afternoon meal.

Observing the pastoral Tramore countryside, White had been listening to his wife tell how several of their goats had almost broken through a barrier, when he felt a sudden sharp pain in his head, slumping forward to the table, scattering plates, cups, and saucers to the floor.

The former Governor of Roanoke lay dead.

Part One, Chapter Four

1595-1597

The February morning was dark and extremely cold,
particularly when powerful western winds raked the land when
they swept-off the ocean. Sir Walter Raleigh walked the length
of the long wharf studying the five ships under his command
and, accompanied by the four captains of the other vessels, was
prepared for a departure on this cold morning to sail early
enough in the season to reach El Dorado and return safely to
England with a hefty sum of Spanish gold.

Provisions and water were stowed. Sails were inspected, and
ample ammunition was protected against water damage. The
winds were prime for sailing, and the crews of all ships were
primed for adventure, plentiful gold, and beautiful Spanish
women. Currently, crews hastily ensured every vessel was fully
prepared to make the journey, planned to take almost a year.

Raleigh and his captains made their rounds of each ship,
following Raleigh's strict demands for naval superiority. In turn,
each ship's captain assured Raleigh that they considered any
and all obstacles, including the potential for crossing lanes with
Spanish vessels. Each stated he was confident the he and the
crew would deftly handle any situation. Assured himself at this
juncture that all was ready, Raleigh commanded all captains to
prepare to make sail.

Within the hour, the five vessels, sails unfurled, departed from
Wareham, due south of Sherborne, Raleigh's castle in Dorset,
and to the south between the westward Dorchester and Poole
to the east. The ships, aided by strong winds, sailed quickly past
the small peninsula known as the Bill of Portland, into the broad

Celtic Sea, aiming for the Atlantic Ocean, seeking adventure and the enemy's fortune.

*****

On the North American continent, near the shores of Pawtuxet, the Pawtuxet Tribe of Native Americans happily welcomed the birth of the chief's newborn child, a boy. In celebration, extra fish were caught for the enjoyment of all in the village, and some fish would be offered to the gods of the earth, water, sky, and fire as thanks for the boy's safe arrival among the villagers. The infant boy was named Tisquantum, meaning 'seeker of truths'.

*****

Toward the end of July, 1595, Sir Walter Raleigh and his five ships landed and captured the city of San Jose, on the Island of Trinidad. Following the successful capture and placing the city under his control, Raleigh allowed the crews to enjoy the spoils of war. His actions were an act of war since Trinidad was part of Spain's claims in the New World. Raleigh sought to take control of the entire island for England.

Following pillage and rest, Raleigh established control leaving men behind to maintain order, and continued on his journey for El Dorado and Manoa. He was not dissuaded by a captive named Antonio de Berrio, a senior Spaniard in San Jose, who informed Raleigh there was no such place. When asked how De Berrio knew, the captive Spaniard told his captors that he himself had spent time seeking El Dorado. He never found it.

Raleigh set out, and spent several more weeks exploring the Orinoco River, traveling almost 400 miles of its length before deciding to rest, refurbish, and return to England before truly inclement weather arrived in the Atlantic, hampering a safe return. Disappointed about the expedition, Raleigh made peace with a tribe of Topiawari Natives, assuring protection against Spain in return for friendship and peace.

Raleigh was sure the Queen would be satisfied by his capture of the entire Island of Trinidad for England. With new provisions at the ready, the expedition stopped briefly at San Jose before making way to England.

Raleigh was stunned to discover that news of his expedition reached home before he did, and was further embarrassed to find the entire journey was already regarded to be a grand failure. Even the Queen, his staunchest supporter, yet angered by his secret marriage to Bess, declared the trip a failure. Further, any additional junkets to the non-existent El Dorado would be funded by Raleigh himself.

*****

By 1596, Lord Burghley seriously began engaging the Queen with discussions about a cessation of the war with Spain.

"Royal finances are terribly strained, Highness," the trusted advisor declared. "The surpluses originating from the Armada victory are gone. The war has continued endlessly for eleven years." Burghley poured a goblet of wine.

"We have subsidized King Henry IV of France, the Dutch, and Raleigh's Follies. His latest outing turned-up no gold, only some rocks and an island in the Caribbean. We cannot colonize Trinidad without funds. We are unable to colonize North America, the most readily available source for every resource we need and want." He quaffed the wine, pouring anew.

"The markets we could furnish are unspeakably massive. We must, Your Highness, figure a method of settling in North America. The key to England's future lay there." He drank again.

His son, Robert, sat silently near his father, waiting for the Queen's ultimate and unquestionable decision. For her part, Queen Elizabeth turned to look through a window, as if her answer lay there on the wind or sky.

"Your Highness," Burghley continued, "I respectfully request that you permit me to begin a new set of talks with Parma." The Queen continued her gaze out the window, contemplating she had listened to Lord Burghley's sage advise for almost forty years. He had proved right most of the time. She stood, and with each movement, the crinoline fabric of her burgundy gown produced rustling sounds like autumn leaves crinkled underfoot.

   Spring had come to England, but it was a cold, wet, inhospitable season this year, seeming much more like late autumn or early winter. A fire burned in the hearth at Nonesuch Palace, in Surrey, south of London. The Queen stood before the fire, continuing her stare through the window, where a hard rain fell as it had for several days.

"My father's greatest mistake was the French War that raged three years until 1546. I yet recall his ranting to the rafters about the bloody costs of war, and I, too, remember, how that war ravaged the national treasury. That surplus resulted directly from the dissolution of the Catholic monasteries. I help the Dutch to help the English. Spain threatened our sovereignty in a most seriously near-assault last time.

"That is why the Armada was sent to England. Only able sea captains and severe weather destroyed both Spain's chances and opportunities. I may be a woman, but I have the strength, determination, and absolute divine right of God to bear-up to *any* burden that threatens or affronts my kingdom and our people.

"I have not been the Queen of England by being fearful. I shall not start being fearful now." She turned back to face the two Cecil's at her table. Burghley understood the look on her face was one of stern resoluteness. He sensed an ultimatum coming. He poured more wine.

"I want to strike at the very heart of Spanish power. Formulate the necessary troops into an army. Strike Cadiz! Sever the Spanish powerhead from its vile nest of spidery tendrils. Send Raleigh and Devereux to lead the attack."

The Queen returned to the table, seating herself, directing both men to sit. Burghley knew the unyielding voice. His son was learning it repeatedly, even though he was already in his mid-forties. He had already experienced every nuance of the Queen's persona. Briefly pondering a question to ask, Robert Cecil negated the effort, understanding that the only question at this intersection of decision and performing was, "how many men, and how long a campaign?" The senior Burghley, aware the decision was made, nodded silently, making notations. He looked to the Queen.

"So be it, Your Highness. I begin forthwith." Nodding to his son, they stood, bowed, and departed as a page opened the door, and the monarch was left in private thought. The door closed.

Outside the warm room, the heat of the beneficial fire dissipated rapidly. Rain was audible outside. Away from the room, father took son into confidence near a window to cover his voice.

"We must amass a force to strike supremely at Cadiz by summer in efforts to finally quell Spanish threats while saving what funds remain in the national treasury."

"Affirmed," son replied firmly. "Shall I round-up the army, father?" The older Cecil nodded.

"Yea, and I shall send word to both Raleigh and Devereux to see me immediately." Burghley looked around quickly. "You know what to do. The decision for choosing both those men could be perceived several ways." The younger Cecil chuckled.

"Win or lose, you mean, father?"

"Yes, Robert, and in more ways than one, depending on how one looks at the situation, I daresay." A page bowed as he turned the corner carrying a document, heading to the Queen's War Room.

"Go to it, Robert. We meet later for dinner." Father and son parted ways at the window. The Cadiz Campaign was underway.

*****

Spring did finally arrive, or so it seemed after the incessant rain and winds yielded to mild temperatures and sunny days. In East Anglia, that sense of newness was shared at the Norwich farm of Richard Plascomb.

Now a young man of twenty-two, Richard often stood alone on his father's farm watching the setting sun as it faded westward across the water. With each passing day as the earth rotated, Richard increasingly considered what lay at the distant end across the water. He believed his opportunities awaited him. It was a feeling he could not dismiss. He understood how the earth of the farm worked. Yet his ardent youthful yearnings for something more, something bigger, and more promising beyond sprouting veggies for daily living, one season after the other, pulled like a gravitational force upon his curious mind and youthful sense of adventure.

Thus, when the call for men to fight in the English Army against Spain spread through the shires, Richard answered the call. His mother cried; father approved, much to his muted private concerns. How could he blame his son for serving his queen? Plascomb senior knew a man had to leave home to make his own somewhere, somehow, in the world. As Edward Plascomb viewed life, there were no guarantees beyond Anglican prayer and hard work for good crops. Every man has a destiny that awaits him.

Richard Plascomb departed home with the other young men who decided something more than meager, daily, farm life awaited them somewhere beyond England's shores. Richard soon found himself sailing with a military company to the Netherlands. Among the men in his company, Richard met another young man named John Smith, who told Richard his father advised him to, "study, because your future depends upon it." Smith, from Lincolnshire, northwest of East Anglia, laughed, telling Plascomb he joined so he could study the world first-hand. He wanted adventure. Though six years apart in age, the pair shared the excitement of something new. They became fast friends as their vessel sailed across the North Sea to Holland.

*****

Spring turned to summer. Some things in life are guaranteed, yet ephemeral. That summer, in Lowton, a town west of Manchester, in Lancashire, near Morcambe Bay, the Mather Family, known locally as strict Puritans, ushered-in the birth of their son, naming him Richard Mather.

*****

That same summer of 1596 found Raleigh and Devereux attacking Cadiz, Spain. Fighting valiantly, their forces smashed the Cadiz stronghold, vanquishing Spanish forces, and taking the entire city under English control. Sacking the city commenced after victory was confirmed on the twenty-second of June.

Robert Devereux, Second Earl of Essex, was now at the height of his power and fortune, but hubris exacts a price at a place and time unknown to him with the fatal flaw. Now just twenty-nine-years-old, Devereux relished in his present subjugation of Cadiz while contemplating his next conquest, the position sought by Robert Cecil.

*****

Thomas Smythe, now in the thirty-ninth spring of his life in 1597, welcomed Edward Sandys, Member of Parliament, to his place of business on Baker Street, London, on a surprisingly warm April morning. Mr. Smythe, a very wealthy business man, currently held the position of Governor of the Muscovy Company, a stock trading company established in 1554. Sandys, only three years younger than Smythe, was sure he had come to the right man in Sandys, a man who would listen to his plans for establishing new settlements, and, if his position was rationally plausible, new English colonies in North America. Smythe admitted Sandys to his private meeting room, inviting him to have a seat.

"Mr. Sandys, I know of your diligent work in Parliament, and I understand you are one of those types of men who prefer to work from the shadows. That said, what brings you to the Muscovy Company on this glorious day?" Sandys sat forward.

"Mr. Smythe, I shall be direct. There be neither cloak nor sword in my visit today, I assure you. First, I thank you for your time, and I speculate to look for your money." Smythe laughed out-loud.

"My good Sandys, spoken like a true Member of Parliament, though they don't usually tell you that upfront, I daresay! Shall I have a new tax appraised of me?" Both men shared the humorous moment.

"Goodness, no, Mr. Smythe. I seek investment funds and sources in this endeavor I seek to discuss with you." The word investment instantly seized Smythe's attention.

"Investment, you say, Sir? In what regard, may I inquire?" Sandys nodded.

"I am here to speak with you in regard to establishing new markets abroad for English goods." Smythe cocked his head.

"But, of what markets do you speak, Mr. Sandys? England has no colonies abroad with whom she maintains a proprietary nature for selectivity in regards to direct or indirect trade. That is to say, anything beyond Raleigh's Follies in Trinidad." Sandys agreed.

"What a boondoggle that misadventure was, Sir. A great cost to the national treasury."

"Agreed, Mr. Sandys, and it's too soon to know anything about the island we now control. Hence, of what markets do you speak?"

"Mr. Smythe, I am proposing that we gather the correct gentlemen to form an investment group specifically for the purpose of establishing new settlements -perhaps even actual colonies- in North America." The statement made Smythe sit-up straight.

"North America?"

"Yes, Mr. Smythe, North America. We have attempted to establish settlements over the previous dozen years, and all have failed for one reason or another. I subscribe to the belief that with a substantial investment in supplies and willing settlers, we may establish highly successful colonies in North America. The profit potential is unlimited. Imagine a collection of colonies fully dependent on our English goods.

"In return, we acquire new, unknown natural resources, enlarging our existing markets here at home. The market for goods traveling between two worlds -old and new- would repay investors very profitably, and faster than they might ever imagine.

"When one colony is started, another can follow. Growth is incomprehensible, along with profit potential. What many of us presently consider true wealth would become mere pocket funds when compared to what we might reap after we sow."

Smythe listened, saying nothing, but his fingers quietly drummed the table as he contemplated Sandy's words. Presently, he looked across the table, thoughts of profit racing through his mind.

"What of Spain?" Sandy's shook his head.

"Spain is done as a European power. We defeated her forces soundly at Cadiz nearly a year ago, capturing their stores of gold and silver. King Philip IV is rumored very ill. Their war in the Netherlands continues, but Spanish resources are drained continuously to support their efforts against the Dutch." Sandys felt compelled to stand, pushed by an unknown force greater than himself, attempting to sell his idea to the profit-eager Smythe. He felt as though he was running a campaign for a seat in the Parliament. He paced the floor, energized by his ideas and their plausibility in a market-driven world.

"Mr. Smythe, this is England's time as *the* select nation by the choice of the divine. New markets will escalate demands for English goods in an entirely new arena. I, myself, would front my investment portion if we could start a new stock company for the specific purpose of developing colonies in America."

"I think your idea timely and progressive simultaneously, Mr. Sandys. The proposal is excellent. I suspect, as investment ideas come and go, someone is going to think of this idea."

"Correct, Mr. Smythe, and it may as well be us!" Smythe seemed very interested, but cautious.

"Where do you propose this first new settlement, Mr. Sandys?"

"The place called Virginia, so named by Raleigh himself. It contains vestiges of the Roanoke settlement mystery of seven years passed. The late Governor White described the climate as hospitable, land arable, and ocean access plentiful. Imagine an entire colony demanding English goods. In return, they send back what we need and want to expand home markets. Of course, we do not know fully what is there, but that would change with time." Smythe stood now, walking around the table to shake his guest's hand.

"I like your ideas, Sandys. Tell you what, say. Devise a business plan and return in a fortnight. Meanwhile, I shall speak with my associates to gather as much support as I am able. We go forward from that point if I think we may venture forth with this idea, Mr. Sandys. I like it. It has excellent profit potential. So, a fortnight, then?"

"Two weeks, Mr. Smythe?"

"Yes, sir, a fortnight it is. I tell you what, too, Mr. Sandys. While I gather financial support, I request that you gather political support in Parliament. The combined power of the two forces will help us forge a real campaign for success." The men shook hands.

"I am truly glad I decided to speak with you, Mr. Smythe." Smythe chuckled.

"Not as pleased as I am, I assure you, Mr. Sandys." Bidding his guest a good day, Sandys departed, stepping-out to a sun-filled Baker Street.

In his office, Smythe calculated the successful possibilities of new markets in America. He recalled the Muscovy Company had opened Dutch markets to mercantilist enterprises. Sandys was correct in his approach. New American markets would open vast new markets to colonies fully dependent on English goods, including the most basic staple products like tea and stamps.

Smythe considered his own strategies for a new stock company for colonizing America as he arranged to meet colleagues for a business lunch at a nearby pub.

Part One, Chapter Five

1597-1599

During a temporary lull in the fighting in the Netherlands, Richard Plascomb slept on the same ground where he fought, and he did it happily. Warm spring weather had come to the Low Countries, and interest in fighting was waning on both sides.

In the recent weeks, Richard, mud-faced and caked with dirt and soil from fighting, was introduced to Maurice Orange, successor to Prince William I of Orange, assassinated in 1584 by a Catholic fanatic. Richard, never dreaming of meeting a world leader, was respectful, and proud of the dirt that covered him, telling Maurice Orange that, "he was covered with the dirt of freedom." Orange completely agreed.

Somewhere, in the middle of a dream, John Smith roused Plascomb.

"Food, Richard! We eat! Awaken, or it surely shall be gone." Shaking himself conscious, Richard was introduced to a newcomer to the outfit of the 'Liberation Army, as the men had come to refer to themselves fighting in Holland to support the Dutch. The new man transferred the previous day after fighting further north for nearly a solid month. Agreeing to Smith's recommendation, the two men offered the new man some of their provisions. Initially, the man was perceived as disagreeable, mean-spirited, and ready for a fight at any moment. Yet, as soldiers in the same army, provisions were shared. The young man, hungry as anyone in war, thanked the pair for their human kindness in the midst of atrocity, introducing himself as Miles Standish.

*****

"And, so shall you be also known as Member of Parliament from Dorset," said Queen Elizabeth to Sir Walter Raleigh, almost one year following his highly successful takeover of Cadiz. "Rise, Sir Walter."

Raleigh was back in the Queen's best graces and fullest favor. As a result, his personal wealth had multiplied significantly. His role as Commander of English Forces that took Fayal, an island in the Azores, off the northwest Spanish coast, represented Raleigh's capstone in a brilliant campaign against the enemy.

Following the Queen's announcement of Raleigh's place in Parliament, Raleigh, along with his wife, Elizabeth, or Bess, and a sizable group of dignitaries, including members of the royal family, enjoyed a royal reception that afternoon in Raleigh's honor.

Toward the rear of the room near the quartet playing some of the Queen's favorite melodies, two men stood talking quietly as the celebratory event segued from official to that of a less formal, friendlier reception. William Dorsey and Charles Lanish, both Members of Parliament, watched conspiratorially as the, "braggard, self-possessed, and invincible" Raleigh accepted accolades from all many guests.

"What do you think, Mr. Lanish?" inquired Dorsey about the guest of honor, presently making his way around the large reception hall, guided by the Queen herself, who made introductions, laughed, and selected the most favored for conversation. Lanish sneered.

"I can tell you this, Mr. Dorsey, and straightaway. I know that, one day, our forever-queen shall die. Come that day, as surely

47

as we stand here about to congratulate the victor as the Queen makes her rounds, the fortunes of that bombastic, narcissistic, and egotistical Raleigh will be altered ad infinitum." Lanish looked to his associate. "Does that answer your interrogatory properly?" Dorsey laughed.

"And rather completely, Mr. Lanish."

"Good," was Lanish's simple response, but Dorsey sought more details. Lanish looked around the room, keenly observing the guests as to whom was secretly watching whom.

"I already have interested parties planting seeds of destruction for Sir Walter with none other than King James of Scotland. The day our virgin queen departs this world for the next, King James will travel south to become King of England. When that glorious event comes to fruition, Mr. Dorsey, I can assure you Raleigh's days will be done. They are numbered as we converse." The royal party approached.

Within moments, Queen Elizabeth greeted the men and their wives graciously, introducing them to the newest Member of Parliament from Dorset. Both men offered Raleigh their most sincere bows without offering their hands. Dorsey moved to cover the insult.

"Of course, Sir Raleigh, Her Royal Highness is correct. Your esteemed service to England and the Crown has surely reached every ear in all of England, and perhaps Scotland as well," Dorsey stated with the most decidedly verbal surgery he could muster so quickly without being even superficially obvious in the circle of deceit. Lanish sought to enter his support.

"We look to your entry to Parliament, Sir Walter," he stated officially.

"Thank you, Mr. Lanish," Raleigh offered in return. "I tell you, I shall seek your qualified leadership and knowledgeable guidance in conducting our Majesty's business for the betterment of all Englishmen and our country. Your kindness is thankfully received." Lanish smiled.

"Of course, Sir Walter," he replied graciously. "Serve a queen, serve a king. Service is what we do in Parliament. You shall see for yourself very soon." The Queen, seeing someone, interrupted.

"There is Lady Gwendolyn. You must meet her, Sir Walter. Goodness knows how many years she has remaining on this earth. Do come." The small group bowed as Queen Elizabeth turned, leading Raleigh to the special guest. Dorsey watched.

"How much time on this earth, indeed," he snickered wickedly, turning to Lanish, smiling gregariously so as not to appear in any controversy.

"All good things in their time, Mr. Lanish. Even the best plants require the proper time before harvest."

"Agreed, Mr. Dorsey," came the agreeable reply, while their wives requested some refreshments.

*****

In the town of Coventry, located in the western-central county of Warwickshire, west of the Avon River, John Davenport was born on 15 April. His parents quietly welcomed their new son into their pious Puritan household.

*****

Robert Devereux was unable to attend the reception for Sir Walter Raleigh because he was on a special mission assigned by Lord Burghley at the Queen's direction to intercept a vast shipment of Spanish gold in the Azores in summer 1597. Months of high security planning had gone into the endeavor, based on information from a reliable source within the Dutch diplomatic corps in the Netherlands.

Whether bad weather or misguided sailing was to blame, Devereux could only watch hopelessly through his spyglass as the Spanish vessels carrying the gold sailed below the horizon, at least twelve hours ahead of him, and with no chance of catching them. Thus, he had failed in his royal mission. Devereux was now forced to turn back to England after a stop-over to rest the crew and replenish supplies and provisions.

Angry with himself as much as the Spanish, who may have been tipped-off about the planned interception, Devereux banged the railing with his clenched fist, causing his spyglass to fall into the ocean, only increasing his heightened state of anger and frustration.

*****

Thomas Smythe and Edwin Sandys revisited their plan to form a stock company selling shares for investment in North American colonies. Sandys was thoroughly pleased that Smythe had found a good number of, "gentlemen of respectable means," who agreed an entirely new world of profit motivation awaited them.

Sandys agreed to study a series of maps that Smythe acquired in efforts to devise a plan of proper latitude and longitude for the first settlement. Additionally, Smythe assured Sandys that a charter for the company was already in progress, and would require at least a year of planning and negotiations with the Crown. The maps were laid-out for close inspection, and the men began talking earnestly about the first new settlement and the future stock company.

* * * * *

Robert Devereux, Second Earl of Essex, found himself much out of the Queen's favor in the New Year of 1598. Beyond the most personal holiday celebrations, he had remained steadfastly aloof socially due to his severe embarrassment at Court regarding his botched attempt to capture Spanish gold the previous summer. He never was able to discover if the Spanish were alerted, despite paying significant bribes to loosen tight tongues.

Now, in late February, a new year progressing daily, Devereux mentally worked on plans to wipe-clean his stained slate and begin anew, particularly since he was called to Court in London. Perhaps a new adventure awaited him. He was determined to undermine Robert Cecil. This would be his year of successes, he thought, making his way to the Queen.

* * * * *

In Austerfield, the Bradford family greeted a new day. Now approaching his eighth birthday, young William Bradford entered his mother's room to awaken her. There was breakfast to be had before farm work began.

William was used to being without a father he never knew since his father died when William was only sixteen months old. His grandfather and several uncles served as male figures for the boy, but mother always made breakfast each and every day. When William called to his mother, she did not reply to

51

repeated calls. Undaunted, William found a small woolen blanket, wrapped himself in it, and sat at the foot of his mother's bed to wait for his mother to awaken. It was quite cold in the house.

Outside, the sun had risen, and William's grandfather and Uncle John had arrived to start the daily farm chores.

"Odd," commented grandfather James Bradford, when he looked to the roof of the thatched cottage and studied it briefly.

"What's that now, Father?" asked his son, John, now looking to the roof himself where James pointed.

"It's just odd that there's no smoke rising from the hearth. Alice has no fire burning. She's always got one going by now," he said, looking to his son.

"You're right, father. Come, let us see what's happening." Knocking at the door, calling, "Alice!" The banging on the door woke William, who had fallen asleep. He blinked as the door was pushed open and the men entered, able to see the boy sitting on the bed. The house was very cold.

"Now, William, is your mother having a late sleep, boy?" his uncle asked as grandfather looked around the small cottage.

"Yes, Uncle John," William replied. I tried to wake her, but she's very tired. I'm hungry." Uncle John picked William up as James tended to his daughter-in-law. He jumped back instantly when he touched her.

"Jesus, Mary, and Joseph," he said clearly enough for the other two to hear. John, nephew in his arms, turned back to his father. The men traded a look of wide-eyed disbelief. John immediately understood, shaking his head. Grandfather quickly modulated his voice.

"Now, John, if you would be so kind as to get a roaring fire going in the hearth. William, dress and help your uncle." Grandfather looked to son after William ran to his tiny quarters.

"Light a fire. Feed the boy. I'll fetch the family and the Vicar."

"Right, and what do I say to the boy?"

"Nothing for now until I return. Keep him busy and out of this room."

"I'm ready, Uncle John!" William called, returning, but not before his uncle blocked his entry to the room, taking his hand, leading him to start the fire.

Outside, grandfather quickly mounted and rode swiftly to town. William's mother, Alice, had died in her sleep during the night. William's uncles and aunts would raise him.

*****

At the palace in London, Devereux joined the Queen, Lord Burghley, and Robert Cecil, already in discussion dealing with the protracted warring with Spain, and the slow, yet relentless series of uprisings in Ireland, led mostly by Thomas O'Neill, Earl of Tyrone.

Typically late, a page announced the Earl, and Devereux entered. Burghley, who had been speaking, cast a casual glance to Devereux without ceasing his discussion. The Queen cast him a cold, cast-off stare, while Robert Cecil flatly ignored the Earl, maintaining his focus on his father's discussion. Devereux seated himself and poured wine into a goblet.

"Therefore," Lord Burghley was saying, "I urge negotiations with Spain for our benefit, Highness," he concluded. Queen Elizabeth turned to Robert Cecil.

"What is your input, Earl of Salisbury?"

Cecil replied instantly that he agreed with his father's position, adding, "there is a potential for a Spanish-French alliance and settlement that would pit us against both countries, Highness. We must avoid this scenario without question. The treasury is continually depleted over the war coasts. A two-front engagement would severely weaken our hegemony on land and sea, where our true power is growing unchecked.

"The Dutch may have to fend for themselves if this war continues much longer." The Queen nodded, quietly pondering everything she had heard. After forty years of ruling, she understood her realm. She turned to Lord Burghley.

"Initiate the appropriate matters for negotiations for a settlement through the usual channels, Lord Burghley. Those avenues of opportunity will be the most advantageous, at least at the onset of talks."

"Perhaps," Devereux said, but was swiftly reproached by the Queen.

"Robert Devereux, Earl of Essex, I do not recall seeking your voice in the matter at-hand. *Perhaps*," The Queen stated with particular emphasis, "one should be on time if one wishes to be included in the conversation. Undeterred, Devereux plowed ahead, obviously unphased by the rebuff.

"I merely sought to offer my opinion on foreign affairs," he stated, looking to those at the table. Robert Cecil moved not a muscle. Lord Burghley stared ahead, immobile. The Queen appeared to stare through the Earl of Essex.

"Mr. Devereux, if I want your opinion, I shall give it to you," she said icily, her stare absolutely glacial. "If one is so interested in mastering foreign affairs on land, perhaps one should master them first at sea."

The direct reference to his failed mission from the previous summer before the most trusted members of the privy council was an affront Devereux refused to accept. He sat seething quietly as the Queen returned to Lord Burghley and her entire countenance changed.

"And what else do we have to discuss, Lord Burghley?" she asked with almost delirious charm and cheer.

Devereux, used to having his way, stood so sharply, he knocked-over the chair in which he had sat. Letting it lie there, storming to the door as a page opened it, and hearing Burghley speaking as if Devereux had never been there.

"Thomas Smythe has petitioned the Crown for a patent on a new stock company establishing settlements and colonies in North America."

Devereux slapped a page across the head, ordering him to upright the chair as he charged out the door. The boy, rubbing his head, fixed the chair, and was stopped by Lord Burghley.

"Are you alright, boy?" The page nodded, rubbing his head.

"Aye, your Lordship. It will be fine in a while." With a nod, Cecil motioned for the page to rejoin the others. Studying the boy as he sat along the wall rubbing his head, the Queen made a decision.

"We shall not forget this day," she spoke calculatingly while she observed the young page, replaying the entire incident in her mind for future reference.

Later, in the hall after the meeting, the young page whose head was slapped asked an older page why, when the Queen says something, she says, "we?"

"it's simple, really," the older page said. "Whenever the Queen says, "we," it means she is speaking for God and herself. All monarch's do that." He laughed. "Believe me, they will *not* forget, either."

*****

In the Netherlands, the unit in which John Smith, Richard Plascomb, and Miles Standish were serving, came under the command of Sir Ferdinando Georges. During a period of unexpected quiet, Georges received fresh troops. When they arrived, Georges offered those who had served at least a year in the outfit the choice of remaining, transferring to a different unit, or returning to civilian life. Choices were to be made and reported in-person to unit leaders within two days.

The three friends sat discussing their options and ideas. Smith said he was remaining since he had nothing to return to in Willoughby. Standish had also chosen to stay, declaring himself a, "professional soldier." He relished the attack.

Richard, though, was of a different mindset. His lack of enthusiasm increased over the previous months. True, he wanted adventure, but constant killing in battles was not what he considered adventurous. He wanted travel, women, excitement.

"The excitement of battle wanes quickly," he explained. Standish laughed.

"Are you kidding, Plascomb? That's what I live for!" he exclaimed. "Hunt the bastards down and destroy them, I say!" he crowed proudly, looking to Smith, who nodded.

"It has its moments, I'll say, but a little loving excitement would also be welcoming, as opposed to all this death every day. I'll stay so long as I'm paid, or until I become bored." He shrugged.

"Then, I'll move-on, but where?" he asked rhetorically, shrugging his shoulders again. "I don't know," he said, looking across to Plascomb.

"War requires a special kind of man to stick with it, I suspect. He's got to enjoy the more brutal aspects of life. Also, a complete disregard for human lives and private property helps. I don't believe that's you, Richard. You've got to do what you see fit for yourself. We all may cross paths again in the future. Who's to say? But I'll say this.

"Even if you leave today, when you arrive at home, or wherever you are going, the desire for broader horizons shall always be with you." Standish had been sharpening a knife while Smith talked. He spoke.

"The difference between us and you, Plascomb, is that we know what we want. You, on the other hand, are yet seeking." Smith agreed.

"I know a settled life isn't for me. I'm like Standish. You, though, Richard, may need to settle-down." He laughed. "Look at it this way, you've survived two years in battle. Maybe the odds have to be changed."

"That says a lot in itself," Standish said, putting away his razor-sharp knife, standing to sheath it in its belt holder. "Go home, Richard. We'll meet again. It's a small world." Standish walked over to a soldier who called to him. Smith turned to Plascomb.

"Aye, Richard, if you think you should depart, then do so. You may escape a worse fate than awaits you here in Holland." Smith stood, patting Plascomb's shoulder.

"Follow your conscience, Richard. If you're not here when I return, I'll know why." Plascomb nodded as Smith walked out of view, but Richard could hear him calling someone.

Sitting alone, Plascomb's mind raced with the measurement of possibilities against the knowledge of absolutes. Why, he thought, was hindsight always so much clearer than looking ahead? A sound interrupted his attention.

A man appeared before him holding a pot of black ink. Another man stood next to him with a list of names. Behind both men stood a group of about twenty fresh-faced soldiers who clearly were replacements.

"Plascomb, Richard," the first man stated, holding the list. "Two years good service. Stay, transfer, or depart?" The decision had to be made now. Considerations, calculations, hopes, fears, and dreams all rested on the next single word Plascomb issued. The men waited. The seconds felt strangely like hours.

"Depart," Richard said plainly, exhaling deeply. It was done. The man with the list nodded to him holding the ink pot.

"Stand, Plascomb," he directed. When Richard stood, the man dipped a brush made of pine leaves into the ink, shook-off the excess, and marked Richard's uniform shirt on his left shoulder inset.

"You are marked for departure, Plascomb. Thank you for your loyal service to the Crown." He turned to another young man. "This is Elijah Smith, your replacement. Give him your weapon and meet at the food shelter to depart in fifteen minutes."

"Aye, Sir," Plascomb replied, handing his weapon to the new man and shaking hands with him. The group continued moving, calling names.

Fifteen minutes later, Richard Plascomb was in a group of about sixty others who decided the same way, returning to wherever it was each called home somewhere in England.

Later that afternoon, when tea was served, both Smith and Standish discovered Richard had, indeed, gone home. They raised a small cider to toast him.

*****

Summer's progression continued as it had for a millennium. The latest information from Lord Burghley to Queen Elizabeth revealed that the secret negotiations were proving to be both significant and worthwhile.

The most recent meeting on the fifth of August found the Queen supporting Burghley's position and its continued dedication. Late on the morning of August 8, the Queen, reading in the rose garden of her Greenwich Castle, London, was alerted to the presence of a servant holding-up her skirts as she ran along the path to the seating area.

"Your Highness!" the young servant cried, running. "Highness!" she called again, causing the Queen to drop her book. She stood. The girl arrived, breathless.

"Your Highness!" She repeated, catching her breath.

"Speak, girl! What is this activity all about?"

"Highness, it is Lord Burghley! Lord Burghley is dead, Your Highness!" The pair made their way to the castle.

Matters of state continue, even without those deemed most astute and able in such matters. By September, 1598, one month after Lord Burghley's death, Queen Elizabeth sat in a meeting discussing conclusions to the war with Spain. Hiding her feelings of absolute loss at Burghley's death, the Queen carried-on business as if Burghley had merely stepped from the room momentarily.

To her right sat Robert Cecil, Earl of Salisbury, and Burghley's capable son. Now thirty-five, Cecil had eclipsed the conspiring Rebert Devereux for the position for which he was thoroughly trained. Sitting across from Cecil was Robert Devereux, Earl of Essex. Currently, there were matters beyond Spain that had to be addressed.

In Ireland, where a targeted and pointed effort by the Crown to eliminate Catholicism from that country by reshaping it to match the Church of England, were increasingly failing. Uprisings had increased to outright revolts, led by Hugh O'Neill, Earl of Tyrone. The discussion among the gathered centered on the best way to subdue the Irish threat. The decision was made to send Devereux as Lord Lieutenant, and head of an English military force to subjugate the Irish activist leaders and subdue the uprisings. Lastly, John Whitgift, Archbishop of Canterbury, would sweep into the country with his assistants to Anglicize the church in Ireland.

Elizabeth, who had been good in mood and disposition lately, once again welcomed Devereux into her close circle. For his part, the brash Earl remained on his best behavior, accepting the Queen's good graces and his newest assignment to Ireland. A knock on the door interrupted the talks.

"Avanti," the Queen called, obviously in an Italian mood today. It suited her, and both men enjoyed the graceful manner in which her Highness conducted state business so capriciously. An older page approached, bowed, and offered the Queen a silver plate upon which a folded paper lay.

"Your Highness, it comes from the master at arms. A messenger just arrived."

"Thank you, boy. You are excused." The page bowed and departed while Elizabeth unfolded the paper, reading what was written. The astonished look on her face told of something important.

"Gentlemen, let me be the first to inform you that King Philip II of Spain has died." Both men sat straight at the news. "He died two days ago, on 13 September 1598." The Queen turned to Cecil.

"Mr. Cecil, perhaps the king's death shall see you to obtaining peace with his son, King Philip III." Cecil stood.

"I go immediately," Your Highness." Turning to Devereux, Cecil stated, "amass your forces, Sir, and sail at the ready. God be with you." Devereux stood and the men shook hands. A bow to the Queen saw Cecil depart. Also bowing, Devereux said he was preparing to depart, but not before the Queen offered a comment.

"Do not fail me again, Robert, Earl of Essex. Too much rides on this endeavor."

"I offer my most sincere and able determination to succeed, Highness." The Queen nodded.

"Thank you. You may go to your business." Bowing again, the Earl took his leave.

When the room was quiet again, Queen Elizabeth excused all the pages sitting along the wall waiting for an assignment. When they had gone, she walked over to the window observing the leaves changing to fall colors and mourned for Lord Burghley.

*****

By April, 1599, Robert Cecil, Earl of Salisbury, learned that Devereux's attempts to quell Irish uprisings were unsuccessful. Resistance was stronger than anticipated. The counterbalance to the Irish frustration was success with peace talks with Spain. Answering a knock at his door, Cecil was greeted by the master guard, accompanied by a young man.

"Mr. Cecil, a good day to you," the guard said. "Please excuse the interruption to your important duties, but I have your new secretary with me." He introduced the young man.

"Mr. Cecil, please meet George Calvert, your new secretary." Cecil and Calvert shook hands.

"Excellent that! I can use some help around here. Welcome, George."

"Thank you, Mr. Cecil," Calvert replied.

"Mr. Calvert was born twenty years ago years ago, in Kipling, Yorkshire. He took his BA at Cambridge only two years ago. We believe he will be an excellent secretary, Sir."

"Thank you, Mr. Edwards," Cecil said, accepting papers from the man, and admitting Calvert. Wishing Calvert good luck, the master guard departed. Cecil engaged Calvert in the workings of his new situation.

Part One, Chapter Six

1599-1600

Richard Plascomb, now returned six months to his family's farm, took a fancy to the daughter of a family who arrived after his initial departure to war. Noticing her at regular church services, he was determined to speak with her father. On second thought, he thought it prudent to at least get her name first.

Two months later, Richard, now twenty-five, took his wife, Cecelia Route-Plascomb, sixteen, into their marriage bed to consummate their Anglican wedding vows. The excitement of war and travel yielded to a greater exciting force neither he nor Cecelia had known previously.

*****

When Martin Luther nailed his ninety-five theses to the door of the Wittenberg Castle church in 1517, he was an angry man. He had grown tired of the Catholic Church selling indulgences, a way for the wealthy to essentially buy their way into Heaven. Luther also rejected many clergy practices, and deemed the Church corrupt and antithetical to God. Luther wanted his say, a lone voice against the established, powerful, and monolithic Catholic Church. He got his way, and then some. His actions ignited demands for reforming the Church across Europe. His lone protest spurred the start the birth of Protestantism and a landmark span of time called the Reformation.

Now, eighty-three years following the Reformation's first shockwaves, reverberations continued throughout European churches, pushed by religious seekers eager to formulate their evolving faiths across Europe, England, Ireland, and Scotland.

In England, continued shifts between Catholicism and Protestantism, based solely on the ruling monarch's choice, scattered church doctrines like leaves in a strong gust of autumn wind. Henry VIII initiated the seismic break with Rome, establishing himself as the ultimate head of the Anglican Church, a Protestant faith.

His son, Edward Vi, was perceived as the king who would prove England was a country chosen by God. Yet, when Edward died at the age of fifteen, in 1553, the Protestant ideal also died. His half-sister, Mary, then ascended to the English throne, returning the country and its people to the Catholic Church.

Five years later, in 1558, Mary was imprisoned, and her half-sister, Elizabeth, became Queen of England, restoring Protestantism as the official religion. Those Protestants who fled under Mary's rule and severe persecutions returned to England as word of Elizabeth's religious decision was established.

Elizabeth quickly sought to quell religious fervor throughout England and Ireland, still under English control. Some who returned from the Continent had been involved in different, new, sometimes radical forms of worship. They brought all those alien ideas back to England. Where Mary's rise to the throne was viewed as England not being a country chosen directly by God, Elizabeth's rule renewed the national belief that God had chosen England as an elect nation, a belief that would eventually be carried to the American colonies.

In Elizabeth's first year of reign, the Act of Supremacy placed her as the "supreme governor" of the Church of England. Also, the Act of Uniformity ensured that Anglican worship would follow the Book of Common Prayer. Still, evolving religious ideas started by the Reformation continued well into Elizabeth's reign, and it was during this period that Puritanism began to take a serious hold throughout England.

   William Brewster, now thirty-three-years-old, had been working as the head bailiff at Scrooby, Nottinghamshire, having returned to his father's home eleven years earlier. He also became the Scrooby Congregation's Puritan leader and minister. Presently, he was hosting a small dinner with select men of the Scrooby community, several of whom had made inquiries about Puritanism. He held-up a book named, 'Advertisements', published in 1566, thirty-four years earlier.

"This book was written by then Archbishop of Canterbury Matthew Parker. In it, he describes the demand for uniformity in the liturgy as demanded by Queen Elizabeth." He placed the book back on the table.

"The name Puritan truly is a derogatory term," he plainly stated, glancing at the six other men around his table. "With continued switching from Catholicism to Protestantism and back again, many ministers took the liberty of doing away with the many elaborate vestments of the Church, taking to wear what they chose to minister. They also made changes to liturgical practices.

"Hence, the Archbishop's book, designed to reign-in all clerics, did not achieve its objectives. Many continued to refute the book's demands for uniformity. Those who refused to wear the required vestments were collectively and scornfully called 'Precisians', or, more plainly, 'Puritans'.

"Martin Luther possessed no idea how revolutionary his theses were when he vented them in anger. A simple monk as he was, he gave birth to a new manner of worship beyond the idolatrous, as well as the morally and financially corrupt

Catholic Church." Again, Brewster looked around the rough wooden table at his guests, thoroughly rubbing his already graying beard. A young man of about fifteen years also looked around at the men.

"It seems right unfair to belittle a group for thinking differently," he noted for all. Several older, more reasonable men, knowledgeable in the ways of the world, laughed softly, or gave each other understanding nods. Brewster patted the young man's forearm.

"Such is the manner of things, lad. Those who do not conform to the will of the majority will suffer for their individuality."

"But what of us here at Scrooby?" asked an older gentleman. "We do not conform to the dictates of that book." Brewster nodded affirmatively.

"You are correct, Mr. Wiltshire. We do not. Ever since that book was published, many have simply disregarded it. Some, contrarily, have accepted some forms of episcopacy." Another guest had a question.

"By episcopacy, Mr. Brewster, you mean rule by bishops, correct?"

"Yes," Brewster responded. "However, many more have elected to establish their own presbytery, complete with a separate congregation that deals directly with God." The youngest man at the table spoke again.

"You mean they have actually separated from the Church of England?" His tone indicated one of divine wrath.

Nodding, Brewster replied, "aye, they have, indeed. They are the true separatists. They break from the parish system, establish individual congregations, elect ministers by consent, and self-govern through the church, a true presbytery."

"And a theocracy, government by religion," one man observed.

"Aye," Brewster replied, adding, "where the elect rule and the Bible governs." The young man was working to understand all this talk.

"What of retribution, Mr. Brewster?"

"We are on the other side of the country, too far from London and Canterbury to worry, at least for the time being, that is," Brewster said speculatively, rubbing his beard.

"What of Whitgift?" one man asked. "The Archbishop of Canterbury."

"What of him?" Brewster asked.

"I refer to persecutions," the same man replied. "Persecutions like those during Mary's bloody times against Protestants?"

"No," Brewster responded thoughtfully. "The Queen and Whitgift have not taken that destructive path. As conservative as the queen is, she does see the Separatists -and Puritans in general- as a political threat. They have imprisoned a few but martyred none.

"Whitgift's predecessor, Edmund Grindal, refused to stop the prophesizing, where Puritan clergy, leaders, and laity could discuss the Bible. The queen relieved him of his office and installed Whitgift in his place, and who did stop them to the best of his abilities." Brewster drank some mead.

"But, with Grindal's death some seventeen years ago, as well as the deaths of other prominent Puritan leaders, any further church reformation under Queen Elizabeth has effectively stopped. Yet Puritan thought continues to grow throughout England."

"Are we Separatists?" the young man asked. The majority shook their heads.

"No, we are not," his host replied firmly. We, Puritans all, aspire to remain within the Church of England, but with our own manners of worship. We seek change, reforms, from within the church. We do not profess to break with it.

"So long as the Crown and its representatives do not involve themselves in our affairs, we shall continue on our selected path. At this time, we are quietly here in Nottinghamshire, out of sight and minds of London and its bureaucracy."

"Time will tell," bellowed a guest from the other end of the rough wooden table. "We have many friends in Parliament - Puritan friends- and they maintain our positions on all government affairs." A different man offered a speculation.

"Perhaps James will prove more conciliatory to the Puritan position when he takes the throne." A fifth man laughed scornfully.

"*If* he ever takes it!" he scoffed. "Good Queen Bess seems ready and poised to rule forever and a day!"

"Every man has his last day," another man offered. "Just as Edward and his father, Henry. The only difference among all of us is how short or long a time we have before that day arrives." Affirmative nods and verbal ascents of agreement moved 'round the table.

"James is of a Calvinist theology," Brewster stated for all. "He did sign the Negative Confession in 1581. If you recall, it favored our Puritan position that God alone selects the few for eternal redemption, and nothing can be done to change that predestination." More supportive, "ayes" sounded.

"So," the youngest said contemplatively. "Time shall tell, will it not?"

"Aye, it shall," Brewster said. "You're learning, lad." The others around the table laughed as they began eating their mutton stew.

*****

Sir Robert Devereux sat scowling at the copy of a weak, unfavorable truce he received from Hugh O'Neill, Earl of Tyrone, and acknowledged leader of the Irish revolts against forcing the Irish to accept the Church England over Catholicism. Picking up the seemingly worthless parchment, he paced the room.

"I would thrust it into the hearth if it be lit!" he hollered across the room to his aide, who sat quietly observing, listening, and calculating how to remain out of the line of fire when the Earl might, in his fits and bouts with anger, begin hurling objects in reach against the opposite wall.

"Every letter I send to the Queen with ideas regarding strategy and appointments is rejected! Instead, Robert Cecil governs me, the Lord Lieutenant of Ireland! I detest that sniveling prat!" he railed, dismissing his aide to think. Pacing a few minutes longer, Devereux stopped briefly to stare upon the verdant lush greenery of spring in Ireland. Devereux decided to return to England in a sincere effort to win-back the Queen's good graces and favor, although this decision meant he would be leaving his assigned post without permission. He fathomed no other alternative to circumvent the infuriating Robert Cecil and address Her Highness directly. Throwing the damnable truce to the table's surface, the Earl started to prepare for his venture to Windsor, the Queen's summer residence.

*****

Richard Plascomb met his father at the center of their freshly plowed field, ready to plant autumn vegetables, including cabbage, Richard's favorite, especially the way Cecelia cooked it. Presently, the sun felt warm and pleasant as the men, preparing to seed, heard a sweet voice calling to them. Turning, they discovered Cecelia approaching, a mug of mead for each man. Richard sighed at the site of Cecelia's blonde hair blowing in the late spring winds.

"Aye, you're a wonderful lass," Richard complemented his beautiful wife when she reached them. Richard's father also thanked his dutiful daughter-in-law for the refreshment.

" Tis time for dinner, you two," she said, smiling at them, her hands on her slender hips.

"Go eat father, and I'll start to sow. I'll come in after a row or two." Finishing his mead mixed with beer, Edward agreed, carrying the empty mugs into the cottage while the young couple talked in the sun.

They watched Edward enter the cottage, closing the door. Richard watched Cecelia more than his father. A sudden breeze blew the blouse from Cecelia's right shoulder. She automatically moved to fix it, but Richard intervened.

"No," he said in a low voice. "Leave it." Taking hold of her small waist, Richard pulled her lithe frame to his own sturdy one for a passionate kiss. After it, Cecelia giggled, and rubbed the front of Richard's farming pants. The most fundamental Puritan rule is to never lose self-control, but young love is stronger than religion. It measures sin, if at all, its own ways.

"Aye, Mr. Plascomb," Cecelia teased. "I'm beginning to wonder what kinds of seeds you're looking to sow in this field on this beautiful spring day in late May." They kissed again, Richard kissing along Cecelia's supple neck. She arched her back, now pressing her lower body to her husband's hardness, yielding to its unquestionable presence. Richard cast a quick glance to the cottage in the distance, assured his father was enjoying more mead and good food prepared by Richard's mother.

Richard plunged his face between Cecelia's white breasts, fully exposing them to the warm sun. In turn, Cecelia pushed Richard's head down, grabbing his dark brown hair.

"Shall we sow some seeds of our own in your field, wife?" Breathlessly, both fumbled to be released, sinking to the warm earth, where in the warm sun on a bed of earth, did Richard and Cecelia sow different seeds in late spring on a sunny English morning.

*****

Prior to her departure for the summer to Windsor, Queen Elizabeth announced to Parliament the appointment of Sir

Walter Raleigh as Governor of the Isle of Jersey. The island was located southeast of the Channel Islands, off the northwestern French coast, west of Cherbourg.

A reception followed at Greenwich. Once again, Raleigh received the Queen's grace and full support, much to the continued ire and discontent of many in the charmingly receptive crowd. Murmured jeers were drowned-out by receptive cheers, and the stilettos of envy were verbally sharpened in quiet groups. Following the reception, the Queen and her Court departed for Windsor.

*****

Several days after Raleigh's reception, Edward Sandys completed an address to a group of potential investors for a new stock company to be called the East India Company.

Following his presentation that promised significant profit from colonization based on new markets for English goods and services, land speculation, and an ever-growing demand for English goods, ultimately leading to an enlarged English empire, Sandys introduced the highly-praised English geographer, Richard Hakluyt to the assembled investors.

Hakluyt, portly and near-waddling when he walked, thanked the crowd for its warm reception.

"Gentlemen, there has been much said and speculated about the potential for what awaits anyone at the opposite end of the great Atlantic Ocean on the Continent of North America. Though Spain controls some of this land, their colonizing model is not one England must emulate.

"This is partly true because Spain has overextended itself and is reaping the losses. There is no question that assured and rapid financial gain awaits those who invest in the first, real, and successful establishment of English settlements and colonies in North America." A boisterous round of applause sounded for the weighty geographer.

"Of course, there are other reasons for colonizing. We seek a passage to the Orient through North America. And, yes, we seek also to balance, if not exceed, Spanish influence in the region. Now is the time to heed the call to invest while the costs are minimal, and the gains phenomenal." More cheering erupted, allowing Hakluyt to pause before delivering his closing statement.

"Gentlemen of reason, intellect, taste, and financial influence, the investment is yours, but, so, too, shall the handsome profits be yours, and yours alone!" If the crowd was previously enthusiastic, they were standing to cheer and applaud. Sandys shook hands with Hakluyt.

"Excellent, Richard!" he praised quickly before offering to answer questions from the assembled. " Smythe will be thrilled to hear the good news about the investment reception," he said, taking questions.

*****

That same May, 1600, John Smith had worked his way to Italy aboard a merchant vessel sailing for Italy. He departed from the fighting against Spain eight months earlier because he was, "bored with the same old war effort." Upon leaving, he accepted a job on the merchant vessel to find new adventures abroad.

In Italy he briefly loved a woman in Naples for several weeks before heading to northeast Italy. There, he joined the Austrian Fighting Forces in the Long War against the Turks. Once again, Smith discovered adventure in war, establishing himself as an excellent soldier good enough to be promoted to the rank of Captain in the Austrian Forces.

*****

Edwin Sandys met again with Thomas Smythe once more in July, 1600, in their efforts to start the East India Company. Though the investors were eager for profits, Sandys explained, they were more interested in quick profiteering as opposed to a slower, more steady growth.

Smythe agreed that such short-sighted financial expectations could be more problematic in the long-range planning of growing colonies, as well as newer ones. But he also added that it was important to get things started and deal with issues once they were operating.

Enough funds were invested to initiate the company. All Smythe had to do was obtain the company charter from the Queen, and he had an audience with her in July at Windsor Castle.

*****

The roses were in bloom at Windsor. English rain has a dutiful purpose after all, the preponderance of spectacular roses. The rose garden was a bounty of a massive colorful display of highly scented roses, exquisite enough to sweetly perfume the air and enliven the senses of everyone spent any time at Windsor Castle in the final week of June.

Queen Elizabeth was enjoying lunch with ladies of her Court, when a page approached the party, assembled leisurely at a long table in the rose garden. Noticing the page immediately, the Queen did not concern herself. But when the Captain of the Guard appeared shortly after the page, looking as if he were attempting to catch-up with the boy, the Queen did take keen notice. She stood, silencing her ladies. Rounding the table, the Queen was within eight feet of the page, who bowed.

"Your Highness," he said, but was interrupted by the Captain.

"Halt, boy!" came the call. All, including the page, turned. The page turned back to the Queen, wide-eyed, unsure of what was happening. The Captain arrived, bowed.

"It's alright, boy," he said, facing the Queen. "Your Highness, the Earl of Essex is here. He just arrived. I suspect he sent the page to advise you." The Queen's eyes flashed surprise.

"Essex! Here? How? He is in Ireland, failing miserably!" The ladies at the table sat in numb silence. The page started shaking. For a moment, the trilling song of a robin filled the summer air.

"I assure you, Your Highness, the Earl is here. He is waiting in the vestibule meeting hall. The Queen turned to the ladies.

"Carry-on," she directed, gathering her skirts, heading to the castle.

"Come with me," she demanded of the Captain, stopping so suddenly the man nearly rammed into her. She addressed the page.

"Boy, tell the Earl to meet me in the royal drawing room." The page bowed and ran-off ahead of the pair. The Captain followed silently, considering the Queen was moving at a furious pace for her sixty-seven years. He understood, instinctively, she was quite angry, but not the degree of her ire. He did not wait long before realizing how angry she actually was. They stopped. She turned to him.

"Captain, you assemble a group of guards. Meet me in the hearth room as quickly as possible. I want to arrive before Devereux."

"Excuse me, Your Highness, but you directed the page to meet with the Earl in the drawing room." The Queen stopped again.

"Captain, are you, too, questioning my commands?" The Captain withered, assuring he was merely confused about two rooms for the meeting. They walked again, the Queen elaborating excitedly but directly.

"Captain, I want the Earl drawn to one room while I gather my thoughts -clearly- in another. I do not want it to appear that I am coming to his presence. He shall be brought unto mine." They approached an entryway where two guards moved to attention.

"Start with these two. Replace them now," she commanded, moving into the castle with the Captain and the two stunned guards in tow, where they arrived at a T-junction.

"Retrieve the other guards. Have them outside the hearth room in five minutes. You knock twice and enter. Do not wait for me to reply to your knock. Understand?" The Captain replied he did.

"Good, that signals me you are at the ready." The Captain repeated the order and retreated. The Queen aimed for the hearth room.

"I do so hope the Earl of Essex enjoyed a peaceful journey because the sea is about to become rougher than any storm he may have endured previously," the Queen hissed aloud through her teeth as she moved to the room. Inside, the same page awaited. She eyed him.

"Is the Earl in the drawing room, boy?" she asked calmly and in proper royal fashion. The page assured the Queen all she wanted had been done. She gently held the boy's face in her aging hand.

"My half-brother, Edward, looked like you when he was your age. What are you, ten?" The boy's eyes grew wide.

"Highness, why I'm full eleven as of yesterday!" Elizabet smiled.

"God love you, boy. May your life be as full as mine, but may it be filled more with love than calculating." The boy looked confused.

"Highness?" Slightly laughing, the Queen patted the page's youthful face, thinking of her long dead half-brother, Edward, who died just a few years older than the page.

"Never mind, young one. Do this for me. Bring the Earl here, and walk, do not run, in the castle."

"Yes, Highness," came the reply as the Queen opened the door for him, watching him walk along the hall. He waved as he turned at the junction and stopped. When he heard the hearth room door close, he ran to fetch the Earl.

The Queen, seated upon her cathedra near the great hearth, called, "enter!" when the rapping on the door sounded. The page entered, announced Essex, and the Earl entered. At that same moment, the Captain knocked and entered the room from an opposite door, accompanied by six guards. A second group of guards entered from the same door as the Earl, who now stood surrounded. The Queen directed the page to wait in the hall. Devereux spoke.

"You Highness, do you- "but he was cut-off swiftly and surprisingly by Elizabeth.

"Who commanded you to speak!? The Queen demanded, stepping from her cathedra to the table in the room that held documents. Locating the the one she sought, the Queen unrolled it.

"This is my order that you report to Ireland as Lord Lieutenant as of the year previous to this one." He voice had returned to a patient, haunting, threatening tone. "Tell me, Lord Lieutenant, who is in charge of Ireland while you stand here before me at Windsor?" The Earl was at a loss.

"Your Highness, I came only to vindicate myself in your eyes in order to – "

"Who!" the Queen railed, throwing the parchment to the table, where it automatically rolled-up and rolled-off the table. "Leave it," she directed when the Captain moved to retrieve it.

"I repeat, who is in charge in Ireland as you stand here, your feeble attempts to subdue the Irish riots failing miserably in establishing the Church of England?"

The Earl stood speechless, and the Queen realized this was the first time the haughty, boastful, and prideful Earl of Essex was ever so silent. She favored him as much as Raleigh, but he refused to yield to her authority.

"You have deserted your post, Robert Devereux, Second Earl of Essex, against orders of your Queen to maintain your position. What say you, Earl of Essex?"

"I did as I thought best, Highness," he responded pleadingly, yet with a tone the Queen found disagreeable.

"You believe yourself a natural power and native not to be controlled, Earl of Essex. But you are not above the law. You are under obligation and service to me!" the Queen shouted. "I am the ruler of England and Ireland, Earl. You are not." It was here where the Earl forever changed the course of his relationship with his royal cousin. At times, silence is golden. It can also be foretelling. The Earl turned his back upon the Queen in silent anger.

She seemed to fly at him in one explosive move, slapping him across his face so hard it knocked him off-balance and nearly off his feet. He grabbed the table to stop himself from falling.

"How dare you!" The Queen hissed, glaring at him. Inside, the Queen was torn by the thoughts that danced through her head at that moment. This man was her cousin. But she had always governed her country from logic, not emotion, and she was not about the change course now.

"It is at this moment forward, Robert Devereux, Second Earl of Essex, you are removed from all offices bestowed by the Crown. Your income is stripped. You are confined to house arrest!

Captain, see that those orders are duly recorded within the hour and carried out forthwith."

"Yes, Your Highness" the Captain responded at attention. Devereux was seized, and the orders repeated to the guards. The Earl was dragged roughly, calling for the Queen's forgiveness. As quickly as it all started, it ended. The door closed; the calls withdrew along the halls. With quiet restored to the room and her head, the Queen sat upon her cathedra and wept for her cousin.

Three weeks after the incident, the Queen welcomed Edwin Sandys and Thomas Smythe to Windsor for discussions about their new stock company called the East India Company.

The Queen and Robert Cecil listened attentively. Cecil's secretary, the young George Calvert, also attended the meeting, listening with great interest. The pair described their ideas to infuse private capital into colonizing North America. After several hours of talks and questions, Queen Elizabeth honored the request for a royal charter for the new company, assigning Thomas Smythe Governor of the new enterprise. George Calvert recorded the event, and began to understand how owning land equated to having significant power.

Part One, Chapter Seven

1600-1601

Summer passed to autumn and fleetingly, winter arrived. By Christmas, 1600, the world was really no different than it had been, except in the lives of those alive at the Christmas tide.

Nearly penniless, politically isolated, and angry at the loss of everything, Robert Devereux, cousin to the Queen on his mother's side, had taken to risky behaviors. His latest schemes involved the instigation of a riot in London meant to cause a slight degree of anarchy. He spent his lonely holidays plotting revenge with a group of individuals who always lived outside lawful boundaries.

Thomas Smythe enjoyed splendid holidays, complete with a grand dinner held in honor of stockholders of the East India Company. All talk over dinner and the evening was of the superb return on investments made to establish settlements and colonies in America.

Cecelia Plascomb was receiving a positive return on her and Richard's loss of self-control back in the cabbage field the previous May. Their baby was due in February, as best as she could figure.

*****

The New Year burst-forth with good wishes and hopes for a better year for all. Yet, little over a month into the new year, on 8 February, 1601, a riotous crowd of almost three hundred hooligans rampaged through London's streets, complaining and ranting against the Queen and the illegitimate claims of her right to rule.

The ruffians were quickly subdued by authorities, yet several hours were needed to quell the social eruption and the violent actions of those involved. Authorities were stunned upon discovering the rebel leader to be none other than Robert Devereux, former Second Earl of Essex. On this discovery, word was rushed to Greenwich seeking royal advice about the delicate situation. Devereux was being held along with members of his gang of ruffians until word returned from Greenwich. Included in the report and request were information stating that the former Earl surrendered to authorities, and he was quite apologetic about the entire affair. Everyone, including the lamentable former earl, awaited word from the Queen. Word of the riot and those involved spread swiftly, arriving at Greenwich Castle before official reports. As is the case with such social occurrences, the story grew as it passed from one to another.

The Queen was at Greenwich, hosting a reception for Sir Walter Raleigh, naming him as Member of Parliament, this time for Cornwall, located at the furthest southwest, wind-swept corner of England. Once again, the glittering splendid Court and special guests engaged in the social pleasantries of one more link in the successful chain of incomprehensible events for Sir Walter Raleigh. His wife, Elizabeth, also called Bess, like the Queen, joined him with the Queen as she presented him to the French and Dutch ambassadors and their wives. Raleigh portrayed the graceful polished embodiment of masculine strength as he danced easily to a French madrigal with his wife. Following the introductory dance, all guests gathered on the dance floor to enjoy the celebratory music.

Speaking in fluent French with the French ambassador, Elizabeth was quietly approached by a guard, who handed her a note. Accepting it, she read it, folded it, and glanced quickly across the large crowded room, sighting the Captain of the

Guard. Elizabeth turned to the ambassador, speaking fluent French.

"Ambassador Florusy, please excuse me, as matters of state intervene at the most inopportune moments." Bowing, the ambassador turned to another guest as the Queen walked to the Guard Captain. Stepping out the room for privacy, she accepted and read the note before refolding it and handing it back.

"First, burn that note. Second, Mr. Devereux is determined to test my hand at every opportunity. Where is he now?" The Captain replied he was in London central with a sheriff. Music floated from the large crowded hall as the Queen considered options, turning back to the Captain.

"This is treason, plain and simple, Captain. My order is that Devereux shall be removed to the Tower of London immediately and prepared for a trial on charges of treason. Notify the judges, and be sure that Sir Francis Bacon is one of them. He will have the most...philosophical perspective. That is all, Captain."

"As you command, Highness," he replied, and departed after bowing. Standing a few moments by herself, Queen Elizabeth sighed deeply, readjusting her attitude away from the stress to the enjoyment she had at the reception. She turned to see Thomas Smythe in the doorway.

"Your Highness," he said, bowing, awaiting his monarch's acknowledgement.

"Look up, Mr. Smythe. Are you enjoying the festivities?"

"Indeed, Your Highness, and I am always grateful to be included in such enjoyable memorable moments."

"There will be other memorable events, Mr. Smythe, and perhaps even more personal, shall we say?" Smythe studied the Queen's enigmatic smile.

"May I inquire, Highness, as to the nature of such events?" Smythe asked as they reentered the hall.

"Does one require a reason, Mr. Smythe?"

"No, Highness, curiosity rendered me briefly senseless."

"Worry not, Mr. Smythe. Time shall make all known to all to know."

"You Highness, I would like to name the first settlement to be called Virginia, in your honor." The Queen pondered briefly.

"Your sincerity is to be held in high esteem, Mr. Smythe. Allow me to consider the proposal," the Queen replied, turning to the Dutch ambassador. Bowing, Smythe took his leave, passing William Dorsey and Charles Lanish, like Smythe, from Parliament. Greeting both men, Smythe commented positively on the reception. Neither man smiled.

"Indeed," Dorsey replied with a distinct tone of malfeasance.

"My wife had to be here," Lanish commented, waving to someone in the hall. Smythe, sensing personal hostilities, continued on his way through the crowd.

*****

Upstairs from the reception, Robert Cecil, Earl of Salisbury, took some decidedly quiet minutes out of everyone's sights to finalize his letter to King James of Scotland. Cecil picked-up the letter and, crossing the room, read it aloud for clarity before forwarding it.

Oatlands Palace

Your Royal Majesty King James VI of Scotland,

   I write with confidence of your good health. As Queen Elizabeth's most trusted advisor, and son of the late Lord Burghley, I write to assure you that I offer my humble truthful insights and loyal service at which time it becomes fact that you shall ascend to the throne of England.

   Though guaranteed that Her Highness shall enjoy many more fruitful years on the throne, man can only plan for the future, not predict it.

   Therein, God's Will on all matters remain in His hands. I look forward to serving you as trusted advisor with my utmost respect and sincerity.

Your most humble servant to the Crown,

Robert Cecil, Earl of Salisbury
Advisor to HRH Elizabeth I

Content with the letter's message, brevity, and tone, Cecil established his personal future course. He might not be able to predict the future as he aptly wrote, but no plant grows without seeds planted at the correct time. Now, he had to work to see his plan come to fruition at the proper time.

Cecil folded the letter and called for a page, sealing the letter with wax bearing his initial embosser. The page waited for orders.

"Take this letter to the Captain of the Guard, boy. Tell him it goes to King James VI of Scotland from this royal household. There is no rush. Understand?"

"Yes, Mr. Cecil," the page replied. Cecil laughed.

"Right, then, off with you, rascal," Cecil said, laughing all the more, making the page laugh, heading to the door to discharge his assignment. Music floated in when the door opened. Checking himself in a looking glass, Robert Cecil returned, unmissed, to the festive reception.

*****

While Sir Walter Raleigh enjoyed yet another success, Richard Plascomb found it difficult to concentrate on shoeing his horse because the midwife was in the cottage with Cecelia, her mother, and Richard's mother. Foolishly trying to hurry, he dropped a tool on his big toe, and the pain was keen through the worn boot. It was one of those pains so intense, it made the individual feel as if he would vomit. Richard decided to slow-down.

He spun around when the barn door opened, but only his father entered, carrying some equipment. Edward, born in 1546, had just turned fifty-five, a long life for a farmer. Laughing

87

at his son's heightened edginess, Edward patted Richard's shoulder.

"Aye, son, you're a sight tighter than a freshly tanned hide!" he exclaimed, laughing again. "Relax, Richard, the midwife said it was a false birth. Your Cecelia yet has several weeks to go."

Turning glumly back to the horse he had been shoeing, Richard asked his father if it was always this maddening.

"Did you mean the shoeing or the waiting, son?" Edward laughed, fully knowing what Richard meant, but the humor made them both laugh.

"I meant the waiting, father, of course."

"Aye, I know. And aye, at first. But, it only proves you did everything right!" he bellowed, laughing all the more. Richard had to laugh as well, but he felt like the next several weeks would pass exceedingly slowly.

*****

On February 20, 1601, the Queen was notified that the judges had reached a decision in the case of one Robert Devereux. He was found guilty of one count of treason.

The Captain of the Guard, announced in the throne room, entered quietly. Though at first, he spoke not, Elizabeth read his countenance and instinctively knew when she accepted the Court's decision parchment.

"He is guilty, is he not, Captain?" the Queen asked, unrolling the document. The Captain cleared his throat.

"He is, You Highness. I state it only because you asked me." The Queen surveyed the document in her hands.

"I see this is the decree for death as the result of being found guilty of treason."

"It is, Your Highness." A hallowed silence seemed to forcibly pull the oxygen out of the otherwise sunny, airy room. The last time Elizabeth held a similar document in her hands, it, too, only required her signature for the death of her half-sister, Mary, Queen of Scotland and England. Now she had another equally demanding decision to make. She crossed to a table laden with official documents.

"Captain, you may take your leave of me while I consider my duties to my people and my country. Tell me, though, Captain. Was Sir Francis Bacon as philosophical as I considered he would be?" The Captain nodded solemnly.

"Yes, Your Highness, but only in his perceptions, not his decision." The Queen nodded slowly.

Thank you, Captain. I dismiss you until I require your presence once more to deliver this document." The Captain bowed and departed.

Briefly studying the death document, Elizabeth allowed it to roll-up and lie on the table. Leaving it there to think, she sat on the loneliest chair in all the realm.

*****

Four days later, Queen Elizabeth, anguishing over the looming decision, sat once more in the noiseless throne room, hearing only the fire crackling in the hearth, and shifting her glances between a window and the death warrant before her.

Queen Elizabeth had always ruled with the distinct ability to hide her personal grievances and feelings, thereby ruling with an emotionless keenness. A robin's song filtered into the window, catching her attention momentarily. Picking-up her quill, she inserted it into the ink bottle, and affixed her royal signature to the document, dating it, so the act would be carried out the following day at two o'clock in the afternoon, on 25 February. The Captain accepted the document and it was properly delivered for its purpose.

*****

Robert Devereux surveyed the sizable crowd as he was led to the gallows that freezing cold afternoon in late February, but he did not see his royal cousin. Military drums rattled a somber repeated beat as the black hood was placed over the condemned man's head, and a rough heavy noose was positioned around his neck.

Devereux's heart pounded in his chest. Where did it all go wrong, he thought as his mind raced as rapidly as his heart. He started hyperventilating as the Anglican priest started payers, then panic seized him entirely. Prayers did not prevent him from vomiting.

All of Robert Devereux's concerns and fears coalesced when a sudden jolt below him made him feel like he was falling, but not for very long.

Robert Devereux did not see his royal cousin that fateful February afternoon because she and her Court had departed before noon for a long weekend at Oatlands Castle, her residence in Surrey, southwest of London.

*****

That same somber day in late February came to a grey, dark close at the Plascomb farm in Norwich, along with the sound of shrill cries of a previously unheard voice in the cottage that filled the space in the room beyond where Richard sat with his father before their small warming hearth.

Richard jumped-up nervously when the newest round of cries was accompanied by the delighted women's voices in the tiny bedroom. Behind the closed door, the midwife, and Richard's and Cecelia's mothers were crowded into the room where the birth had just happened. Richard pushed his ear against the thick wooden door.

"All must be well, father!" he whispered loudly, straining to hear everything.

"Aye, Richard, I believe so as well," Edward replied, almost as nervously as Richard guessed. The door flew open with the new father standing in the doorway, his ear against the air.

"You naughty spy!" teased his mother-in-law.

"Tis a boy child!" the midwife exclaimed happily, moving aside to allow Richard's mother to pull him into the crowded room where the midwife was finishing Cecelia's clean-up, so she could look her best, and try to feel the same.

Husband embraced wife and infant son together. Then, and with a nod from his wife, took the tiny bundle into his arms.

"He's all ours, Cecelia!" he exclaimed joyously, staring at the little bundle of new life.

"That he is, Richard, made from the dirt of the earth," Cecelia replied, smiling. Smiling back at Cecelia, Richard recalled that spring day in the field where the infant was conceived. "What shall we name him?" Richard thought.

"What of Christian?" Cecelia suggested, and Richard nodded.

"Christian, Christian Plascomb," he repeated several times before agreeing with his wife.

"Tis a fine name, indeed," Richard's father said, motioning for the women to follow him.

"We'll make a special dinner," both grandmothers said simultaneously, laughing, closing the bedroom door to allow the new parents and child to unite and relax before the hard work began.

Part One, Chapter Eight

1602

On the fifth day of the New Year, the Earl of Southampton offered a glass of sherry to Bartholomew Gosnold, thirty-two-year-old lawyer, and son of a line of well-to-do squires. Accepting the glass, Gosnold gratefully stated his thanks.

"Thank you for accepting my invitation, Mr. Gosnold. That sherry will warm you presently on this freezing winter day in January." Gosnold laughed as he sipped.

'You're are correct, Earl. As cold and absolutely dreary as it is outside, this sherry is already working its polite magic."

"Excellent, Sir," the Earl said, leading his guest to a large table where a large map of North America's eastern shore was spread-out. "I invited you because Mr. Thomas Smythe personally recommended you for this venture, or should I say adventure?"

"Either way, it sounds wonderful, Earl. I accept the challenge. I require only the particulars and the finances to begin...*our* adventure."

"Very good, Mr. Gosnold," the Earl replied, pointing to the map. "Your objective is to land here, the northeast coast of North America, and explore the area. Lay some English claims as well," the Earl said almost as an afterthought.

"Your second objective is to establish a trading post in the New World. That is primary. This, according to Smythe, will help jump-start the entire settlement and colonizing project." Gosnold nodded.

"I've heard that Smythe has been losing investors from his new East India Company." The Earl agreed, picking-up his glass.

"Unfortunately, the initial shine of rapid profits has lost some of its glitter, due mainly to problems connected to obtaining the royal charter. Investors want a return on their investments."

"And the Crown acts when it chooses," Gosnold added, and the Earl agreed.

"Yes, investors are not content to wait-out the Crown for long-term conditions. It is clear they subscribe to an invest now, profit now mindset."

"Which carries its own set of problems," Gosnold offered.

"Beyond that," the Earl said, "Smythe and I believe new information about the continent and its riches will call the investors back to the holy grail of investment, and they shall realize the dreams of profit in the short-term," the Earl said, looking again to the map, pointing to the area of interest once more.

"The local area is relatively unknown, so do your best to all you are able. A geographer will be sent with your crew and exploring party. He will record land mass, surface features. Bring back many samples of the best the area has to offer us."

"And my ship?"

"She's called 'Concord', add she's fitted with the best riggings, masts, and sails. You'll also have a fresh crew, all honest and reliable, and all hand-picked by Smythe and me. She's currently being tested for seaworthiness in Falmouth where the weather is better. You shall also have a duplicate of this map and several others. Your geographer will make newer ones for all of us."

"We sail from Falmouth as well?"

"Yes, and your departure date is 24 March, or about a little over eight weeks away. I shall personally provide you the necessary funds to pay the crew and purchase all your provisions. You, too, shall be handsomely paid for your dedication and services as captain and leader of the expedition upon your successful return." Gosnold considered.

"And if I do not return?"

"Then, Mr. Gosnold, our contract is null and void. Yet I believe you shall return successfully. Mr. Smythe told me of your superior ship work in the Azores with the late Robert Devereux." Gosnold's face took a negative turn.

"Bad business that, I mean of last year." The Earl nodded slowly.

"Yes, and if he was the Queen's own cousin, what does that say for the average man?"

"I shudder to consider it, Earl. Rest Mr. Devereux's soul all the same. The men's glasses 'clinked', drinking to the late Second Earl of Essex.

"Stay for lunch, Mr. Gosnold, please. We can fully discuss all our plans." With Gonold's acceptance, the Earl directed his servants to prepare a lunch for two. The Earl poured more sherry.

*****

On 10 March, 1602, in a crowded noisy meeting of the States-General of the Netherlands, Amsterdam, a leading investor addressed a broader group of investors before the final vote determining whether or not to start a new joint-stock company to be called the Dutch East India Company.

"Gentleman, this investment company, which will or will *not* be started based on the forthcoming final vote, promises to enhance each investor's financial standing significantly if properly managed. It's charter, a copy of which each of you shall be granted, promises to regulate, promote, and protect Dutch business ventures while, at the same time, funding our war with Spain." One man stood.

"Does said charter give us a monopoly?" he shouted to the speaker.

"It does!" came the speaker's loud firm call. "Further, the same charter allows us free customs passage, authority to raise a navy and an army, build forts, colonize where we want, sign treaties, administer justice, and coin money!" This news created a stir in the audience.

"We currently have men making contacts at the Cape of Good Hope, in Southern Africa. We also have plans to colonize and open markets in Molucca, Tidore, Banda, and Japan. These are all new markets in the Far East!" Murmurs echoed throughout the large crowd, all eager for new markets and plentiful profits.

"But what I require at this moment is your vote! Do we move forward or not? You have the *final* say! Therefore," the speaker said, holding a gavel above his head, ready to pound it.

"All against, raise your hand and shout, "nay!" Heads turned, owl-like, scanning the crowd for negative votes. No one voted against.

"Then, that done, all in favor, raise your hand and shout, "Yea!"" Several hundred hands shot skyward, and the resounding, "Aye!" was deafening. The gavel fell. Applause and cheers rang-out.

"Let the Dutch East India Company begin!" yelled the speaker above the shouting investors.

*****

John Winthrop, now fourteen-years-old, started his matriculation, or enrollment at Trinity College, Cambridge. The son of a very wealthy family living at Groton Manor, in Edwardstone, Suffolk, John had developed the manner of haughty will, giving directions to those he deemed not to be on the same social level as he. Otherwise, he was quiet and introverted, perhaps partly due to his mother's pious religious positions. His declared study was to be law.

*****

John Smith accepted orders to travel to Transylvania in the spring of 1602. As the Dutch-Spanish War for Dutch Independence continued, so did the Long War between Hungarians and the Turks. The European countryside captured Smith's senses, but he remained ever-mindful of the dangers surrounding him in war. Assigned to a Hungarian prince, Smith arrived in Transylvania the previous March, and was leading a team of men through some foothills in search of a band of Turks rumored to be there.

Venturing several miles beyond a suggested perimeter in pursuit of retreating Turks, Smith and his men were ambushed by a rear Turkish guard that had out-flanked them, turning around behind Smith and his men. One of Smith's men was killed instantly. Smith turned to holler orders, but a single bullet from a volley of shots slammed Smith to the ground, knocking him unconscious.

*****

Bartholomew Gosnold bid his wife, Mary, goodbye, and sailed from the southwest English port town of Falmouth, Cornwall, on 26 March, only two days after the initial sail date.

Now, on 7 April, two weeks after departing, Gosnold was grateful to providence for good weather and excellent winds. Speaking with his geographer, Richard Hakluyt, Gosnold admired the maps that lined the table in the geographer's spacious cabin. Hakluyt laughed, adjusting a measuring device.

"You lead for the present, Captain, and I shall draw for the future." Now, Gosnold laughed.

"Is that why your cabin is larger than mine?" he asked humorously.

"Perhaps, Captain, as the maps require much space. At any rate, they are my charge. The men and ship are yours."

"Agreed, map maker, but I must survey on deck. Work your future visual magic. Good day." Hakluyt replied in-kind, and Gosnold ascended to mid-decks to inspect wind and water and the crew. Hakluyt prepared his instruments.

*****

John Smith awoke to find himself in irons and chains. The black irons connected his wrists and ankles to a set of chains linking him to a stone wall. Sudden, sharp, loud voices stirred him even more. Others shifted and moved upon hearing the approaching voices. Sitting-up as best he could, Smith felt a sharp pain in his shoulder. The bullet, he thought. Some of the men he knew, others he didn't.

Two men, one a Turk, the other Smith guessed to be Caucasian, perhaps Russian, entered the dark cell. The Russian held a whip; the Turk, a gun. A wounded stranger next to Smith moaned in pain. The Turk said something Smith couldn't understand, but it was about the injured man. The Turk quickly scanned the room, obviously counting the number in the cell, then shot the wounded mand dead, point-blank.

"Well, he injured no more," the Russian said with a heavy accent with a nasty smile, laughing with the Turk who had a toothless mouth, and who also suddenly pointed the gun at Smith's face.

"No! No!" the Russian pleaded. "Good English man. Only little wounded! Good worker when heal!" Smith's mouth had gone bone dry. The gun was lowered.

"I give good discount!" the Russian added, repeating it in Turkish. The Turk shrugged, kicking men, tilting their faces upwards to look at them. Smith figured he was guessing ages, fixing prices. Many were quite young, Smith thought, following the Turk's path of observations. Their dirty, yet skinny frames and hairless faces belied their youth, and the Turk was nodding, approving. The Turk selected the younger men immediately, while the Russian called to someone. Four sizable Russian soldiers entered, unlocking the chains of those selected. They were too weak to struggle and were taken out.

Another round of choices was starting; Smith was selected. The Russian opened his chains, speaking to him in his heavily-accented English.

"Smith, you lucky man today. Welcome to our slave market. You will work in a Turkish colony is southeast Russia. Your life is now set as a slave," the Russian told Smith, chuckling. Smith spit in his face. For his action, he and several nearby men were whipped ten lashes and carried out. Soon, the ten men and boys were shackled together in a cart heading from Smith didn't know to somewhere in southeast Russia. Smith knew he had to remain calm, remembering everywhere they passed.

*****

Almost halfway around the world to the west, Captain Gosnold logged into his captain's record:

On 14th May 1602, Concord sail'd up the southeast land of North America and moor'd at an area so rich and abundant with fresh, giant cod, which we cook'd eagerly for a splendid dinner, that I officially nam'd it Cape Cod. The abundance here is unquestionable and prime for English colonization. Mr. Hakluyt is already measuring and drawing.

Concord's crew stepped onto land for the first time in seven weeks, and into a very new world. It was wild, untamed, and lush. The measure of available timber was enough to erect whole cities. The crew explored most of their first day, returning to their vessel to sleep safely after the superb meal of cod, salted meats, and mead mixed with beer, planning for specimen collecting the following day.

Yet as the explorers' excited voices carried through the woods that day, they had no idea they were continually observed. In fact, they were sighted long before their mooring, and the news of their arrival was quickly passed along the Native message routes, ranging from southeast Maine to the territory south. Several tribes gathered to discuss the arrival with their chiefs.

The following morning, Concord rounded the Cape to Nantucket Sound. Hakluyt marveled at the earth's proportions in this magnificent pristine region. Commenting on an island to the eastward side of the coast, the geographer sketched it roughly for added detail later.

"What shall we name it, Captain?" Gosnold thought about it, also found joy in the small island's natural beauty.

"It appears like a private vineyard of such supreme proportions," Gosnold replied. "I know, we shall name it after my infant daughter who died four years passed. We shall name the island Martha's Vineyard!" The mapmaker wrote it on the map in-progress.

"Martha's Vineyard it is, Captain."

Concord continued its sailing to Buzzard's Bay, Gosnold naming it Elizabeth's Island, for Queen Elizabeth. After several more days of exploration and collecting, Gosnold set anchor at Cuttyhunk Island to build the trading post. With an eager crew and hospitable weather, the crew began setting camp.

A rough post was erected by the end of the first week in June. The crew originally planned to stay as long as possible, but skirmishes with hostile natives, and concerns about a shortage of supplies and provisions to keep the crew of thirty-two through the winter, the crew elected to return to England.

Cod was salted for passage home. Small trees were collected. Seedlings and seeds were gathered, labeled and stored, and fur samples were gathered. All the while, Hakluyt continued mapping.

Concord and her entire crew set sail for England on 17 June 1602.

*****

Gosnold and his crew arrived at Falmouth, Cornwall, on 23 July 1602.By the middle of August, Gosnold met with Thomas Smythe, who informed him that the Earl of Southampton was imprisoned in the Tower due to his involvement in the uprising led by Essex the previous year. The news stunned Gosnold.

"Sir Robert Cecil himself pleaded to Her Highness for mercy, and she granted it in the form of a reduction of sentence of death to life in prison," Smythe said. Smythe sought to change the subject to the expedition.

Smythe eagerly studied the samples of fur, trees, seeds, soil, and plants Gosnold collected. He listened to Gosnold's details of the abundance of cod, wildlife, and natural resources. He was disappointed that the trading post was abandoned, and news about hostile natives was unsettling.

"Nonetheless," Smythe said decisively, "we must present these samples to Her Highness. I cannot determine why she requires so much time to grant a charter. Investors are losing interest." Gosnold understood.

"There are those already saying that our venture is a failure, but I see it otherwise, Captain Gosnold."

"There are always detractors, Mr. Smythe. 'Tis always easier to criticize that create." Smythe agreed.

"Captain John Smith should be made aware of these samples as well," Gosnold suggested, but Smythe shook his head.

"Captain Smith is fighting the Turks in the Long War with the Hapsburgs. There's no telling when -or if- he'll return." The decision was made to show the Queen the abundance of materials and resources awaiting English colonization in hopes of securing the requested charter for the East India Company.

*****

Southeast Russia proved it had a short summer. By late September, 1602, John Smith started to experience the quickly approaching Russian cold as he broke rocks with nearly a hundred other men of all ages and nationalities. The hard-physical labor enabled Smith to stay warm, but his shoulder wound was also proving slow in healing, due to absence of medical care.

Smith also realized he was the only Englishman in the slave camp. He mentally plotted his escape anew each day. He understood he had to escape, traveling back across the Russian-Romanian border to make it back to the prince, in Transylvania, in western Romania.

Smith discovered he was in Kagul, located just on the other side of the border he had to cross. The slave camp faced east-west. Smith deduced this by observing the sun's rise and setting each day. It was already beginning to set earlier each afternoon. To his northwest lay the Carpathian Mountains. To his east, less than a hundred miles away, was the Black Sea. Smith decided a land escape would be his best method. This meant he had to escape through the rear gate, following the setting sun's direction. He could skirt the southern portion of the Transylvanian Alps, making his way back to Prince Hugard, in Lupeni, Romania.

Smith's immediate sergeant was a wild-eyed abusive Turk with a fast whip and a general mean-streak. He was swarthy, about forty, contemptible, and absolutely played favorites among his charges.

Slaves he beat usually remained absent several days to recover. Those who rendered sexual favors returned with new clothes and extra blankets, but were warned not to share them. Slavery makes strange bedfellows, Smith pondered, clothed only in the flimsy tattered rags he'd worn every day since his arrival. There would be no new clothes or extra blankets for John Smith.

He said nothing negative to the nightly favorites who returned each morning, proud of their warmth and a good meal because war and prison are really the same thing, except that, in war, you're allowed to be killed. Instead, Smith calculated several of the favorites were his avenue of escape. The two young slaves, both Europeans, Smith studied typically left at night and returned together the next morning. They always had extra everything. They were clean. Smith began to plot.

*****

King James VI of Scotland sat with several favorites in Edinburgh Castle with wine and a great fire in the hearth in the Christmas Season, opening the most recent communication from Robert Cecil, Earl of Salisbury, in London. The letter offered best wishes for the royal couple in the season of Christmastide. The King looked across to Robert Carr, Earl of Somerset, the king's most favorite.

"The Earl extends best wishes for Christmas to the queen and me," he said sarcastically, loosely waving the letter. "My most favored, Robert, *do* remind me to offer the queen good Christmas wishes from the Earl of Salisbury if you be so kind."

"I shall, your Majesty," Carr replied, grinning handsomely, aware of the king's disdain for his wife, Anne of Denmark, whom the king married when he was twenty-three, and she fourteen. The rift started when she converted to Catholicism several years after they married.

"Good," the king replied. "I shall be sure to pass the word to the heifer." The men in the room laughed along with the king at the merriment. James was always more comfortable in male company.

"The Earl also says, "blah, blah, blah, and, I summarize, "all is well in England." As it should be," the King said, flipping the letter to a nearby table. A servant entered to pour more wine, departing after he finished. King James raised his goblet.

"Let us enjoy what I think shall be our last Christmas in Scotland, my men." Glistening silver goblets went aloft.

"After all, forty-four years is a long-enough reign for a queen. England requires a king once more."

"Here, here!" the group of four men called, and all drank. Christmas 1602 awaited a mere three days hence.

Part One, Chapter Nine

1602-1603

John Smith felt himself withering away. He had the knowledge and experience required to survive war and wilderness, but no one, he fathomed, could ever be prepared for the experience of a slave camp. Not even prison could compare to this wretched existence.

Rocks could not be broken in eighteen inches of snow, so the laborers were taken into the leading Turk's sumptuous quarters to clean. Smith didn't mind. It was pleasantly warm, and the opportunity offered him a chance to better-acquaint himself with his surroundings. Luckily, he was assigned to work with one the Turk's favored, young, sex slaves, one of the two he shrewdly befriended over several months.

The youth's name was Maluk. He was dark like a Turk, but his light eyes underscored his mixed-race. Smith seemed to sense that Maluk also wanted to escape, and he possessed a thorough knowledge of the palace layout. Having no common language between them, they devised hand signals, utterances, and eye contact to communicate.

Their group had been assigned to cleaning the large, front, entry hall, marble stairs leading to a second floor, and the bannisters. Above Smith and Maluk, a half-dozen slaves were cleaning the wide stairs and wooden bannisters. Allowed to talk, loud talking bounced off the marble walls richly decorated with expensive tapestries.

Even the guard holding the whip as in good spirits, and Smith soon learned why after the guard slipped into a room on the second floor every few minutes. Maluk gestured to Smith; it was drinking. Smith nodded. There must be alcohol in that room, Smith thought, counting the twenty-two stairs leading to the second floor, wondering how many he could bound with one leap. Maluk was right. When he and Smith climbed the stairs, Smith noted rooms lining both sides of the ornate hall. Passing him, the guard smelled of some type of drink. This could be the day, Smith thought excitedly, studying his surroundings even more determinedly.

Looking for available weapons, Smith found none. Instead, he heard hollering from the hallway above. The Turk appeared, rubbing his head as if he'd just awoken from a nap. Seeing Maluk, the Turk laughed, called to him, beckoning him up the stairs. He and Smith traded looks and nodded. At the top of the stairs, the giant Turk grabbed Maluk, tossing him over his broad shoulders, slapping his bottom, laughing, and disappearing down the hall. Smith heard a door slam shut. Smith moved.

Running across the wide entryway, he tore a large tapestry off the wall. Upstairs, Smith crossed the wide hall to the room where the guard had been drinking, discovering a bountiful table of elaborate foods. Luckily, the guard was sleeping in a chair. Grabbing a long knife, Smith plunged the knife into the guard's chest, shoving a potato into his mouth when he screamed, jamming it in as far as possible. He removed the knife and returned to the tapestry.

Cutting away the brocade rope that fastened the tapestry to the wall, Smith figured it to be about fourteen feet long, and its strength and quality would do the job. He ran to the top of the stairs. In the food room, the other slaves were eating voraciously. Smith could hear noises from one of the rooms.

Alone in the large hall, Smith discovered a tether in the hall to the left, the same direction the Turk had carried Maluk. At this

107

close proximity, Smith heard the familiar sounds of passion underway. The Turk grunted, pig-like, engrossed in his business. But at the rate the bed was hitting the wall, Smith decided he didn't have much time.

With the rope secured, Smith ran it along the base of the wall to the stairs, draping the remaining length down the stairs. If he stood in the corner below the stairs, he could remain unseen. The stairs were part of a wall that formed a right angle with another wall supporting the second floor. The corner was ideal for hiding as flatly against the wall as possible.

Smith ran to the front door, where no other guards stood. Freedom was a few minutes away. Back in the food room, the slaves were yet gorging themselves. Smith ran in, his index finger over his mouth. He pointed outside, rapidly, several times. Obviously understanding, the men started searching for blankets, coverlets, anything to keep themselves warm. They began running out after stuffing their pockets with available food, down the stairs and out to freedom. One man was dressed like a Russian Army captain. Another wore three coats, all his pockets packed with food. Smith followed when he thought he heard the Turk in the hall.

Running to the bottom of the stairs, Smith hid in the corner, holding the rope, waiting for the right moment. The front door was wide open, and the cold air alerted the Turk that something was very wrong. Wearing only a towel around his thick waist, Smith could hear him atop the stairs. He awoke when he saw the open door, slaves running away, and felt the frigid air. He began screaming, eyes wild. Smith counted his footsteps down the stairs, abruptly pulling the rope as tightly as he could.

The Turk suddenly saw the same rope, but it was too late to change his forward momentum because was moving too quickly. Making a failed attempt to grab the bannister, the Turk hurled downward, forward, air-born, crashing to the marble stairs half-way down, bouncing, landing on the floor in a disheveled heap. Smith heard the Turk's neck snap when he crashed. He moved not. Maluk, dressed in the Turk's oversized, yet warm clothes, appeared atop the stairs.

Running up, Smith shoved food in the boy's pockets, clapped his shoulder, and pointed to the door. With a single nod, Maluk ran down the stairs and out the door, never looking backwards. Quickly, Smith found warm clothes, packed himself plenty of food in a sack, and headed down stairs.

At the door, Smith spit on the Turk and closed the door, heading westward in hip-deep Russian snow.

*****

The Anglican priest made the sign of the cross over the head of the infant being held over the baptismal font in the narthex of the local church in Essex, England. Holy oil was placed on the infant's forehead, tiny lips, and heart, also in the sign of the cross. Now, on 18 February, 1603, Israel Stoughton was initiated into the life of one of Christ's own, baptized in the Church of England.

The priest blessed the parents, the family, and those in attendance at the baptism to celebrate a new child following in the path of the faithful, baptized in the Christian life.

*****

King James VI of Scotland accepted the most recent communication from Richmond Castle, a royal residence, from Robert Cecil, Secretary of State for Queen Elizabeth.

14 March 1603
Your Majesty, King James VI of Scotland,

I write to you again, but his time with disturbing news. It was on this very morning that Her Royal Highness has taken ill. Though she claims her wellness, she remains in a constant state of vacillation between a mood of deep melancholy and reproachable self-blame.

The Queen says she deeply regrets the death of her half-sister, Mary, a decision she claims was pushed by Lord Burghley, Duke of Norfolk, in 1587. Her Highness also feels despondent for the execution of her cousin, Robert Devereux, Second Earl of Essex.

Too, she blames herself for the recent terrible harvests that have scourged the country, the almost unstoppable inflation, and high rates of unemployment both in and around London.

We pray, of course, for a full recovery, yet, at the moment, all seems most tenuous. The Queen's physician is in attendance here at Richmond Castle, and remains here until Her Highness recovers. Parliament has not been advised at this time in order to refrain from imparting any panic. You understand how royal illnesses only spread rumor and propaganda among the populace.

I personally have the situation at Richmond Castle and London under control. I shall advise you further about this dark period as we progress to its ultimate success.

Your Loyal Servant,
Robert Cecil, Earl of Salisbury

King James read the letter aloud to Robert Carr and Robert Villiers, another favorite. When he finished, he studied the letter a few moments before speaking. When he did, he was curious since something in the letter held his attention. James was excellent at pitting nobles against one another, thereby setting traps for anyone at a turn. Handing the letter to Carr, the favorite asked the king what bothered him about the letter, beyond the jarring news of the Queen's illness. James shifted in his chair.

"The Earl's specific use of the phrase, "its ultimate success." The Earl is either quite diabolical, or he extremely dedicated to my aunt, the Queen. His inference could mean my aunt's recovery or my ascension to the throne of England." Carr nodded.

"He's very good," Carr commented, handing Villiers the letter as King James stood, pacing the room, hands clasped behind him.

"Anything can happen, Carr. My aunt is approaching seventy this coming September. I tell you," he said, turning to his two favorites. "I direct you both to start a slow, yet progressive plan to move to London. I want all to be smooth should we be required to go to London if the worst happens." Carr and Villiers stood, Villiers placing the letter on a table.

"At least Salisbury is advising you, Majesty," Carr noted, much to the king's agreement.

"You're right, of course, Carr. I would be unknowing if not for Cecil's letter. Who knows when word would otherwise arrive?" Villiers postulated.

"Cecil does have Her Highness' ear on all matters, Majesty. He is her closest advisor."

"Are you nominating him, George?" the king asked, embarrassing his favorite.

"Of course not, Majesty!" he replied, but laughed. "I was unaware Cecil was running for anything." The King laughed.

"They are all running, George, running all the time for all they can get. Go plan. We discuss plans over dinner at seven." Bowing, both men took their leave of their king as he quietly considered his near future.

*****

It took John Smith seven weeks to make his return to the Transylvanian Palace of Prince Hugard, in Lupeni, Romania. He arrived hungry, tired, but thankful in the third week of March, 1603. The entire household was astounded to learn of Smith's return. But from where? He disappeared almost one year ago, taken for dead.

Prince Hugard, joyously relieved, made arrangements for Smith to be cleaned, fed, and doctored. Rest would follow. A celebration was planned for his return. Following a hot bath and food, yet still exhausted, Smith collapsed into a deep, motionless sleep.

*****

Robert Cecil was called to the Queen's bedchamber on the morning of 24 March, 1603. Climbing the stone steps he'd walked for more than twenty-five years, he turned onto the hall, where a nurse outside the bed chamber curtsied as she

112

quietly cried. A lady-in-waiting brushed the young nurse aside, entering the room.

"The doctor's inside, Mr. Cecil," she told him. Thanking her, he knocked, and was granted entrance. The Queen's ladies waited at a window across the room. The doctor set eyes with Cecil, and slowly, grimly shook his head, remaining silent.

The Queen lay in her bed under many covers. Cecil always understood she had always been a sensible humane woman who refused to marry so as to not reduce any of her God-given right to rule absolutely. Always firm in the control of state, his Queen now lay on the portal to infinity.

Presently, Queen Elizabeth's eyes opened and, seeing Cecil, weakly reached to him. Her lips moved, but no sound was emitted. Kneeling at her bedside, Cecil asked what she had said.

"King?" she said hoarsely.

"Your Highness, your royal nephew, King James VI of Scotland, is planning a transition party to arrive here. Shall you await his arrival for all our sakes?" he asked, his voice wavering.

But the Queen only shook her head slowly. She would not be waiting. Offering a flashing smile and a sudden look of complete lucidity, as if she was ready to rule strongly again, her eyes closed, and her last earthly breath was released.

Queen Elizabeth I, daughter of King Henry VIII and Ann Boleyn, and who ruled England and Ireland for nearly forty-five years, lay dead, the last in the line of rulers form the House of Tudor.

Like the waves created by a rock tossed into placid water, news of the death of Queen Elizabeth I moved outward from

Richmond Castle to all points in England, Scotland, Ireland, and the Continent.

On 5 April, 1603, King James VI of Scotland, House of Stuart, traveled south to London to ascend to the throne of England as King James I. As devastated as they were at the death of 'Good Queen Bess', the English populace looked to their future with hope and a renewed feeling of national pride.

Following the grand funeral for the Queen, all of England awaited as James prepared for his coronation to be held at Westminster Abbey on 25 July, 1603.

*****

Winter's cold façade faded with spring's highly anticipated arrival in April, 1603. Thirteen months had passed since Christian Plascomb's birth in February, 1601. Now, he was walking and doing a little talking.

His proud paternal grandfather, Edward, handed his handsome blond-headed grandson back to his mother for feeding. Meanwhile, he and Richard put on their caps, making their way back to the fields to finish plowing, setting seeds for the newest summer and fall crops.

"I'll get the horse, Richard, if you'll fetch the plow," Edward said. Outside, the two men walked to the small barn where several horses, cows, chickens, roosters, and several sheep roamed at-will.

Edward ventured left to the barn, and Richard, right, to their tool shed. Since the horse had to be led-out after its harness was applied, Richard waited outside with the plow, where he contemplated the great garden with its bounty of fresh growth for the entire family. He recollected the day he and Cecelia

114

made love in the warm dirt that day in May, smiling to himself in the carnal beauty of the unexpected, the unorthodox act in the most natural of places, the place to which all ultimately return. The fiery union brought forth their beautiful son. He laughed to himself. He was happy.

Self-control should be maintained, he thought. But if that was true, who would ever have children? Richard's thoughts were interrupted when he realized he'd been waiting quite some time for his father's approach with the horse. Laying the plow on the ground, Richard headed to the barn, calling to his father. Inside, he heard the horse whinnying. Entering, he called again to his father, turning a corner to the left, leading to the stalls. He stopped instantly.

"Father!" he called loudly upon finding his father lying motionless on the dirt floor.

"Father!" he shouted, kneeling, holding his father's limp head. Richard called again several times, but with no purpose. Edward Plascomb, Richard's father of fifty-seven years, had fallen dead.

*****

John Smith was handsomely rewarded by the prince who hired him to lead his troops. The prince greatly admired Smith's survival skills, in addition to his strength, bravery, and military skills. Subsequently, in mid-April, flush with gold as his reward, Smith resigned his position. It was time to move-on.

His shoulder healed successfully, and he knew he was lucky and grateful. By the start of the third week in April, Smith was aboard a merchant ship heading to Algiers, on the northern coast of Africa. He decided to visit a place he'd never visited. The sun was as bright as the shiny gold coins divided among his few bags. Behind him lay war and history. Ahead of him waited a new life.

*****

Puritans were a growing presence in Parliament, and to illustrate their intent that all shall live accordance with Puritan thought, religion, and lifestyle, they publicly published the names of all fornicators and clerics they decided drank too much.

Puritans held that the Church of England had the wrong ministries, the wrong message of salvation, and improper ceremonies. They sought to reform the Church from within its boundaries, as opposed from breaking away completely.

Separatists, though, such as the independent congregation of Scrooby, near York, in Nottinghamshire, and which met at the home of William Brewster, actually broke from the Anglican Church, or Church of England. Such Separatist congregations made their own rules and governed their churches in the manner they decided best. Separatists also welcomed the pending coronation of King James I, known to hold very conservative Calvinist religious views.

Puritan members of Parliament started organizing their demands to present them to the new king during the 'honeymoon' period immediately following a coronation, when good will and evenhandedness seemed unlimited to both sides of an argument. In the meanwhile, Puritan religious fervor continued to spread quickly through England.

*****

Universities, including Cambridge and Oxford, were led, and lectures given, by Puritans. Against this wave of religious zeal to

116

gain control of Parliament, particularly in the House of Commons, and rule citizens lives through Puritan religious thought and positions, Anglicans were aghast.

It was unfathomable that the fundamental will of the Puritans was to control government and an entire society through religious beliefs. Subsequently, Anglicans awaited nervously, and Puritans assured a true adherent to the only true faith, Puritan, and born of Protestants, was to be crowned king in several months.

For as many reasons as there were citizens, all of England waited the pending coronation of King James I of England in hopes of solving many problems.

*****

On their farm outside Norwich, in East Anglia, Richard and Cecelia Plascomb went about the business of daily life during the interim between the Queen's death and the pending coronation in July, only two months away. They had never met the queen, and they were confident they wouldn't ever meet the new king.

All they knew about the monarchy was that it leveled too many taxes for no apparent reason than enriching their treasury and themselves. Parliament only argued endlessly, and the growing conflict about to what degree how much religion should run the country was no more than political rubbish and a waste of Plascomb hard-earned money, what little they managed of it to keep after buying feed, fabric, and the foodstuffs they could not grow on the farm.

Richard was confounded despite the fact that as his mother's son, she inherited only one-third of her late husband's farm.

Richard inherited the additional two-thirds by law. But he needed more land, but there were no funds to buy them.

At twenty-nine-years-old, Richard could not achieve to the degree of his father which, taking stock of the farm, wasn't much. Yet taxes were rising, and farm profits were not keeping-up with costs. But a farm was land, and land was always expensive.

He thought about all his problems that, he realized with a laugh, weren't real problems. Instead, he understood, they were his earthly wants, overpowering him. Yet he wanted more for the family. As far as religion was concerned, Richard enjoyed his Anglican faith. He thought Puritans, called such, and rather snidely, for their ardent demands for church as they saw fit for everyone, was one group of souls attempting to dictate their religious beliefs upon the masses, like it or not. Richard couldn't accept that way of governing. Intolerance was rearing its serpentine head in many forms in the Parliament.

The tools stored, Richard closed the shed's door as a familiar voice called him. It was Christian, now over two years old, and running everywhere. Scoping-up his son in his arms, he kissed him, waving to Cecelia, standing in the cottage's front door.

"Just checking the horses and cows!" he called, carrying his tow-headed son. Waving back, Cecelia retreated inside.

In the kitchen, Cecelia had made Richard's favorite dinner, Sheppard's Pie. She was planning to tell him their little family was about to grow again by one, possibly by November, as best as she could calculate, rubbing her slightly swollen stomach. Smiling as she removed the dinner from their hearth, Cecelia considered names just for the fun of it. Her mother-in-law continued knitting, realizing the good news that would be forthcoming over her son's favorite dinner.

Part One, Chapter Ten

1603

James Williams, merchant tailor of London, and his wife, Alice Pemberton, daughter of two well-known, London, trading families, announced the birth of their son, named Roger Williams, in the first week of May, 1603. To celebrate their news, they held several large social gatherings following Roger's baptism in the Anglican Church in London. A life in the trading business was being carefully planned for Roger.

*****

In June, 1603, Thomas Smythe stood staring out his bedroom window at his estate home. Keenly aware of business opportunities, Smythe experienced great disquiet after learning of the start of the Dutch East India Company fifteen months ago. Fully aware of Holland's role as the leading Renaissance center for art, music, literature, and government, in addition world exploration, he now had to contend with the possibility that the Dutch would venture to colonize North America before the English.

He thought it strange, yet entirely plausible, to have to fight the Dutch for North American land claims after aiding in their war against Spain. His wife's voice broke his concentration. His musings released, he smiled warmly.

"Sorry, my Dear. I suspect I was away in thought," he told her as she adjusted several layers of his black and purple velvet robes.

"You were in deep thought, Thomas, or, on this day, should I say, Sir Thomas?" she asked, smiling proudly at him. Smythe laughed good-naturedly, recalling a conversation he had with

Queen Elizabeth two years earlier at Sir Walter Raleigh's inception as a Member of Parliament for Cornwall.

"Well, Dear, perhaps, in several hours, Sir will be completely appropriate." He looked at his wife. "How much has changed in such a short time," he said, adjusting his robes." His wife asked what he meant. He shrugged.

"I suppose things change all the time," he replied wistfully, leading his wife for the ride to Whitehall for his knighting ceremony.

The day was 20 June, 1603, and Thomas Smythe, now forty-six, Governor of the Muscovy Company and French Company, and developer of the East India Company, was experiencing an investment slow-down due to slow colonization plans. However, on the same date, in a small frame of time, much had changed.

Queen Elizabeth died less than three months earlier, on 24 March. King James VI of Scotland succeeded her on the English throne as King James I soon thereafter. Also, Sir Walter Raleigh had fallen from royal favor, Robert Devereux was dead, and Thomas Smythe was being knighted on this day by King James I. A knock upon the door revealed a servant with a terrible wide-eyed look.

"Whatever is it, Agnes?" Mrs. Smythe asked, looking quickly to her husband, who also noticed their servant's dreadful appearance. Agnes started crying uncontrollably. Mrs. Smythe comforted her.

"Oh!" Agnes gasped between sobs. "Sir and Lady, word has just come that the plague has broken-out, but we're not sure where. The word's spreading rapidly!" The Smythes looked at one another, aghast.

"God, no!" Smythe whispered loudly. "Not again!" The three moved to go downstairs to meet with the messenger.

*****

King James I, now thirty-seven-years-old, became king of Scotland when he was one year of age, referred to as a 'cradle king'. James was always pro-English. England and Scotland remained two separate sovereign countries, yet were more often at odds than not.

First, as a youth, then as a teenage king, James remained basically friendless, and had only minimal contact with women, and never associated with individuals outside royal court. At sixteen, he was kidnapped by William Ruthven, Earl of Gowrie, and held until he escaped the following June, 1583. Soon after, he declared himself of age and ruled himself with no regents.

In addition to his kidnapping, James was also forced to denounce his cousin-favorite, Esme-Stuart, a French Catholic, and his mother, Mary, former queen of Scotland, and her beheading in 1587, all before James turned twenty-one. Thus, James was well acquainted with political intrigue as he prepared for his coronation as King of England. He was eager to bring peace at home and abroad. His early struggles forced him to learn through experience. He was unprepared; however, for his coronation's postponement until the plague passed.

Sources confirmed the 1603 plague started in Hungerford, Wiltshire, roughly seventy miles west of London. For that reason, the coronation was postponed for safety reasons, and no firm date could be offered so long as plague existed. James ruled regardless, and matters of state quickly hampered him. Having decided to maintain Robert Cecil as his closest advisor and Secretary of State, King James met with him to discuss domestic religious issues, particularly what was referred to as 'the Puritan issue', which was spreading rapidly across England. The king asked where the name Puritan originated.

"Majesty, the name Puritan began as a derogatory and abusive term for those who seek reform in the Church of England beyond the limits set by Queen Elizabeth I. Their demands to eradicate vestments, the Book of Common Prayer, the sigh of the cross, all church hierarchy, a presbytery ruling, as well as other demands, first led many to call them Precisians, for their rigidness, then Puritans. That name took hold as the name for their religious movement, which is now splintering into multiple factions, each seeking different demands." King James shook his head.

"Mr. Cecil, think of how many wars have been fought over religion. Consider the number of lives lost, and all over a set of private beliefs. I daresay the country would be better-off if people kept their ideas about God to themselves, as it should be, and stopped thrusting their beliefs upon the masses as ultimatums." Cecil considered this observation.

"But, Majesty, what is to prevent them from saying the same about your decisions in regard to the Church of England?" The king's response was immediate and forceful.

"There are two fast and hard reasons, Cecil. First is that as king, I alone am the unquestioned head of the Church of England, the official religion of England, Reformation or no Reformation. Second, I lay rightful claim to the Divine Right of Kings to make any claim I deem necessary.

"But, let us arrive at the purpose for today's discussion. What do these Puritans want from me? What is this petition you mentioned?" Cecil shifted in his chair, quickly learning the king's

122

approach to discussions. He wanted all the information with little banter.

"As I stated, Majesty, the movement is splintering into factions. Consider a spectrum. The Presbyterians are all the way left, Church of England to the right. In the center are the Puritan factions seeking different demands. Puritans seek reform from within the Church. Separatists have already broken from the Church, wanting nothing to do with it. Then, there are the Millenarians, who hold the end times are quite near." The king stared at Cecil.

"My instincts tell me you jest not, Mr. Cecil." Cecil said he was serious.

"Their petition bears a thousand signatures, and they are collecting it to be presented to you. It sates- "

"Never mind what it says," the king interrupted, standing, pacing. "Set a meeting for a fortnight. We shall settle all this directly with the group." The king looked out a window.

"All this nonsense about God. There are wars in progress, new colonies to establish, royal charters for new stock companies waiting to be granted, and I am sitting here having to deal with the most private matters of peoples' lives. Very well, the people must be heard. Is there anything more, Salisbury?"

"Yes, Majesty, the situation with the war with Spain."

"Of course, I knew something pressing was awaiting our discussion. Now that the tempest of religion is settled for the time being, allow me five minutes to reflect while you prepare the discussion," King James said, leaning against a window's wall overlooking the garden at Hampton Court.

123

"I wonder if my aunt ever stood at this very window contemplating her next moves, feeling as isolated as I do for all of England?" Cecil knew but remained silent. The king studied the blooms in the east garden. "If only a king's life could be so wonderful as a garden," the king said quietly, maintaining his gaze below.

*****

Standing near a window, King James re-read the petition obtained from the Millenarian Puritans. Even his private mutterings sounded angry to Cecil, sitting at the table, awaiting a response. "Why, exactly, do they object to these things, Salisbury?" the king asked testily.

"Which, Majesty?" King James scoffed bitterly.

"All of them, really!" came the reply as the king sat at the table, shaking his head in complete disbelief. "Demands, but not a single reason supporting their position on any of them." He placed the parchment on the table, searching for the thousand signatures. They weren't difficult to locate.

"I will say I do not like the contemptible complaints against the established Church of England. What do they have against making the sign of the cross at a baptism? Why do they object to clergy wearing vestments? In the name of the saints in Heaven, why do they object to the use of a wedding ring in marriage?" The king paced anew.

"I object having a wife who converted to Catholicism, but I am not about to do away with her." The king shook his head. "No, their demands are not reforms. They are complaints against a specific group. What is next? Shall we refrain from attending religious services due to objections of clouds in the sky on the

124

fourth Sunday of the month?" Returning to the table, King James forcefully retrieved the petition, shaking it.

"No, this petition is rejected forthwith. However, the matter is not over. This requires a greater discussion than a mere royal decree." James pondered. "Set a conference at Hampton Court in the new year. Be sure it follows the twelve days of Christmas, so as to prevent any further demands, as they are, being added to this ridiculous petition."

"Yes, Majesty." The king asked what month it was.

"June, the middle, Majesty."

"Good, that allows me some seven months to gain additional insight into this disturbing matter. Contact Whitgift in Canterbury. I want to see him here within a fortnight's time specifically regarding this petition. Is he aware of it, do you know?"

"I know not, Majesty, but I am sure he's heard of its existence. Talk of church matters always spread quickly, particularly in these times of change. Will there be anything else, Majesty?"

"No, Salisbury, at least not presently. We are off to Oatlands for a week of hunting. Shall you be joining the party?" the king inquired, walking to the door opened by a page.

"In several days, Sire, following completion of business here."

"Very well, Salisbury. I shall see you at the pheasant hunt on Sunday afternoon. I am informed the weather is splendid." Cecil stood as the king departed the room. Asking the page to close the door, Cecil began his letter to John Whitgift, Archbishop of Canterbury.

*****

News of the Hampton Conference both mollified and excited Puritans in the House of Commons in Parliament, where two members, Sirs Edwin Sandys and Thomas Smythe were in discussion over dinner at Sandys' home. The ladies were in the garden, and the men discussed recent issues. Sandys offered sherry.

"I grant it gives us true support for King James," he told Smythe. "Yet, my focus is, and remains, one of finances and profit for investors." Smythe could only agree.

"I quite understand the tenuous business position we both are in with every investor until the first permanent settlement is established, and the profits came back to investors." The men joined the ladies in the garden until the announcement for dinner.

The death of Queen Elizabeth once more slowed the process of obtaining a royal charter, or patent, for even the first colony. A new level of frustration on the part of eager investors, all prepared to reap unknown financial windfalls, had seen the withdrawal of even more funds from the pool of economic resources originally started over three years earlier, when the East India Company was established. Yet it required royal approval through a patent, also called a charter, before any trading could begin. Time, as it seems, is money.

"I am of the opinion it will take some time for King James to work through the bureaucracy in English politics," Sandys surmised as his servant entered the garden, announcing the first course to be served in ten minutes time.

*****

John Carr was announced in Robert Cecil's castle quarters. Immediately, Cecil recognized trouble.

"Mr. Cecil, jealousy and avarice are with His Majesty," Carr stated with true concern. Cecil was up.

"You mean Lanish and Dorsey?" he asked. Carr nodded.

"We must interrupt whatever they are planting against someone." Cecil looked for the letter to Whitgift to show the king as a ruse.

"Let's go," Cecil said, leading the way out, breezing past the pages jumping to attention as the pair swept from the room.

A page announced the pair, surprising the two men. Dorsey abruptly stood, followed by Lanish. They nodded their recognition of Cecil and Carr, begging the king's permission to depart. Once gone, Cecil presented the king with his letter to John Whitgift. In turn, King James said he didn't need to see it. He was expecting the Archbishop in several days.

"Majesty," Carr said carefully. "Your two previous guests are known to be malicious scoundrels." The king only nodded, pouring wine.

"Somerset," the king said, "I hear many, but listen to only half of them. Thank you for the input. If both of you are done, I seek to read and think before the evening meal." The pair took their leave.

In the hall, Carr said he had an idea. Advising Cecil to go ahead, Carr called a page, requesting he take a paper to Mr. Cecil's quarters. Cecil was there when the page arrived. The note read, 'ask the page of the discussion in the room with

Lanish and Dorsey'. Cecil inquired, assuring the page he was helping His Majesty.

In a quavering voice, the page replied that, "they talked of Sir Walter Raleigh, Master, and none of it good, Sir." Thanking the lad, Cecil offered him a coin. Accepting it greedily, yet thankfully, the page departed. Cecil sighed. He'd inform Carr at the dinner.

*****

On 2 July, 1603, Thomas Hooker, now fifteen years of age, born in 1588, in Leicester, England, and being of Puritan beliefs at home, made his entry to Cambridge University, where an even stronger Puritan influence pervaded the quad and the campus. His new studies, he believed would influence him for many years after their completion.

*****

Justice, at times, is not what it claims to be. On 5 July, 1603, Sir Walter Raleigh was no longer to be called Sir. Further, he was immediately stripped of every office granted him by Queen Elizabeth. His fortune dissipated in the span of several human breaths.

He, his wife, and sons were also arrested, Raleigh for treason, the family, "just because." All were taken to a suite of apartments in the Tower of London. Raleigh worked to calm his shocked family as he also attempted to figure out what had gone so terribly wrong.

*****

Richard Plascomb toiled in summer heat as his crops grew to maturity in mid-August. The plow had broken; it was unrepairable. He would be required to but a new one for the next season. The broken one was his father's, so he planned to store it for sentimental reasons.

Richard continued to think about his father, yet fewer times than in the past, and more now from memories than from absolute loss. Harvest was approaching soon, but he had to bring in the cows for evening milking, feed the three horses and chickens, and slop the pigs. He had so much to do all the time. He wished there were more hours in the days.

He could tell afternoon sun was beginning to set lower daily. Another season was approaching its finale. Hopefully, a profit could be realized to allow for the new plow and more fabric for Cecelia and his mother. The plow would reduce profits, but he'd have them to buy the plow, an absolute necessity on a farm.

Four weeks later, in mid-September, a daughter was born to Richard and Cecelia. They named her Ellen. They celebrated with a roast chicken dinner, cooked by both grandmothers. The Plascomb family was growing, and Christian was curious about the new arrival. He' never heard so much noise from something so small, going about the house much of the time with his hands covering his ears, much to his parents' humor. They understood.

*****

William Dorsey sat stoically during the third day of the trial of Walter Raleigh on charges of treason in the Great Hall at Winchester. The trial was moved to Winchester because plague had erupted in London.

Dorsey sat distantly from his colleague, Lanish, to prevent any possible taint or question of impropriety. Others responsible for Raleigh's fall from the celestial heights of royal grace sat blended into the packed court as testimony of evidence was offered forthrightly by Sir Edward Coke. Anyone listening to all the proceedings over the previous three days would consider the evidence -even the best of what Coke declared- was circumstantial at best.

Yes, Raleigh had engaged in privateering, but all funds were submitted to the queen at haste. True, he had monopolies in the wine and cloth trades, but both were sanctioned by the queen at her discretion. He paid his required taxes. His alleged plan to kill the king and his children, and establish Arabella Stuart, James' cousin, to the English throne, were alleged in a letter by Raleigh's supposed co-conspirator, Henry Brooke, Lord Cobham.

Raleigh's counsel advised that Cobham was the "only" witness, and all evidence was conjecture, hearsay, and, thus, were not true liabilities.

There was a rest, or break, taken while the judges of the King's Bench conferred on merits of evidence. Despite the cold November day, Raleigh retreated to the Westminster garden. Fresh air would revive him, he thought. In a secluded room in the east wing, Robert Cecil and Robert Carr observed Raleigh in the dreary mist and coldness of the late morning hour. Cecil addressed Carr.

"The verity of any matter is lost to that which bears the invisible imprint of royal imperator," Cecil said quietly, pulling his scarf closer to his neck. Carr maintained his silence, and Cecil suspected his own position was correct. He decided to engage his own silence, suggesting they return to the court.

Upon entering the court where all manner of chatter resulted in a buzzing hum to the ears from all the talking going on in every space, one of the judges spotted Carr, who, seating himself alongside Cecil, furtively touched his right index finger to a point just below his left ear, moving his finger along his neck to the midpoint, as if scratching an itch. The same judge returned to the deliberations.

"I suspect a good meal on this night," Carr said socially, adding, "as cold as it is this November." Cecil only nodded, all attention suddenly focused on the judges' panel. The announcement for all to resume was made. Cecil was stunned. It hadn't even been fifteen minutes since the break was announced!

Cecil understood these kinds of trials. They usually never favored the defendant under any circumstances. People were returning; Raleigh returned to the box. A hush descended quickly when the accused appeared calmly. He briefly caught Cecil's eyes. Suddenly, Carr stood and left the court, stunning Cecil once more. He moved not. There was no telling who was in the court observing whom at this point. Cecil firmly realized any individual could be in Raleigh's unfortunate position. He sighed; waited, but not long. All was quiet. The presiding judge addressed the entire court.

"Walter Raleigh, in light of all the evidence that has been made public here today, this seventeenth day of November, 1603, this court fonds you guilty of high treason." The loud audible gasp from the court led rapidly to loud verbal outcries, quickly halting procedures. The chief judge ordered a silence, but the calls grew louder. A gavel, however imposing in its applied charge, produces only so much sound. The sound of human outrage against injustice is louder. Sheriffs were called; the chief judge continued unabated.

"Walter Raleigh, being found guilty of high treason, you and your family will be held in continuum in the Tower of London until your execution by beheading on twelve December 1603 at the Old Palace Yard. This court is adjourned!"

The feeble gavel fell again with unheard finality. The judges departed as furious outcries only grew louder and more significant. Raleigh was taken away. Cecil thought it best to depart as well. There could be more than one neck at stake, he calculated.

Meanwhile, passing out of the court, Cecil noticed Lanish and Dorsey shaking hands in a waiting area, both wearing callous smiles of dubious victory. Jealousy and avarice know no bounds, Cecil thought to himself, exiting to the wet coldness of an English November afternoon. Once outside, away from the catcalls and shouting, Cecil knew he had to intercede on Raleigh's behalf, but he also had to do it carefully.

Having slightly more than three weeks to speak about it with the king, Cecil considered a piece of his father's sage advice. He had told the young Cecil at one time to, "wear a mask and work invisible." Cecil was determined to do just that.

*****

Richard Plascomb sat counting the remainder of the money he could claim for profit following the sale of his marketable crops. Cecelia sat close to him holding three-month-old Ellen, who fed copiously. Beside her stood Christian, studying she who gained all their mother's attention. Cecelia thoughtfully stroked her son's almost white hair as she watched Richard count, recount, and record what he did finally decide was a correct accounting.

"We need more land," Richard said wearily. "But, with such low profits, it'll be impossible to buy that tract connecting to the farm along the southeast."

"Maybe next year, Richard," Cecelia replied confidently, realizing her husband's annual post-harvest frustrations were returning. She knew instinctively, too, that by Christmas, a mere three weeks away, typically saw the ebbing of Richard's frustrations in the providence of the Holiday season. Cecelia was proud of Richard for negotiating with their neighbor, the

132

Farmer Bunhill, and buying his used plow. The excellent price for which he bought it hardly cut into the profits, saving them a tidy sum. Cecelia said it looked to her that the plow appeared hardly used at all.

"I love you, Richard Plascomb," she said, encapsulating all her feelings about not having 'more' as Richard typically put it. Richard looked for the coins to his wife.

"You love me even though we don't have more?"

"That's one reason why," she replied caringly, nodding to their children. "And these are two additional reasons." She smiled, brightened. "Oh, and Merry Christmas!" Richard offered a look of true surprise.

"What, Christmas already?" he exclaimed so sharply that Ellen jumped. "Sorry, love," he said, picking-up Christian.

"I love you too, Cecelia, and, yes, Merry Christmas." Richard shook his head. "Blimey, Christmas already!" he expressed, looking to Cecelia. "Where does the time go?"

"Tis the tenth of December, Richard!" Cecelia cried, laughing at his forgetfulness, or preoccupation with harvest and selling for some wages. Richard looked to his son.

"Tis nearly time to find a new tree, Christian." The boy smiled, shifting his attention from Ellen to his father.

"Christmas tree," he repeated, clapping his hands. Father and mother smiled at their son, the father's frustrations already ebbing upon learning of Christmastide.

   Ah, woman, the embodiment of balance between strength and harmony. It is that kings should be as wise as you.

*****

Walter Raleigh stood once again before the council of judges almost fifteen pounds lighter than his first appearance. Robert Cecil, Earl of Salisbury, sat as far from the judges as possible, obscured by a tall man sitting in front of him. He had spoken with King James regarding his forty years of knowing Raleigh, and information from his father stretching back further.

The king listened attentively over the dinner they shared at the castle, progressing through multiple courses and chatting guests. The king may have been filled with holiday cheer, telling Cecil he would strongly consider the matter. He had done what he could by wearing his mask and working like a silent shadow behind the scenes. Now he sat in the court awaiting whatever the king had decided as the court came to order and the leading judge spoke.

"This court has received a motion set forth by the good King James I of England to stay this execution. The panel of judges has counseled and a decision is reached. This court has ruled to honor this royal motion. Therein, Mr. Raleigh's execution is stayed until any other time. He is to be remanded to the Tower with his family indefinitely." The gavel banged. "This court is adjourned." The room exploded with cheers for Raleigh. Cecil decided he could stop sweating now. He stood to depart in the spirit of Christmastide.

*****

On Christmas morning, Cecelia welcomed Richard's sisters, Elizabeth and Mary, two and three years younger their brother, respectively, and their husbands and children for Christmas dinner.

Christian had five cousins to play with on this snowy, windy morning. A Christmas bowl had been prepared, a fire roared in the hearth, along with the goose Cecelia made every Christmas. Edward, Mary's husband, said he always looked to enjoy Cecelia's and her mother's Christmas pudding. Glasses filled to their brims, toasts were made around the table as happy Christmas festivities began.

Part One, Chapter Eleven

January 1604 – December 1604

Depending upon one's perspective, a flurry of excitement or trepidation was clearly evident for attending the Hampton Court Conference on opening day on 20 January 1604.

Members of the Church of England, or the Anglican Church, were largely represented by bishops arriving wearing official church vestments, including staffs and miters, the scalloped-shaped hats worn by bishops as a sign of ecclesiastic position. The bishops represented the governance of churches by way of an episcopacy, or a governing body by bishops, providing a colorful splendid display of religious formality and respect due the conference.

Contrarily, Puritan clerical representatives, mostly ministers and select lay men from individual congregations, arrived wearing simple black shirts or clothing displaying no reference to any church office. Puritan delegates to the conference felt confidently bolstered in their reform positions based on the king's well-known stand in support of Calvinist leanings. His deep religious convictions were understood, though unseen in practice by the common people. But faith is hope with optimism, and Puritans from across England arrived at Hampton Court in distinctly self-confident, courageous spirits, prepared to push for newer and more reforms in what they considered a religion too close to Catholicism in doctrine, teachings, and overall permissiveness, based on its openness to all.

Both sets of representatives acknowledged one another with the least in civil decorum and ironic unreligious contempt and mistrust. King James, though, remained ingratiating, gregarious, and affable in his cheerful greetings to all those attendees with whom he engaged. He worked easily in bridging the unspoken chasm between those who supported the religious status quo, and those seeking reforms they maintained had been heavily stifled under the late Queen Elizabeth and John Whitgift, Archbishop of Canterbury. Puritans were keenly aware the aging Whitgift was present at the conference, which could be taken as the first indication of James' position presently known only to himself. Not even Cecil was privy to the king's position.

The Archbishop, Whitgift, opened the conference with a reading from the Common Book of Prayer, much to the surprise of Puritans, who rebuked the book and refused to use it.

"Perhaps His Majesty has forgotten how we seek to move from that prayer book," one Puritan minister whispered to his neighbor, who merely nodded. With the invocation concluded, the king officially opened the conference, leading with some royal observations, most sounding like a reminiscence of a historical path leading to the conference.

*****

John Smith jauntily boarded a Dutch trading vessel departing Tangiers, Africa, setting sail along the sunny northern African coast in the Mediterranean Sea to Alexandria, Egypt. From Alexandria, he planned to visit Cairo. When the crew discovered Smith had fought for the Dutch against the Spanish, they cheered him, making him an honorary shipmate.

Smith had fully regained his health and his shoulder functioned perfectly. A sealed puncture wound was the only remnant of the original wound from being shot in battle. He knew he was lucky. The crew respected him more, allowing Smith to assist with setting sails on the thirty-ton vessel as it

ventured into the westward winds blowing across the
Mediterranean.

The sun, hot and bright, lay ahead; the winds were at his back.
Smith's skin had turned a deep ruddy tan, highlighting his
greying beard. John Smith felt very much at home sailing across
countries and continents.

*****

For three days of discussion, dissent, and argument, King
James remained an almost invisible silent participant in the
Hampton Conference. However, on the third day, he rose to the
forefront forcefully and fully, becoming the leading spokesman
and most significant proponent of rejecting Puritan demands
and reforms. His unanticipated shift from passive listener to
dispenser of final judgement shocked many, surprised some,
and was welcomed by a silent majority. Puritans had clearly
placed their faith in the wrong candidate for support.

"Plainly, Sir," King James stated firmly, almost impatiently,
addressing the Puritan spokesman. "You state you wish to
eradicate the wedding ring in marriage, do away with baptismal
blessings, and, among other demands, abolish all clergy
vestments. All formality of religious service must go away.
Church governing is to be done by the presbytery method, that
is, independent control by ministers, and, according to you,
wearing any rag of choice, joined by hand-picked lay
representatives." The kings voice began rising with additional
force and directness.

"Do away with the bishops!" he railed. "Eradicate all church
hierarchy!" The king snatched-up the Millenary Petition from a
table of documents, waving it in the air. "Am I correct in in my
most initial and fundamental summation of your demands, both

outlined in your petition, as well as the three days of discussion here?" The Puritan spokesman briefly looked to the delegates before addressing the king.

"Your Majesty, in- "

"No, Sir!" the king speedily interrupted. "It was an interrogatory, answerable in a simple 'yes' or 'no'."

"Yes, Your Majesty, you are correct in your summation." King James tossed the petition back to the table.

"I thought so, Sir. Tell me, what shall we do next? Shall we destroy all the cathedrals and churches because your professed adherents to your faith discount them on the opinion that they are grand?

"If your presbytery council disagrees with a royal decree or edict, shall you form an army and declare war upon the Crown?" The question shocked many on both sides of the argument. An audible gasp sounded through the hall. The question posed one of high treason. King James was unaffected.

"Do you see where I am going with all this, Sir?" He turned to the delegates, shouting the same question to them. The king began striding across the floor, his voice searing, intense, bordering on malicious.

"Religious anarchy will be the direct result of continued unchecked reformation of the established church order. That said, the conformity to ecclesiastic matters is paramount in the church in which I am the supreme head. This prattle regarding your desired reforms is denied. They are anathema to the Church of England and the people of this realm. Thus, nonconformity to established Anglican doctrines shall not be tolerated.

"Further, Richard Bancroft shall immediately replace John Whitgift as the Archbishop of Canterbury. His continued support in religious matters was regarded as absolute authority under the direction of my late aunt, Queen Elizabeth.

"Additionally, I urge the committee to draw-up a constitution and canons against all nonconformists. My compromise will be a complete reworking of the Bible, in accordance with Puritan demands for an updated version. Richard Bancroft, with my oversight, shall lead this endeavor." The king stood on the floor between the opposing sides, Puritan leaders in a troubled disappointed silence.

"Have you any further questions?" King James asked the Puritan speaker, and his response was firm enough.

"Your Majesty, you did sign the Negative Confession in 1581, supporting the Puritan position." The king contemplated this, but only briefly.

"Mr. Bloom, have you ever done something in your youthful life that, with fuller insight, and, as is the way of life, greater hindsight, you would have not done?" King James paced like a tiger waiting to pounce. Bloom understood where the king was heading with this logic. What he didn't know was how armed and ready the king was to discredit him before the entire convention. Bloom sought to refrain from boxing himself into a corner. Contrarily, the king, rich in both external eyes and ears, was already aware of Bloom's position. The die had been cast; the Puritan position was seriously deflated. Bloom responded wearily, feeling the looks of castigation from his own behind him.

"You Majesty, I am at a loss to construct a specific event, but, yes, I am sure there was something I may have done, or done differently."

"Of course there is, Mr. Bloom. Man's nature is to make mistakes. I assure you I would not have signed the Negative Confession on this day, nor the day I did in 1581 at the young age of fifteen, and only two years on the throne of Scotland."

"I understand your message, Your Majesty," Bloom responded, understanding the Puritan cause lost. The king strode back to his cathedra.

"Of that I am positive, Mr. Bloom," King James said, turning to face the attendees at his cathedra. "I tell all of you!" he shouted mightily to the rafters, looking at all in attendance. "Experience has taught me to resent Presbyterian clericalism. For I tell you all here today, no bishop, no king!

"The constitution of canons shall be drawn-up. Richard Bancroft shall be installed as the Archbishop of Canterbury. This conference has allowed us to bear witness to that which we hold so dear to the salvation of our souls. Conformity is the word of the day! Conformity to the established Anglican Church is the order of the day! As head of that church, I decree it! And, by the divine right of kings, I expect it and shall have it! These are the words of our Lord. This conference is ended. Go forth in peace and conformity."

King James and his ministers, including Cecil, departed, leaving the valiant and the vanquished to clean-up the details of the day.

*****

141

By March, 1604, the king's message reached the furthest points from London, and Puritans began sensing a new round of persecutions not seen since the reign of Queen Mary, Elizabeth's half-sister, known as Bloody Mary, due to her making martyrs of many Protestants. Congregations throughout England, all independent of the others, began to shape their religious services along varying degrees of the new rule of conformity.

Some merely adopted minor reforms in a specific church. As with all reactions to forced rulings, others deviated more, adopting as many reforms as possible. In Scrooby, the congregation severed all ties with the Church of England, becoming ardent Separatists in complete violation of the king's command.

William Brewster took the demand to conformity as a signal of approaching persecutions. His word to his congregation was to practice their religion as they saw fit. They were so many miles away from the centers of power that they would never be confronted with problems. But Brewster was unaware of the will of King James I.

*****

Parliament convened in March, 1604, to its typical pomp. Members of Parliament, especially those in the House of Commons, were particularly interested in the king's dealings with them as a political body. Many were Puritans, but the king had not been informed of whom they were. He didn't particularly care.

King James took his place in the House of Lords, from where, in his chair, he could see straight through to the Speaker's chair in the House of Commons. Yet the joyful feelings shared between a new Parliament and a new monarch were already strained and tainted for both parties. The king's position on religious matters set the stage for additional political difficulties. Parliament does not forget. As Parliament convened, its members were already angry, and the king was unmoved as much to Puritans' existence as he was to the level of Parliamentary irritability.

Cecil understood this but remained silent, allowing the king to feel hostility on his home front. The opening ceremony passed with a chilling formality. When King James entered his request for a special fund for supporting the Crown, members later refused. The iciness that opened the new session became glacial when the king, deciding he'd had enough, thanked this, "large advisory council" for his tour. He also looked forward to another at, "some point in the future." When the king and his entourage departed Parliament, anger erupted into a vocal cacophony.

*****

Summer arrived, and with it came the dreaded yellow fever. John Winthrop, now sixteen, was severely ill with fever at Trinity College, Cambridge. Beyond his illness, Winthrop disliked university. He felt, "despised and neglected" because he was not socially adept, looked down on others less fortunate, and eschewed the "pointless comradery" of his peers. He realized he'd been deprived of, "youthful joys" living as he did at Groton Manor, friendless and wealthy.

During his recuperation from the fever, Winthrop experienced a religious awakening. He felt transcended, believing he'd been specifically selected by God -a living saint- and he was to live a better life leading others. Winthrop decided to leave university at the end of term and return to Groton Manor. He was very excited about informing his mother, Anne, a very pious woman,

143

of his religious experience. He would finish studying law in the solitude of the sprawling manor house. He sat to write to his mother of his decisions.

*****

King James laughed mockingly when his favorite, John Carr, sitting with his other favorite, George Villiers, and Robert Cecil at their weekly conference, informed him that Parliament refused his request for support for the Crown. Carr continued.

"Parliament holds the position that you and Queen Anne spend money lavishly." That was when the king laughed.

"Carr, Carr," cajoled the king, pouring wine. "What's a king supposed to do? It is my duty to collect and spend as I see fit." He sipped, leaning forward in his chair.

"Very well gentlemen, if they won't squeeze my goose, then I shall cook theirs." He sat back. "I want a tax and customs duties levied against all merchants, both domestic and from abroad." He looked around the table. "If there are further problems with that decree, take it to the courts.

"And, while we are on this question of royal prerogatives, I intend to reinstitute the issuance of Crown patents, despite Parliament's disapproval of what it calls royal monopolies. Plan effectively, gentlemen. I understand there are a number of businessmen quite interested in investing in establishing colonies in North America." King James sighed, looked through a window to the spring day.

"If there are no additional squabbles with Parliament, or other pressing problems, Salisbury, is Sir Thomas Smythe awaiting our meeting?" Cecil nodded.

"He is, Sire. He awaits in the hall outside this room."

"Excellent, Salisbury," the king said, turning to his favorites. "You both should be informed. I have selected Sir Thomas as my special ambassador to the Czar of Russia." Both men said the choice was excellent.

"Agreed," said the king cheerfully, asking a page to announce Sir Robert. When he was announced, Smythe entered, following protocol, and accepted his seat at the table.

Sir Thomas Smythe was about to learn how his new assignment was about to slow his path to achieving a patent for the East India Company and a settlement in Virginia even more.

*****

When King James announced Richard Bancroft as Archbishop of Canterbury at the contentious conference in January, he had no idea the ailing Whitgift would die in February. On 10 December, 1604, adorned in all the formal vestments of his new office, Bancroft bravely approached the massive oak doors of Canterbury Cathedral, his bishop's staff in-hand. Sweat seeped from under his white miter, despite the cold day. Behind him waited a double-line of multiple attendants to the ceremony.

Standing in front of the great doors, Bancroft lifted his staff, and, using its base, banged resolutely on the doors three times, then waited. A loud voice from within the Cathedral called in response, "In the name of the Lord, God, who are you and pray tell why you have come to this hallowed ground?" Bancroft took a mighty breath, shouting back in response.

"In the name of the Almighty in Heaven, I, Richard Bancroft, have come to secure the office of Archbishop of Canterbury for

145

the preservation of the faith, the saving of souls throughout this land, and the resurrection of the dead and life everlasting!"

Within five seconds, the great wooden bars upon the doors inside the cathedral were heard being removed, the mighty doors opened. Bancroft preceded several dozen acolytes, some holding lit candles on tall pillars, others bearing ancient Bibles. They were followed by several dozen bishops and priests, all making the long ceremonial walk up the center aisle of Canterbury Cathedral in order that Richard Bancroft begin his official installation of the seventy-fourth Archbishop of Canterbury. The pipe organ player started playing, filling the cathedral with awe-inspiring music initiating the highly ritualistic ceremony.

The king carefully observed all in his ambit, aware that he and Bancroft were of the same mind on all religious matters. The call to religious conformity would be held to a stricter set of controls then they were even under Elizabeth.

*****

16 December, 1604 arrived for Richard Plascomb with the sound he was growing familiar to hearing, the first cries of a new child. Edmund Plascomb entered the world early on that cold December morning before the day's first light was apparent on the East Anglia landscape.

The year's harvest, better than the previous, allowed more profit that would now be reinvested to feed a growing family once more. Despite his joy over his new son, Richard also felt the strains of wanting that something 'more' that he and Cecelia agreed they'd otherwise be content to live without. Richard wasn't so sure now. He sat waiting to meet his new son while the midwife completed her work in the room with Cecelia and the two mothers.

146

Holding Ellen, now fifteen months, and waking Christian, two months shy of four years, he told him there was another new person, "who wasn't here yesterday." The boy jumped from the bed, having to be held from barging into the birth room. While the three waited for an inviting word, Richard, pleased of a new birth, contemplated his life half-over. Here he was, turning thirty-one in the next year, yet still on the farm where he, too, was born. In all that time, he hadn't grown in stature or profits. He wondered how he could make a better life for his growing family.

As the mind plays tricks on people, Richard suddenly thought about John Smith and Miles Standish. Had seven years already passed? They had! His thoughts raced about the passage of time, war, and family. He wondered what ever happened to those men he fought with. How had providence treated them? Did they survive the war? He hoped they did. He recalled Smith's words to him. "The desire for broader horizons shall not leave you, Richard Plascomb." Richard actually nodded when he had this remembrance. But his wanderings were interrupted by Christian.

"Father, time for a new Christmas tree?" Father studied son a moment.

"Yes, it is, Christian. What makes you ask?" His son pointed to the closed door before them.

"New voice in house again." Richard smiled benevolently. "How clever, my boy! Yes, there is a new voice, isn't there?" He tussled his son's white hair. "I can't wait to tell your mother what you told me," Richard said, laughing at the child's connection of Christmas with a new baby. The midwife opened the door with a grand smile.

"Come! Come all!" she entreated gleefully. "Aye, Christian, no running!" she called, turning to Richard, winking. "Another good job, Mr. Plascomb. All's well in here, I tell you truthfully. He's a healthy one too!" she said, taking Ellen. The three looked upon the newest Plascomb man to the family on a cold December morning before the solstice.

*****

A healthy and bronzed John Smith bounded down to the docks at Great Yarmouth with plans to head to the Yare River, roughly thirty miles due east of Norwich in the East Anglia region of England. Attempts by the captain of the Trevia to beat a storm to Gravesend, in the southeast, failed, and sever winds sweeping from the southwest forced the forty-ton vessel slightly more north to Great Yarmouth. Smith didn't care, though because he was back home in England after many years of adventure and travel.

After a few days rest in Great Yarmouth, Smith told the Trevia's Captain he planned to sail up the Yare to Norwich, then travel to see associates in Thetford, Newmarket, Cambridge, and be back in London by Christmas. Smith and the captain, who sailed all the way from Alexandria, made their way to one of the many crowded taverns ling the busy Great Yarmouth wharf.

*****

Miles Standish remained fighting with the Dutch and English against Spain in the Netherlands. Not yet twenty-one, Standish certified himself as a professional soldier, being drawn to the work and thrill of warring and soldering.

Now an officer due to his bravery and bravado, the brash Standish led his men on scouting ventures most considered highly dangerous. He possessed an uncanny sense of tracking, developing his skills of locating enemy soldiers with fatal results for the enemy.

Part One, Chapter Twelve

January 1605 – June 1606

Slightly more than a year following the Puritan rejection at the Hampton Conference in January, 1604, fifteen-year-old William Bradford sat in the small, tight-knit Scrooby congregation, solemnly listening to the unforgiving sermon being given by Minister William Brewster, whose density of words could make any listener fearful.

"So, we attempted to purify the Church of England from its vanity, its excesses, and its *corruption* of God's Holy word, but we failed." Brewster closely observed his congregants, rendering his message in deliberate, purposeful measure.

"Instead, they vilify us, by first calling us Precisians, now Puritans for being too extreme in our demands for church reform. We are criticized because a Puritan believes that *no works* will save any man from the fires of Hell!" Here, young master Bradford sensed a second stern study of gathering forces as the minister's voice increased in intense volume.

"Being Puritans as we are, then, requires a much greater demand and a greater purity and stricter obedience to God's word and His will!" Brewster shouted, pointing to the ceiling but looking at his wide-eyed flock. "Not our will, but His!

"We must reject the compromises made by others in everyday life in our efforts to be who we must be, children of God, lest we desire to burn in Hell for all eternity!" Brewster shouted, his cavernous voice ricocheting off the walls of the simple undecorated chapel.

"Scripture is the law by which we should be living every day because God's laws are all that are needed to..." here Brewster wiped his right hand across his left sleeve as if trying to wipe, or rip, something from it. "God's laws are all we need to wipe and rid ourselves of the *sin* we yet carry from Adam and Eve, this sin which we cannot rid ourselves of without a life-long effort to move away from sin to a life of grace and righteousness each and every day!" Brewster leaned forward in the pulpit.

"You all should be worried about your miserable existence. You have not been elected to visible sainthood because you are *mired* in dirty unforgiven sin! And you will *not* be forgiven -ever- until and unless God Himself chooses to gift you with His saving grace!

"Only then can you be elected to walk as a living saint as I to salvation because few achieve the ability to illustrate behavior that serves God every day -never ending!" Young Bradford felt his chest cavity vibrate from its depths as Minister Brewster excoriated his flock with prophesies of gloom and doom and unattainable living perfection.

"Remember that you are so stained by sin that you can never please the Almighty! Repent in your soul! Repent in your life, and maybe -*maybe*- God will bless you with the rare ability to walk in grace. Those Puritans who believe the second coming is upon us are wrong because only God Himself knows when Gabriel's trumpet shall sound across the heavens, announcing the end, collecting the sacred, the forgiven, and the walking saints!"

"We, here at Scrooby, must work to save your souls from eternal *damnation*! Let the Millenarians worry about the second coming! You bear a greater burden, the rescue of your own souls from the fires of eternal burning!" The minister scanned his congregation, lowering his voice for the first time in a while.

"Thus, live a life guided by, lived for, and aimed at pleasing only God." Brewster leaned forward a second time, his voice even lower. "Your eternal life depends upon it."

Brewster stepped from the pulpit, thus ending the service. Puritans held that no instruments should be played, and no music would be heard in church. Members departed quietly, the men shaking Brewster's hand, while all women nodded complacently, knowledgeable of their places in subjugation to their husbands.

William Bradford returned to his uncle's house determined to live the life described in the minister's searing sermon in order to be saved from the eternal damnation that was otherwise guaranteed to be waiting for him at death.

*****

George Calvert was maintained as secretary to Robert Cecil. Calvert, initially puzzled by the vast differences between King James and Queen Elizabeth -gender aside- quickly adapted to changes at Court and the manner in which the new monarch handled State business.

Calvert, now regularly included in the most intricate State discussions, watched silently as the king openly fawned over his favorites, always young handsome males. To Calvert, this display answered his questions about how many young English men became young rich men of privilege, including titles of nobility. Calver remained silent, observing. He also felt an intrinsic glee when the king oft times referred to his most trusted advisors as no more that secretaries, much like Calvert himself.

Calvert truly missed the late queen's direct, yet humane approach to everything. She possessed an acute ability to juggle the public and personal, separate them, and operate simultaneously in both spheres. Conversely, King James worked just enough to maintain order, and he relentlessly kept his true convictions to himself, like, Calvert thought, a strategic game of cards. The king wanted to be holding the winning hand at game's end in every situation, and Calvert couldn't blame him because George Calvert was doing the same thing. After almost six years of working in the innermost circles of the center of all power, Calvert understood how everything functioned, including the king's spoken mistrust of Parliament.

Calvert held fast to his belief that it was time for him to move outward, beyond the influence and shadow of Robert Cecil, whom he respected immensely, and begin exerting influences of his own. Calvert had set his sights on a position as a Member of Parliament in the House of Commons, assigned by the king himself. But all his plans rested on the axis of his ability to maintain his greatest secret, one which would ruin his life if known. George Calvert was Catholic.

All these thoughts tumbled through Calvert's mind as he listened to the Catholic priest state the final blessings over the tiny head of the Calvert's' first-born son, named Cecelius. Calvert, his wife, and several family members blessed themselves as the baptism ceremony arrived at its quiet, peaceful conclusion. Outside the Calvert home, where the baptism was secretly performed for security reasons, the May sunshine caused the young Cecelius to react to the sudden harsh light in his tiny face. But the air was worm, the day splendid, and the Calvert family thanked the priest as he took his leave. Their son was now a part of God's saved family.

*****

John Winthrop, now seventeen-years-old, and living back at Groton Manor, in Suffolk, England, and much to the pleasure of his mother, was married to his first wife, Mary Forth, who, at the time of the April wedding, was five years older than John, who divided his time at the manor studying law and tending to his new wife.

"I have been chosen by God to be a living saint," he told Mary, who thrived on her husband's expressed piety. Very soon after the wedding date, Mary realized she was with child. The family was pleased for the new couple.

*****

Richard Plascomb was, once again, monitoring rapid crop growth by the middle of June. He felt better having paid-off the used plow, which, by his estimation, was hardly used. He'd saved a goodly amount by electing not to buy a new one. In addition to farming and caring for livestock, Richard began erecting an addition to the small cottage to house all the children.

Gathering rocks daily, typically large boulders, all would be fitted together with mortar between them to secure them in place. Christian occasionally accompanied his father on these outings, and Richard took time to impart to his growing son, now four years, about the trees he climbed, the river where he swam in summer, and how the woods had grown since he was a boy on the same farm.

But it was on this fine June morning, too early for Christian to be awake, though the sun was rising, just only now eclipsing the eastern East Anglia horizon to Richard's right. He knew it would be a hot day, for there was not a cloud in the lightening sky. He returned with his second load of good-sized rocks, dumping them onto the earth where they would erect the remainder of the already half-erected room, when Cecelia came running, calling to him in a most-troubling manner. He dropped the wheelbarrow and ran to meet her.

"Richard!" she shouted, yet running, but closer. They met halfway between the new addition and the front door.

"Cecelia!"

"Come at once, Richard!" she entreated, pulling at his sleeves.

"Is it the children?" he shouted, but his wife, now pulling him along, only shook her head.

"No, 'tis your mum!" she answered breathlessly as they entered the cottage. Inside, Christian stood by his grandmother's bed where she lied motionless. He smiled upon seeing his parents.

"Granmum sleeping," he said confidently as his parents and maternal grandmother swept into the tiny room.

"Yes, Christian, she is that," his father replied, somewhat factually, looking at his mother lying across her bed on her left side. Taking her hand, Richard found it cold, too cold for a summer day or night.

"She'd just finished a cup of tea," Cecelia said, catching her breath. "She told me she felt tired; she wanted to lie down. I turned away with the beaker, hearing her moan. I tossed the beaker and came in here. She was like this. Oh. Richard!" Cecelia began crying unconsolably, Christian became aware of something wrong. Cecelia's mother also started crying into her apron. Torn between four demands, Richard steeled himself.

"Cecelia," he said so quietly that everyone stood still, focused on him alone. "Take Christian to the other room. Mind the children whilst I care for things in here. It is a as we think.

"Will granmum be alright?" Christian asked, looking to all the adults currently moving him from the room.

"Of course, son," Cecelia told him. "She's gone to see Jesus," she added, closing the door behind her. The boy asked if Jesus would like her. Cecelia worked to compose herself.

"He will, and very much," she answered, looking around for something to do.

"He will love her very much," Cecelia's mother added, taking the boy into her caring fold.

It is not so much a tendency but a bad habit of humans, who otherwise are so adept at reason and its unemotional considerations, to take for granted those we proclaim to love so dearly. Only at the moment of death do we isolate ourselves in the memory of the departed, wishing we could have had the opportunity to say those kindly, caring words that no longer shall resonate between two people. Time, the final arbiter, halts forward progression for one, leaving others temporarily halted in their frantic, foolish, and desperate desires to right the

155

wrongs left undone before it was too late. Opportunity merely knocks; death claims for eternity.

Anger is a club we wield without hesitation, while the expression of human tenderness is questioned at every turn for sincerity, intent, and objective. Those who profess tenderness and caring are viewed like an obtuse angle, somehow seeking something out of the ordinary and being out of place. They are foolish, soft-hearted, or obscure. It is no wonder death wreaks havoc on the living. They face the crumbling wall of repressed stilted tenderness they withheld for all the wrong reasons.

Richard, his eyes filled with tears, settled his loving mother aright on her mattress, covering her with her favorite woolen blanket all the way to her small straw pillow.

Stepping out of the room, closing the door, he quietly nodded, telling Cecelia and her mother that he was off to fetch the vicar, but not before asking Christian if he wanted to ride to the village. The boy agreed instantly. Together, father and son departed on one of the young, strong horses. Once more, death had come to the Plascomb farm. Richard's mother, Ann Harden-Plascomb, would be laid to rest alongside her husband, Edward, in the local Anglican church cemetery.

*****

In early September, Sir Thomas opened a letter from Sir Edwin Sandys in his office at the Czar's palace in Russia.

17 August 1605

My Dear Sir Thomas,

I write with the sincere confidence you are in good health and spirits in Russia at the service of King James I. Your details of Russian life are amazing. How different cultures are across continents. On the topic of continents, our continent of particular and mutual interest is again the subject of international speculation.

I have recently learned that the Frenchman, Samuel de Champlain has recently returned from an expedition of the northeastern coast of North America. Additional information contains details about his excursions to the same areas where our mutual business interests for colonization are focused. I am sincerely troubled by growing speculation that it is only a matter of time before we are outdone by other countries to colonize that rich unchartered land.

It is with this thought that I -and investors- anticipate your return to England in efforts to renew and solidify our interests. Our investors are once again eager for involvement, especially when word of French exploration of the region was announced.

In other domestic matters, our fellow Puritans across England are sensing a definite squeeze by the Crown in requirements to religious conformity to the Church of England. In fact, one William Brewster, a minister at Scrooby, Nottinghamshire, was brought-up to the Court of High Commission on charges of being disobedient in religious matters. It is said that Brewster ran a Separatist congregation at Scrooby. Thus, the Crown is, without question, pursuing its doctrine of religious conformity. Outlying shires are not evading the Crown's grasp as they did under Elizabeth.

Parliament, though, supports the Puritan position based on the claim that since the Constitutions and Canons against non-conformists was not ratified by Parliament, they do not carry the force of law. Brewster, for all his troubles, was finally released returning to Scrooby. He and other Separatists remain adamant they shall not conform, yet prison cannot be far-off for many, should the king choose to tighten the conformity vice.

For their part in this game of religious cat-and-mouse, the Puritans have taken again to publishing the manes of all fornicators and drunken Anglican clerics. The more Anglicans they can name, the better they think. They seem determined, too, however misguidedly, of inflicting their own brand of moralism on the entire English society. It is as if peoples' privacy is meant for public disclosure as a form of punishment. I see it as vengeance unleashed. Where could such terrible actions take us as a people? Perhaps these moral inflictions shall subside. Anglicans do outnumber Puritans by a great majority. At times, I understand why the Puritans rate such social lashings, since no one likes being told what to do, or how to live his life. These efforts seem to be their driving force.

To close, we look for your safe, healthy, and imminent return to our shores, your home. Our investors await a renewed and reinvigorated determination to obtain royal patents. King James has once again solidly secured royal monopolies on patents and charters, again to the complete disdain of Parliament. Therein we shall surely fare well in our endeavors to secure patents for colonization. God speed your safe return.

Your friend and fellow business partner,
Sir Edwin Sandys

Smythe looked through his office window overlooking the Russian city, ready to return to England and the business of colonization. Time was passing too quickly, and the French were on the exploratory move in the same territory he sought to settle over three years earlier.

*****

A frigidly cold February unfolded in the year 1606 at Groton Manor, in Edwardstone, Suffolk, in the eastern region of England.

It was snowing heavily that morning of 12 February as the family midwife, Mrs. Stowbridge, proclaimed the successful birth of John Winthrop the Younger, first child to John and Mary Winthrop. Enjoying tea before departing to her own lodgings along the snow-laden path, Mrs. Stowbridge joined the family in prayer, thanking God for the infant's God-given determination to come unto the world healthy, and despite the terrible cold. Following Mrs. Stowbridge's departure, John Winthrop returned to his law studies while mother and child slept warmly in their room close to the hearth where a servant added more wood.

*****

Sir Thomas Smythe, recently returned from Russia, was at Hampton Court on 10 April 1605, seated next to Sir Edwin Sandys, with whom he talked confidently about this pending conference. They had been assured they would receive the royal patent they had sought almost seven years to start a colony in Virginia, named for the virgin queen, Queen Elizabeth.

Joining them in the meeting were John Popham, Lord Chief Justice, Sir Ferdinando Georges, Captain John Smith, and Bartholomew Gosnold, both brought by Sandys and Smythe. Smith had met the two the previous December in Norwich. Learning of his vast experience with foreign travel and survival skills, they proposed his investment in the company and the

159

position of colony leader. Smith agreed. Gosnold's previous expedition experience merited his involvement.

   The men were discussing the benefits of colonization while they awaited the king's appearance, agreeing that new markets for English goods was a national progression of mercantilism and expanding industry. They stood when Robert Cecil was announced and entered the room, followed by his secretary, George Calvert, carrying a stack of documents.

"Do stand for His Majesty," Cecil joked while Calvert set the documents on the long table, and Cecil welcomed each of the attendees.

"I've heard of you, Captain Smith," he said, shaking hands.

"To the good, I pray, Sir Robert," Smith replied, making Cecil laugh again.

"All good, I assure you, Captain," he said, casting a quick glance to the door where pages sat waiting for orders. "His Majesty is in exemplary good spirits today, gentlemen."

"Treasury doing better?" Sandys asked humorously.

"Not really," Cecil remarked. "He's been entertaining his favorite, John Carr, so he's quite jolly at the moment."

"Excellent," Smythe remarked, pointing to the documents. "Ours?"

"Yes, and well-studied by the king, I will say. He's quite keen on the entire enterprise. Be short, precise, and pointed. I know he wants to do some hunting at Oatlands. He plans to depart as soon as we are finished." A page opened the door, calling to Cecil that the king had turned the corner of the approach hall. The men stood as he king was announced, sweeping into the

160

room wearing hunting regalia. It was well-known that all the Stuarts were avid horsemen and huntsmen. All bowed.

"A good day to all of you!" the king called boisterously. "You may sit, stand, but do not delay. There is serious hunting to be done at Oatlands." King James picked up a map, laying it open across the table. Introductions were made.

"Gentlemen, as firm as I am about hunting, I tell you I am genuinely pleased with all your plans. Sir Georges, please render your position on your patent." The men joined around the king, focusing on the map.

"Majesty, Sir John Popham and I intend to establish a colony here, in the northeast section of the North American continent, on the Kennebec River. Our purposes are to fully exploit the rich fishing described by Mr. Gosnold, who has been to the place. We also intend to utilize this colony as a place to send England's high numbers of poor and unemployed. Overpopulation at home can be successfully addressed by sending those who cannot find work to America."

"Quite literally," the king responded, having an idea. "What about convicts? Can we not send them there as well? Why not?" the king said, answering his own question. "Note that, Calvert," he added, turning to Georges. "What is the name of your colony?"

"Plymouth, Sire." King James nodded, looking to Cecil. "Papers, please, Salisbury." He accepted the document. "Show me the latitudes." Georges pointed, described.

"Our section of this set of patents is for the Plymouth Company. The royal charter calls for authorization for all the lands claimed between thirty-five degrees north and forty-five degrees north

161

latitude." The king studies the map quietly, marking the latitudes on the document.

"Right, then. Sir Smythe?"

Majesty, our segment of the patent is for the Virginia Company of Plymouth. It approximates in equal size to Plymouth Company's grant, about ten thousand square miles. We seek to start a colony between latitudes thirty-eight north and forty-one north latitude.

"Our purposes have been, and remain, the establishment of a permanent colony for the expansion of markets for English goods in the New World. We also plan to erect an outpost against any and all Spanish influences in the region. We believe there may be vast tracts of gold that may be gained by this action.

"The Spanish have been very successful at locating gold. We are sure we can do the same, especially with consideration that the geographic area in question has never been settled, and is quite fertile in many respects." The king nodded as he again marked latitudes on the map.

"All well and good all around," King James announced heartily, admiring the map. "I do understand the expansion of English industry and trade has itself manufactured a somewhat substantial group of aggressive merchants quite eager to sell our goods worldwide."

"Particularly our woolen products, Your Majesty," Calvert interjected, and to which the king readily agreed.

"Absolutely, Calvert," King James replied, taking one of the patents from Cecil, addressing the assembled.

"It is agreed among the parties that the latitude markings are noted in the patents. It is heretofore agreed that in the geographic area of overlap, neither company shall establish a colony within one hundred miles of the other." The king looked to the men gathered around him. Knowing them to be men he knew they would agree. Nonetheless, he asked for confirmation.

"Is there agreement, gentlemen?" A firm, "yes" was the response by each man at the table, shaking hands with each other, affirming their agreement with the king.

"Very well. This patent heretofore allows for the specific land masses, the right to govern the settlements, and proprietary trade with the mother country. Upon my signature to the original documents for each member of each company, and one set for the royal records, my signature puts the patents into the force of law. They shall grant both dignity and prestige of the Crown. Calvert, arrange the documents for my signature." While Calvert arranged documents, King James shared a few additional words encouragement.

"Gentlemen, there is, in England, an understood, if not practicable emphasis on individual enterprise, and a certain freedom to act on one's ideas. This is one such occasion that offers proof to those ends. Ever since Edward VI and his very brief reign, rest his soul, the belief that England is a select nation chosen directly by God Himself remains at the fore of our thinking. It is an idea that shall be taken to the New World, that we *are* God's select nation of people chosen by Him to go forth and multiply, here and abroad in our new home, America. This is our mission." Calvert announced the documents were ready.

"Very well, let us proceed," the king said, making his way to the table, affixing his signature to each document handed him. Cecil offered the signed patents to those in the room after Calvert applied powder to the ink, blowing-off the excess. The king stood. "It is done, gentlemen. Let the colonizing begin." Accepting the men's bows, King James moved to the open door.

"Shall you be joining us at Oatlands, Salisbury?"

"On the morrow, Your Majesty after business is complete here."

"Very well, Salisbury. I am sure there will remain some partridges with your name on them. Very well, a good day, men." The king seemed to rush from the room. The door was closed.

Thoroughly pleased with finally acquiring what had been so long sought, congratulations went around the table as the planning of the new colonies began in earnest.

*****

By late April, the Virginia Company of Plymouth eagerly financed a company ship's highly anticipated expedition to study and survey the coast of the areas defined in the royal charters. Its mission was to provide improved mapping of the region, establish possible landing sites, and determine locations most preferable for settlements. The ship departed on 21 May 1606, expecting to return by the end of July with good weather and blessed seas.

*****

George Calvert and his wife welcomed the birth of their second child, another boy, to the family in the middle of May, 1606. The birth was a prayer-answered event, though Mrs. Calvert experienced some difficulties. The baptism was secretly planned again with the priest to be conducted in a fortnight's time. The child was named Leonard.

164

*****

  Late in June, the Berkeley family of Bruton, Somersetshire, located in southwestern England, welcomed the birth of their new son, William. Though unknown at the time, his entry to the world would have a profound effect on Virginia in years to come.

Part One, Chapter Thirteen

July 1606 – January 1607

John Robinson studied at Corpus Christi College, Cambridge University, and also held a prestigious fellowship at the university. Born in Sturton-le-Steeple, Nottinghamshire, in 1575, the thirty-one-year-old Robinson, along with his wife of only two years, Bridget White, were not mistaken when they arrived in Scrooby in the middle of summer, 1606.

In a discussion with William Brewster, Robinson explained how, though he was ordained in the Anglican Church, he elected to move to the Puritan manner of religious thought. He decided for himself and his wife to move to the Scrooby congregation following the highly public reports of Brewster's charges before the Court of High Commission. Robinson was also moved to act after learning Brewster had been arrested for attempting to leave England. Brewster listened attentively to Robinson's quiet and respectable story and insights.

Following additional talks of exiting the country, Brewster learned from Robinson that Holland had become a center for those seeking religious freedoms. The Dutch, Robinson thoroughly explained, had always been an international center of acceptance to others on many levels, religious thought among those concerns.

Ultimately, Brewster welcomed Robinson and his wife to Scrooby, identifying the potential for sharing ministering duties, allowing Brewster a deserved break. Robinson first began to involve himself with an internal discussion about the possibilities of planning a departure from England for the entire Scrooby congregation. He decided to hand-over his concerns to God, allowing Him to make the decision.

Ousamequin, known as Yellow Feather, sat with his aging chieftain father and Confederation chiefs, all in a discussion with Powhatan, the hereditary chief of the Algonkian Empire. Powhatan was explaining that the centuries of existence had led the Confederation to extend their lands into the Virginia tidewater region.

Yellow Feather, now twenty-six, was well-educated in the ways of the Indian nation's history and culture. When talk turned to the slow but increased visitations by Europeans to the coats of the northeast, Powhatan said he hoped the visits would cease. If that path was not chosen, he said the English were unwelcome. He firmly stated that attempts at settlements should be resisted, ambushed, and raided as needed to drive out the English, and keep them out.

"These are our lands," he said definitively. "The Gods of the Four Corners have bestowed our nations with the bounty of these woodland lands. It is not the right of others to take them from us." Yellow Feather listened attentively as Powhatan explained that the Native Americans would not yield to the coming invasion of ghost settlers, the white men.

*****

William Brewster had decided, by early fall of 1606, through discussions with Robinson, that Scrooby was officially separated -completely broken away – from the Church of England. He announced his unilateral decision during a sermon, making unmistakably clear the Separatist direction he and his congregation were taking.

"There is no room for compromise when the souls of a demanding God are in the balance," he declared softly yet sternly. "My recent arrest for attempting to leave the country illustrates the extent the king will advance in his efforts to *force* religious conformity upon all.

"We Puritans shall neither be coerced to lessons from the Book of Common Prayer, nor shall we perform superfluous motions that mimic both Catholicism and Anglicanism. They remain virtually the same in scope, only the Pope's influence divides them in belief. They are not us, and we not them. Never shall we be in union." He looked severely at the congregation as he contemplated how to address the remaining segment of his message.

"Now comes our time to look to the horizon for the Host of Hosts and His determination about our future. I remain in fervent prayer for all of us seeking His direction and desires for us. Shall we stay, or should we depart? I cannot say until He invokes His voice within me to set the path, be it on land or at sea. Amen!" Brewster shouted so suddenly and loudly that the entire congregation jumped in union. Then, Brewster planted the seed of coming change. "But, rest assured that if we are to depart, pray it is together in union with one another and God's will." Brewster concluded the service.

*****

"I'm not so sure about your idea, Richard," Cecelia said flatly over tea one evening in late September 1606. To underscore her negative feelings about the entire idea, she shook her head with sincere affirmation, making her position on the issue voiced and confirmed. The 'idea' Richard had proposed was reflected in an emigration pamphlet that made its way to Norwich, Richard obtaining a copy. Ever since its arrival the in August, Richard talked about nothing else but Virginia.

The pamphlet read:

Nova Britannia

OFFERING MOST excellent fruites by Planting in Virginia. Exciting all such as be well affected to further the same. Inquire at the listed office.

Under those words, a drawing of a three-master ship, sails and English flag unfurled in the wind over the ocean offered a visual invitation to something new, a completely new world. The pamphlet, offering the opportunity to all emigrants, was printed in London by Samuel Macham.

Richard claimed it was the chance of a lifetime. Cecelia countered by declaring it was a lifetime of chance. In her deepest sense of self, she knew they would go, but not before she protested in self-assured earnestness for the safety of their children and themselves. She had no idea what to expect because East Anglia was all she had ever known. They talked; she refuted. He cajoled; she rejected. He became pig-headed and determined. Cecelia became withdrawn, drawing onto herself and the children, not against their father, but against his ceaseless dreams of 'more'. Ultimately, the decision was Richard's. They sold the farm in October, and Cecelia placidly listened to Richard's extolling of the great profit they garnered from the deal. She only knew their home was gone. Cecelia had her wits, her will, and her children. She required nothing more from her husband.

By December they were on their way to meet those sailing from Gravesend to Virginia. Cecelia could fathom no more than what was questionable, if not disastrous, winter sailing. Instead of a Christmas tree, there would only be harsh, cold water and unknowing results from this misadventure. She reflected upon her in-laws and her mother, who died in late August. They were

169

secure in the ground and safe in Heaven. Perhaps, she thought, the entire family would be joining them.

Contrary to Cecelia's feelings of trepidation, Richard was fully convinced his opportunity to succeed had arrived. The shiny carriage he hired to take them to Gravesend, East of London, was the first in a succession of acquisitions Richard was realizing money could buy.

*****

Following very praiseworthy reports of endless sources of timber, teeming fishes, superb weather, and fertile soil after the return of the Virginia Company's expedition vessel in late July, the directors of the Virginia Company of Plymouth agreed, prior to a Christmas break, to organize an expedition to settle a site on one of the northernmost allowable latitudes in their patent.

Due to its prominent position on the North American continent, they referred to the new settlement as 'The Maine' settlement, deciding to officially name it at a later date. Said date was set for good weather in May, 1607.

*****

Christian Plascomb had never slept at an inn. Wide-eyed and highly curious, he relished the new foods, smells, and sights of many people together at the inn at Gravesend. A hearth, larger than one he'd ever seen, radiated pleasant warmth throughout the spacious, candle-lit, eating room, where a collection of children of all ages met his wonderous blue eyes. They were all as curious as he about the boisterous talk and excited atmosphere among the large crowd. A Christmas tree in the corner of the room to the right of the hearth reminded him of the time of year, but it was the sole sense familiarity he could connect to the holiday. The crowd, décor, and the talk of a new house played on his short attention span as several children ran

170

past his parents' table. The talkative man sitting with his family also held Christian's attention, and his father seemed to know him well. They were currently talking seriously, while his mother tended to Ellen, now three, and Edmund, who was two.

Captain John Smith and Richard Plascomb had met the previous day soon after their arrival at the inn. Richard couldn't forget the bearded face, and Smith said he recalled Plascomb's youthful face. Though Smith was not married, Cecelia felt reassured with the feeling of knowing at least one person in control of the entire operation upon which they had embarked with about a hundred strangers to a foreign land to establish this place called Virginia.

Presently, several men and their families approached the Plascomb table. Standing, Smith made introductions all-around. The tall gentleman was Christopher Newport, Captain of the ship Susan Constant. The second man, short, stocky, but genuinely amicable, was Bartholomew Gosnold, Vice-Admiral of the ship Goodspeed. The third man was John Ratcliffe, Captain of Discovery. Their wives and children were also introduced, relaxing Cecelia's anxiousness. As women instinctively sense that which men do not, Newport's wife, Barbara, worked her way around the now-crowded table to Cecelia as the men talked of problematic winds, and women tended to all the hungry noisy children. Just as Cecelia raised her eyes to Barbara, the attractive brunette woman, who looked to about thirty-five, told Cecelia, "just a moment, please." Turning, she shouted to all within earshot.

"Hear now!" she exclaimed so forcefully that men stopped talking, children stared wide-eyed, and she had the attention of all. The slender woman in full skirts began giving orders.

"You lot," she said, pointing at the men. "To the bar with you whilst we tend to these hungry little ones – shoo!" With a wave of her supple hand, the men moved to the other room as directed. Gosnold's wife laughed, looking to Cecelia.

"Watch and learn, Cecelia. Barbara knows her mothering," she said approvingly, placing a reassuring hand on Cecelia's shoulder. Barbara wasn't done yet as she turned her attention to the older siblings of all the families.

"Now, this rowdy lot," she intoned, referring to the gaggle of tow-headed children, unsure adolescents, and bored moon-eyed teenagers. The age range was quite wide.

"You lot- the older ones – boys and girls - set to seating the little ones at the table - now." They all moved, seating younger children, whether or not they were siblings. Barbara turned to Cecelia.

"You have to know how to handle them, my dear," she told Cecelia, winking. Stopping several serving girls, Barbara ordered beers all around the table, and house dinner to be served as soon as possible to all the children. The servers agreed instantly. Cecelia almost laughed aloud watching Barbara control the show as beers were soon placed around the table. Barbara sat beside Cecelia. Ann Gosnold addressed the older kids standing behind their charges.

"We mothers shall talk. You shall assist the children as needed. You will remain until your dinner arrives. You shall be young ladies and gentlemen. Am I clear as a window?" A chorus of agreement was the immediate response. Food began arriving, and the older siblings helped everyone's children.

"Even the boys help?" Cecelia asked with surprise. The nods from both women reassured Cecelia even more. Mrs. Newport addressed the three women.

"Captain Newport commands the ship at sea, but I command the house on land," she declared righteously, enjoying some beer. "A ship captain's wife spends a great deal of time alone with her children. She must command or suffer mutiny at home."

"Do not ask them to do," added Mrs. Gosnold. "You direct them to do." Barbara agreed affirmatively, turning to Cecelia.

"You appear troubled, dear. I sensed it. Have you ever sailed?" Cecelia shook her head.

"Never. We've lived our whole lives on a small Norwich farm. This is my husband's idea. I'm not I favor of it. That I can tell you, ladies," she said, watching Christian and Ellen eat hungrily with the other children. Also, Cecelia was quite astounded how all the children, all fourteen of them, resembled each other. A majority had nearly white hair, except for several red heads and three brunettes. Most had blue eyes and alabaster skin. Even their helpful smiles were similar. The older kids started sitting to eat as their dinners arrived. More beer followed quickly.

"I'm surprised how the boys help so easily," Cecelia noted. "It's as if they know what to do." The other women laughed as they drank some beer.

"Of course they do, Cecelia," Barbara exclaimed with some amusement. "They only need some direction. They are the other half of the parent equation," she added, studying the older ones. "It will be very soon for some of them, too, from the looks of them."

"It comes naturally if you guide them along," Ann added as their dinners arrived, and the men returned to join in eating.

The women talked while the men planned the voyage once again, reminisced about past war and fighting, and the children settled to eating and quiet talk. Cecelia relaxed after several beers and a good meal. She'd never had the experience of discussions with other women besides her family. It was a new and exciting experience.

By evening's end, everyone was helping children to bed, and looking to some earned sleep. Nerves were on edge because the three ships were departing in the morning. Sleep was difficult for some, easy for others, but even a fitful rest was preferred to none.

The following day was cold but sunny. Final details were checked as all began boarding. Winds were studied; water observed. Winds were questionable, but only setting sail and being on open water would give a true indication of sailing conditions. Embraces were shared as Barbara and Ann boarded their husband's vessels. The Plascombs sailed aboard Discovery with Captain Smith, selected as one of the seven councilors of the new colony. On 30 December, 1606, Sarah Constant, Goodspeed, and Discovery set sail from Gravesend, leaving behind families, memories, and a lifetime for all intrepid enough to dare establishing a new colony and new lives in the far reaches of the North American continent.

*****

Sir Edwin Sandys officially became the director of the East India Company in mid-January 1607. Simultaneously, he joined the Virginia Company at Plymouth. While his activities in the business ventures expanded, Sandys began expanding his influence in Parliament by continuing to represent opposition to King James' policies behind the scenes. Ironically, he managed to balance his position within the king's favor, yet Sandys was content to straddle two worlds.

Company plans to send the colonizing expedition to the 'maine' coast in May remained in effect. A crew was chosen, as had some individuals electing to be settlers. George Popham, Sir John's nephew, was chosen to command the entire voyage and settlement to be called Phippsburg at the mouth of the Sagadahoc River. The Gift of God and the Mary and John would sail together from Plymouth. While Sandys accepted his new position at the East India Company over a celebratory dinner hosted by investors, the crews of the expedition vessels began planning stores, provisions, and exciting new lives abroad.

*****

The Muscovy Company, a joint-stock investment company started in 1554, and governed by Sir Thomas Smythe, had been planning an expedition led by a highly experienced sea captain able to locate a shorter, less-expensive route to the Orient. Cathay, or North China, remained an elusive exotic market for new trade, especially spices, including the most exotic and demanded of all, Piper nigrum, known to Europeans as black pepper. The Dutch had cornered the market on pepper in a fervent competition against the Venetians, making pepper the leading spice in world trade.

The woody plant, a vine in the pepper family, was native to the Oriental tropics. Piper nigrum bears oval, leather-like, glossy, evergreen leaves nearly three inches in length, and its flowers reveal four-inch spikes. The plant's rich, highly-sought fruit is berries borne in long clusters, called peppercorns, roughly a half-inch in diameter. New growth grows green, ripening to a bright red. Berries slowly darken to black as they dry and age. The highly-prized black pepper contains the whole fruit in a ground-up form.

Salt had been the dominant marketable spice until pepper's demand and sudden scarcity caused market prices to skyrocket across the European world. Pepper helped flavor, but it was also used to cover the taste of meats that had passed their best time for consumption.

Company directors believed that if they could identify a faster cheaper route to the Oriental East, they could either gain a monopoly on the pepper market, or, at the least, control pepper market prices through controlled distribution. The new route was first priority.

In a February, 1607 meeting, directors believed they found their captain. He was burly, barrel-chested, speaking with a booming baritone voice. He was neither shy nor quiet. He offered a hearty laugh as quickly as he could describe geographic details of foreign coastlines, or mentally calculate distance and time required to sail between any two named ports the directors named.

His young son, John, his second son, was at the meeting with his father. "Young John," as his father called him, was about nine years of age, and was being apprenticed for a life at sea, and would, one day, be captain of his own ship. Company directors, mostly Puritans, fully supported the captain's ideas, believing that the family was at the very center of any society. They also held that most of England's social ills resulted from poor or weak government of the home and family, for which the man was solely responsible and the word of family law. The mother's only responsibility was caring for children.

Therefore, a worthy endeavor of instructing one's own son in an honorable skill like seamanship could be firmly supported by the majority Puritan company directorship. The directors agreed among themselves. Thus, this bear-like man was a fitting captain for their next expedition. The captain's name was Henry Hudson.

The expedition to locate the new Oriental route would take Hudson and his son westward, around Greenland, then south - somewhere- to Cathay. They were sure Hudson would find the new route. Following details, Hudson agreed to meet with the directors in several days before sailing from St. Ethelburga's Channel on Bishopsgate Street, London. The departure date was planned for 23 April 1607.

*****

While Henry Hudson was signing-on for a sea expedition, the three vessels that started from Plymouth to Virginia were having difficulties of their own. Bad seas and high winds kept the ships lingering off the English coast until early February before open water could be traversed. Other difficulties impinged on the sailing as well.

Aboard the Susan Constant, many watched from the other two ships while two wrapped bodies, one small, the other more adult-like, were dropped from the port side in late January. Feelings of excited anticipation visible at the inn at Gravesend had withered to furious depression and an unspoken sense of despair, predominantly among the women. At this juncture, they had been at sea almost seven weeks. This time had not acclimated everyone to the constant rocking, swaying, and pitching of the ships crossing the mighty, endless, Atlantic Ocean. Sea-sickness was rampant daily. Further, despite the freezing temperatures, mothers permitted children to run the decks to expend their youthful energy, escaping dark cramped quarters below deck. Whole families briefly braved the cold for fresh air in full contrast to the fetid dank smells permeating below.

Scurvy was the second greatest concern, followed by lice, monitored daily with a vigilant attention. Many wondered, but refrained from saying openly, anything negative. Even the

177

youngest children had stopped asking, "are we there yet?" As glad as parents were that the ceaseless questioning ended, the children's loss of enthusiasm spread to the same adults. Many wondered not if they were there, but would they *ever* get there?

Some prayed more openly than others. Puritan families prayed together on deck through wind and cold. Anglican families, more private in worship, prayed privately and fervently, often reading from several shared copies of the Common Book of Prayer. Sunny days, despite the cold, were reason enough for all to give thanks.

Cecelia rocked Edmund and Ellen, while vigilantly observing Christian, who would spend his sixth birthday at sea. Individual days, though, had ceased to be, and, now, only periods of day or night existed. Those two periods offered something guaranteed. Cecelia wondered just how long this journey would actually last.

Part One, Chapter Fourteen

March 1607 – August 1607

Eastern woodland American Natives typically lived in rectangular logged homes with thatched roofs, or roofs made from the bark of trees. Dwellings were arranged in villages covering a wide area, and each village supported around two thousand citizens. Women planted, gardened, harvested, and cared for children. Men hunted, cleared new land for new fields, and warred when necessary. Major crops were maize, beans, and squash. The societies were highly efficient and self-sustaining.

In the southeast there were five civilized tribes; the Creek, Seminole, Cherokee, Chickasaw, and the Choctaw, who tended to live in towns with familiar streets around a central square.

The Iroquois in the northeast were the best-organized confederacy, spanning distances through the northeast as far north as the 'maine' coast. Other tribes included the powerful Powhatan, who were less conciliatory to the 'ghost men', or white men than the Iroquois, who strived to maintain peaceful relations with member tribes, and offered a united front against foreign, or outside tribes. The Iroquois also worked steadfastly to maintain fair working relationships with whites upon arrival to their lands on the North American coast.

Other tribes included the Pequot, Wampanoag, Pawtuxet, Mohegan, Algonquin, Narragansett, Susquehannock's, Pamunkeys, Occaneechi, the Tuscarora, the Massachuset Tribe, and the Abenaki. Similar to European societies, except in religious beliefs and social customs, Native Americans represented a spectrum of people spanning the sociological temperament ranging from peaceful timidness to warring ferocity.

In early March, Yellow Feather tended to the village temples and burial grounds, being diligent about their upkeep and maintenance. He spoke freely with another brave assisting him in their tasks while women began plowing and planting for the new season. Yellow Feather's village was named Pakanoket, located on Narraganset Bay, near the recently-named Cape Cod. As spring unfolded, life began anew in a new season of growth and promise in the village.

Slightly north of Pakanoket, and closer to the southern portion of the 'maine' coast, twelve-year-old Tisquantum, also called Squanto, of the Pawtuxet Tribe, helped his father prepare for a hunt for the village. His summer transition to his tribe's manhood was quickly approaching. Tisquantum would soon experience the initiation rites with other young braves into the tribe's male adult population.

Even further north of Tisquantum's village, fourteen-year-old Samoset, meaning, 'he who walks over much', had undergone his Abenaki initiation rites to manhood two years earlier, and was making his mark as an excellent scout and tracker. His acute sharp observations, ability to sense a prey's presence and track it several hours after it passed was earning him much praise from everyone in the village. Abenaki means 'people of the eastern dawn'.

On this morning, Samoset led a fishing party, and everyone was assured they would eat well. As he helped prepare to start the fishing outing, the March spring found the women and older girls preparing the fields for new crops, especially maize, the main food staple. With fishing tools ready, Samoset and the other braves set-out to in good spirit to catch all the fish they could carry.

*****

One spring evening in mid-April, William Brewster, John Robinson, William Bradford, now seventeen, and a half-dozen church selectmen gathered around Brewster's table in his Scrooby home. The decision to be revealed was whether or not to depart England as a congregation. Privately, Brewster had already made his decision, telling only Robinson. Between them, they agreed to announce the plan at this gathering. Brewster had just stated the full plan, and those around the table sat absorbing the overwhelming enormity of the idea. Brewster expected the initial shock. True, it meant uprooting entire families from a homeland and property most had known their full lives. He studied the faces of those gathered around him.

"Where are we to go, Minister?" asked one selectman, thinking of his farm land, handed down through three generations, and the fourth growing into it.

"Holland," Brewster answered forthrightly.

"Amsterdam," added Robinson. Brewster had additional information to share.

"The Dutch in the Netherlands have long been a haven -open and accepting – to many religious refugees," he said. "They've welcomed Huguenots, Catholics, Protestants, and now, Puritans. The Crown is truly starting to squeeze the vice of religious conformity on all religious denominations."

"Particularly Separatists," Robinson declared, looking to the men around the table so old that its wooden surface had been worn smooth to the hand. "We are no longer in the bygone days of Elizabeth, who said one thing, but let people be. King James, on the other hand, has begun a country-wide scheme to root-out all nonconformists. No longer do we reside beyond the perimeter of accusation and police treachery over religious practice." Brewster Agreed.

"The time has come to plan our move. I plan to announce the decision tomorrow during the service. We may have to depart in discreet groups. We have not enough ships to take all at once." Robinson leaned forward.

"It must appear that all is normal in Scrooby. All sailings will depart from Lincoln in the earliest hours of morning."

"And secretly," Brewster added. "We must be sure the departures are done secretly to be able to move all of Scrooby to Holland. It may require several years, but we don't know. This we must understand and agree to. We sail up the Trent River, cross by land to Lincoln, where a ship awaits us. Upon boarding, the ship will sail down the Witham River to Boston, then enters the North Sea through The Wash, due east of Nottingham in the east."

"It is then a brief crossing to Amsterdam," Robinson stated, nodding to affirm the plan.

"I like it," said young William Bradford from across the table to the surprise of all. Heads turned to him. "The Lord God is calling his people like He did when He called on Moses to lead His people out of Egypt,' he said proudly. The men all smiled with equal pride, especially Brewster.

"Young Bradford, how right you are!" Brewster exclaimed energetically.

"And the young shall lead," Robinson declared, nodding at Brewster.

"Then," Brewster said, "it is decided and agreed. We will depart secretly with those who choose to leave early. The others follow. We depart in middle May to erect our promised land in Holland. Begin talking with your families; decide when you wish to depart. Secrecy is paramount, lest we find ourselves imprisoned." The men agreed quietly yet with a united determination. The meeting ended as all returned to their homes. Once alone, Brewster and Robinson agreed on another issue; William Bradford was a young, upcoming leader in the Scrooby community Separatist congregation. They began making formal plans to depart with the first group in less than four weeks.

*****

Henry Hudson, his son, and his crew of ten strode confidently into St. Ethelburga's Church in London on 19 April 1607. A church and its hallowed atmosphere were a far-cry from the rough-and-tumble, foul-mouthed world of a sailing ship, and it was for that very reason was a welcome respite from the mayhem and pressure of being responsible for a successful ocean venture. St. Ethelburga's Church was surrounded by popular inns and taverns on Bishopsgate Street. Hudson and his crew were introduced to congregants by several Puritan Muscovy Company directors. They also partook in the service and shared communion.

Following the service, the shipmen made their way to the docks to begin final preparations for departure in four days aboard the ship Hopewell. They slept on board, many on the open deck, due to agreeable weather.

Finally, and on schedule, Hopewell and her crew were prayed for by a Puritan minister and blessed an Anglican priest. The crew tossed-off the thick hemp tethers holding them to land, beginning their voyage to find the new route to the Orient.

*****

On a fog-shrouded Tuesday morning on 12 May, the first group from Scrooby crossed land several miles east from their small boat that took them up the Trent River from Nottingham. Repeated calls from mourning doves and other birds cracked the early, foggy, morning silence as the sixty men, women, and children crossed the unexplored English countryside, traversing tall reedy grasses flanked by dense woodlands that surrounded them. Sleeping partridges, startled to alertness by the sudden appearance of intruders, bolted skyward in an explosion of frenetic energy and boisterous calls, startling everyone, accompanied by several screams and shrieks from children. Fright subsided when the group approached Lincoln, where a second boat waited.

William Brewster handed the tillerman a green velvet pouch when he boarded last. The tillerman inspected the contents, nodding to two crewmen, who nodded in return, pushing away from the shore. The ride down the Witham River was silent, except for a prayer spoken by Brewster to boost spirits by calling upon God's will and benevolence for this journey. Acting as look-out, William Bradford prayed to himself, meaning every word. The sun started burning-off the early fog and, as it lifted like a white mist curtain, revealed a massive ship truly worthy of ocean travel. This tangible reality caused several people to weep, faithful in the belief that they were to be delivered to God's new Holy Land.

With a handshake, Brewster thanked the tillerman, for he, too, would be accused of helping escapees if caught. The group moved the ocean vessel, boarding quickly. Keeping Bradford along his side, they boarded last so Bradford could lead a group when Brewster or Robinson stayed in Amsterdam, and one of them remained in Scrooby until the final group's departure. In short time, the vessel's three masts unfurled and moved swiftly from the mouth of the Witham River to The Wash, an inlet in the eastern portion of England shaped like a squared-off capital letter 'U'. The Wash was bordered by Skegness, Holbeach, at the base, and Hunstanton to the east. The ship entered the North Sea in quick time, beginning its southeastern voyage to the Netherlands.

The winds were behind the travelers, the sun now warming the morning enjoyably. Led by Brewster and accompanied by a learning Bradford, the successful departure felt instantly like freedom, and the entire group prayed on deck in warm sunlight. Their Promised Land lay closer with every new prayer.

*****

Ten days following the first group's departure from Scrooby, a different group of travelers, more visible and greatly celebrated, threw-off the hemp ropes, moving from the docks at Gravesend. Sir Ferdinando Georges and George Popham stood waving as the two ships, under the command of George Popham, Sir John's nephew, ventured into the winds that were to take them on an expedition to observe, study, map, and start a settlement called Phippsburg on the 'maine' coast at the mouth of the Sagadahoc River. Muscovy directors, including Smythe, John Popham, and other dignitaries, waved their last to

185

the ships with great fanfare, excitement, and hopes for rapid profits as they made-way under full sail to open water and into history for the Company.

*****

Three thousand miles west of the happy crowd at Gravesend, the Sarah Constant, Goodspeed, and Discovery made preparations for landfall. When Commander Newport determined he had attained the proper latitude, he steered Sarah Constant toward a landform that projected from the mainland like a peninsula.

The weather was mild, and sight of land drew all passengers to the railings from below, marveling at the blessed sight of land - any land! Waves were smaller, the water bluer, the air fresh, and the sun warm and welcome. These elements only made thoughts of standing on firm ground more exciting and inviting.

Drawing closer to land, the pear-shaped peninsula jutted into a large bay that fed into a smaller calmer waterway. Passing into that small water body, Newport named it the James River in honor of King James. Sailing up the wide, newly-named, James River, the trio of vessels sailed almost fifteen miles before Newport spotted a site most preferable for settling. His decision made, Newport aimed for the left bank as crews raised sails and secured them. Behind Newport, Gosnold and Smith followed his lead. The three ships were quickly tethered. Newport informed the other captains of his river-naming decision. They agreed the name was proper for the occasion.

Many had true difficulties walking on land after so long a time at sea. Merely standing also proved problematic. Children found great delight in spills, falls, and wobbly knees, and this fun helped the adults forget their troubles for at least a while.

Men and boys were quickly gathered into a single group by the captains, who divided them into teams. If the voyage was tough, the harder work lay immediately ahead. Trees had to be felled, water boiled for drinking and cooking, shelters erected, game and fish sought for nourishment. That was only the start. Smith, leading his group, jumped atop a rock, cupping his hands over his mouth, and shouting joyously, "welcome all to the colony of Jamestown!" The crowd screamed its approval, and an eager feeling of new adventure overcame the travelers, helping them overcome the calamities and duration of the ocean visit. The work of establishing a new colony was underway.

Women and older girls helped carry foodstuffs from the ships, while other women worked to bathe the children in the cold James River. Land legs slowly returned as the efficient mobility of everyone focusing on the tasks at-hand. Trees fell, laughter rang-out, hammering, energetic conversations, pots and pans banged, and yelps of playing children resounded in the still spring air.

Yet the new arrivals were not as alone as they thought. Unseen but highly present, obscured by their abilities to blend into their environment like deer, natives of the mighty Algonquin empire silently observed the actions of the ghost people. They watched as giant trees started smashing to the forest ground, thundering their way, crashing with malevolent loudness. Lead scouts offered hand signals to communicate with their braves. As soon as the message was finished, scouts departed swiftly and quietly through the dense forest in the cardinal directions to begin passing the message that the ghost people were here again, apparently with plans to remain.

The clash of two distinct worlds and societies, one attempting to lay claim of land by reason of tradition and religion, the other to take it away by reason of God's will and change, was also underway.

*****

Thousands of miles north of the start of Jamestown, Henry Hudson continued his northward journey seeking the new route to the Orient guided by the North Pole. The date entered in his captain's log was 12 June 1607. He and his crew had been at sea for two months, expanding on an oceanic area initially explored by Willem Barents during the previous century.

Hopewell had been steered northward from England, into the North Sea, hugging the rugged, wind-swept Orkney Islands at the northern-most tip of Scotland. Passing them, Hudson steered a northwestern path between the Orkney's to the port, or left, and the more northern Shetland Islands on the right, or starboard side. Hudson, aware that the Shetland Islands lay slightly north of sixty degrees latitude north, he calculated that the Arctic Circle lay only another eight or nine degrees in latitude north.

Days aboard the Hopewell were pleasant with full sun. Nights, though, were extremely cold, even in summer. By mid-May, Hopewell had begun cruising past Iceland to its starboard side. A few days later, they began canvassing the east coast of Greenland. Hudson laughed, explaining to his son, John about the Vikings, who named Greenland to fool other explorers so they could keep Iceland, the more beautiful of the two.

Hopewell passed to the southwest of Reykjavik, Iceland, then northeastward of Ahgmagassalk, Greenland before steering north-northeast along the coast, moving into the Sea of Denmark and across the Arctic Circle. At Greenland's barren northeastern point, east of the northern section of Peary Land,

Hudson headed due east-southeast. By now, it was just passed the middle of June. His travels had taken him and his crew across the Greenland Sea, high above the seventy-five north latitude lines. All of Barent's recordings, coupled with Hudson's knowledge, informed him he was approaching Spitzbergen, which lay due north of Norway's most northern point, itself above the Arctic Circle. Hudson was also aware that the summer solstice was a mere two days away. From that point, days would shorten and darken one minute each day.

All the while, Hudson educated and talked with John, teaching him to use the sextant, the stars, and the sun to denote time. John also learned to calculate sailing time, and how to tell distance using the horizon. His son's favorite task was steering the ship, sometimes have difficulty turning the massive wheel with his small arms, much to the amusement of his father and crewmen.

Another crewman taught John the differences among the many whale species they encountered in their travels. He showed John the black and white killer whales with their tall dorsal fins, white belugas, the barnacle-encrusted grey whales, but John's favorite was the massive blue whale. It was fun to watch the orcas rise and dive rhythmically in unison. The belugas popped their heads above the surface looking like they were surprised to be where they were. The enormous greys lolled above the surface, curling their great bodies to dive deeply again. But when the giant blue whale reached the surface, its huge body imitating a momentary attempt at flight, it lateral fins extended like blunt motionless wings, its underbelly exposed almost joyously to the sky above, John ran barefoot around the main deck, his arms extended, his blond mane waving in the wind like he, too, could take to flight like the giant blue.

If they proved unsuccessful in the next fortnight, Hudson planned to return to England. First, though, he wanted to persevere. He yet had two weeks to find the successful route.

*****

It was a Saturday in mid-August. At the base of a palisade, young members of the Mohegan Tribe were frolicking in the cold water off the maine coast. There was a lull between spring planting and fall harvest. The youth and women took a break, allowing the children to play in the waves at a site near the village.

Atop the eighty-foot palisade, Samoset, now fourteen, and alone with one of his favorite village girls, the same age, just finished enjoying each other's bodies in sexual freedom. Natives had no rules or inhibitions against sex except for married women. Their young bodies, glistening with sweat in hot sun on cool green grass, separated after their latest encounter.

Samoset was now considered a man in the village following his ritualistic practice of the sweat lodge and several additional quest rites. He was permitted all the benefits and expectations of being a man. Standing, he helped the girl stand, drawing her to him, kissing her. Reopening his eyes, smiling at her, his attention was seized when he caught a glimpse of something white, way out on the water near the horizon. Samoset released the girl stepping around her, looking, studying. He quickly realized what he spotted, and closing-in fast, were the tell-tale white sails of ghost ships.

Samoset stole a last quick kiss, looking frantically around for his loincloth, motioning for the girl to dress quickly, telling her what was coming. Looking in fright, the girl dressed, crying-out for Samoset. Love-making turned instantly to responsibility.

190

With her singlet tied, Samoset instructed her to run back to the village to start spreading the word while he alerted those on the beach, who were unaware. The girl nodded and, barefoot in summer, ran from their favorite spot in a clearing into the forest to alert the village.

Turning, Samoset looked down the rocky palisade to his people. Cupping his hands over his mouth, he released a special call signaling danger. Playing stopped; the people looked upward. He called again, his strong voice echoing across the width of sky. Instinctively, several older women looked across the water, pointing, shouting. The call fell upon them a third time, but they were already scooping children, running from the beach.

Realizing his people were alerted, Samoset ran back through the woods to the village after one additional glance to the two approaching ghost ships. He figured them to be about two hours distant. He could report this to the elders of the council. For now, time was on the tribe's side.

Aboard the two ships, the sight of land was a welcome sign that God had willed this expedition. With sails fully taut, fueled by strong winds, the ships closed the gap with each minute. Passengers scrambled up to the deck to see land for the first time in almost seven weeks.

*****

While the Muscovy Company ships closed-in on the maine coast at roughly forty-five degrees latitude, Henry Hudson was forced to abandon his current search for Cathay via the North Pole. Increased ice sheets, reduced provisions, and approaching inclement weather formed the basis for his decision. Presently, the Hopewell was sailing southward in the Norwegian Sea,

191

having recently crossed the latitude indicating the Arctic Circle. Hudson figured another four weeks of sailing before he reached Gravesend, east of London.

*****

In London, seventeen-year-old Theophilus Eaton was introduced to his first business as a merchant in the cloth trade. Only seven years earlier, London's population had increased to almost 85,000 inhabitants. The growth initially started in the 1530's, when King Henry VIII began dissolving the Catholic monasteries, forcing people to move to cities for employment. Further, when the king moved his court to his main residence at Whitehall, the city's Riverside districts experienced a surge in regentrification, significantly altering the city's financial status to that of a high-end area of living.

By 1600, London was handling four-fifths of the entire cloth trade, especially the much-desired, high-quality wool. The sudden collapse of the Antwerp market in the mid-16th Century allowed London's markets to become a major world player in cloth trades. Adding to the profit-making machinery, a proliferation of new joint-stock companies, run by entrepreneurial upstarts such as Theophilus Eaton, born of means, educated, and eager to make their marks in business, made London the world's financial center.

Theophilus, part of the new wave of young businessmen replacing the failing mercantilist ideas of, "export only," with new markets in new colonies and lands, steadfastly began changing the face of London's financial arrangement, fostering new jobs, increased manufacturing, and a visible cadre of rich young men acting as the new lions of industry.

*****

Bartholomew Gosnold found the site of Jamestown to be, "an unhealthy place." He voiced his concerns to John Smith about the growing dissension that seemed to infest colony members within weeks after landing. There were those of the party who were not content to remain within the original confines of Smith's proposed area of settlement. Feeling over-confident about their survival abilities, seemingly unconcerned about Smith's advice regarding potentially hostile natives who had not materialized since the landing two months ago in May, and ardent in their overzealousness, including greed-ridden desires to claim huge tracts of land for themselves, several men had abruptly moved beyond the settlement's borders to stake their claims for riches and becoming land barons. Their wives, of course, following much pleading to reason against the possible dangers, reluctantly and dejectedly gathered their children and departed with their husbands.

James Wilson, his wife, Anne, and their six children aged two months to nine years, was one such family. Surviving the winter crossing, James initially worked the building crew. Strong, efficient, and a man known to state his word forcefully, he belittled Smith as a, "mothering saint" who wanted to keep everyone under his power, while he mapped the area on the numerous scouting sorties he performed with men of the settlement solely to claim the best lands for himself. Anne Wilson was aghast at her husband's bold blatant assertations, but she was prevented from saying anything publicly. The Wilson's soon found themselves at the center of a growing chasm between those who supported Smith, and those more inclined to side with her husband's point of view.

Richard and Cecelia were divided in their own home. Cecelia sided with Mrs. Wilson, while Richard supported James Wilson. Richard, too, had designs on land for the great farm he always wanted. Their disagreements on this issue, which Cecelia called, "the mania for more," was also shared in other small dwellings,

193

some yet in construction. Yet wives' voices were stunted in expressing opinions publicly. The women shared their positions with those wives from whom they sough emotional support they lacked at home over 'more mania'.

Cecelia told Richard she was flatly appalled at his refusal to back Smith, who specifically chose Richard to go on all the scouting sorties.

"I haven't ruled against him, Cecelia, I simply don't want to wait so long to have a large farm and a hefty profit from produce sales." When Cecelia asked who would buy what, they, too, were growing, Richard fell silent. Many families were in the same predicament. But only the wives were aware. Women talked and shared; the men privately plotted their strategies. As much as the problem festered, the divisive issue came to the fore in late July, nearly three weeks after the Wilsons ventured beyond the settlements borders.

Albert Mosely, who initially shared Wilson's viewpoint, decided, or was forced by brute reality, not to be so recalcitrant in a world he, in actuality, did not, and could not control. On the afternoon he came running back into the settlement, Mosley ran directly to Smith's small wattle and thatch lodging, waving to everyone he saw to follow him. His face was ashen, his eyes, "wild in his head," said the widow Gremshaw, whose husband, John, died shortly after landing. Mosley all but fell into the doorway to the floor of Smith's cottage, babbling incoherently, while a sizable curious crowd, including the Plascombs, was now gathered outside the cottage.

Smith dragged the mumbling Mosley fully inside, asking everyone to allow him a minute to sort-out what was happening. He called to Richard and several other able men to assist. Outside, the crowd began trading stories out of thin air, speculating wildly and imaginatively about how Mosley, usually very quiet and reserved, had gone stark raving mad. Mosely's wife, Anne, was called, and arrived with all her children, fearful of all she'd heard running to the cottage. She was pushed by a wave of people to the front of the now-despairing lot, whose stories grew louder and more alarming with the passing moments.

A minute later, Smith, Richard, Charles Wright, and Ian Charles appeared, looking glum and somber, their faces pallid. Smith motioned to Anne to come inside with the children. She entered, and Smith asked that she leave the children outside. When he whispered into her ear, Anne screamed wildly, drew back, and looked about to faint. Ian supported her, leading her inside. Several mothers took her children. A man in the crowd shouted angrily at the men in the doorway.

"What is the problem?"

"Yes!" another man shouted. "We demand to be told of what is happening!" Resounding calls and shouts of agreement were rallied at the men. Smith pressed the air to settle everyone, but the hollering continued.

"Let him speak!" Richard called loudly to the unruly crowd. A quiet grew, and Smith addressed the crowd.

"If you recall, upon beginning to start this settlement, I asked that we all remain together. We yet are new here. We had no idea if we were alone here. It is clear, now...we are not."

"You're a liar!" a man yelled. "You want good land for yourself!" Smith turned to Plascomb, saying something as the crowd gathered new momentum in its argumentative agitated state. It quieted quickly at the sight of Mosley and Anne, who was visibly

195

shaken, crying onto her apron. Her frightened children drew into her, also starting to cry, though they knew not why. Plascomb moved forward with Albert, placing the ill-looking Mosley before the waiting crowd. Many thought him sick, but he nodded to Plascomb and Smith, running his hands nervously around his hat's rim. Maybe he could explain. Mosley cleared his throat.

"I saw the Wilsons this morning, only but a little while past."

"Louder, Mosley!" someone hollered. He started anew, gathering strength. He repeated his sentence, but his mood changed severely.

"Very well, then! Since you are so mean-spirited and downright hateful, if you wish to claim all the land in this territory, then I bid you go do it – today! Go out and stake your claim!" Mosley's attitude change took all by surprise. "Follow James Wilson and his dream filled with self-satisfaction and boundless greed! I said I saw the Wilsons about one hour passed!"

"Where were they?" a man shouted. Mosely smiled unnaturally.

"They were all over, now that you ask!" Heads turned at this response. Murmurings started. You could hear a pin drop from the sudden silence as the crowd worked to understand. Mosley knew they had no idea what he saw then or meant now.

"You have no idea of what I speak, do you?" he asked. "They were all over!" he railed, shaking anew, working to control himself. "James Wilson was on the front section of the great cabin he was building. He had six arrows through him, and he was scalped." No one understood. He gave a quick explanation with hand gestures. People gasped openly. Two women fainted.

Someone vomited loudly. Mosley continued describing the massacre of the entire Wilson family.

"Blood was everywhere. It covered the floor, the walls. It runs yet!" he cried. "Body parts were tossed in every direction, entrails exposed, all scalped, even the children!" People grabbed their children, drawing them in tightly. Mosely said it appeared they all tried to run when everything happened.

"The mother, Anne, and the youngest child were inside, the rest scattered madly. They were naked, cut-up, dead," he said with finality, turning from the crowd to wretch.

Smith called for volunteers to go bury the family in a Christian manner, saying no one should be left to scavenging animals or returning curious looters.

When the burial party returned later that afternoon, the men who participated refused to speak of what greeted them. They, too, were as transformed as Mosely by the experience. All talk of break-away settlers ceased with a powerful silence. As August arrived, a renewed sense of unity provided a sense of community and pride. Wives and husbands returned to mutually agreeable terms. Yet the proudly-felt sense of unity shared among those at Jamestown was driven as much by an unspoken fear as it was by the expressed caring greetings of each person in passing.

Part One, Chapter Fifteen

August 1607 – December 1607

John Rolfe, born in Norfolk, in 1585 was tall, having wavy, dark, brown hair and hazel eyes, and rugged good looks from four years in the sun working aboard various merchant vessels sailing between England and Europe. Just turning twenty-two, Rolfe earned an ample salary from his hard work, yet he desired something more, seeking to achieve a greater sense of accomplishment. On his most recent return voyage to England from Italy, Rolfe considered purchasing his own ship, perhaps even developing a trade route of his own. He decided to save his money for his venture.

*****

Sir Thomas Smythe stood staring out the window to London streets at the Muscovy Company as Captain Henry Hudson detailed the final set of oceanic factors resulting in his decision to return to Gravesend for the sake of the crew's and vessel's safe return. Smythe's eyes closed; he inhaled deeply, slamming his hand down on the window sill.

"There must be a faster route to Cathay!" he exclaimed, his voice tense with frustration. "We have investors ready to invest heavily if we find that route!" Returning to the table, Smythe sat across from Hudson, the captain's skin a dark brown from nearly five months in sunlight, cold air, and forceful winds. A second director leaned forward.

"If we believe, as we do, there is, in fact, a faster route to Cathay and the Orient, then I recommend a second expedition." Hudson, though, shook his head.

"'Tis September, Mr. Grodson," Hudson offered. "Would be best if we let winter play-out. The ice sheets were severe in August. They will be worse now." Impossible, actually," the captain added with a shake of his big bearded head. Grodson nodded.

"Your words are understood and taken in the most serious measure, Captain," he said, turning to Smythe and his fellow directors. "Your call, Sir Thomas."

"I propose a second expedition in April, 1608, only seven months away, in spring because this first venture proceeded so well. To do it, I propose we meet with Captain Hudson again in February to make plans. This will give us the holiday season to increase investor capital. I propose a vote now, majority rule. All against, say, "nay." The room fell silent. Smythe nodded. "All in favor, say, "aye." A resounding "Aye!" made it unanimous.

"Very well, gentlemen, we meet if February to devise our plans," he said, asking Hudson to study his charts and be prepared to offer his proposals at the meeting to be held 15 February 1608, seven months hence.

"Are you in agreement, Captain?" Hudson nodded with certainty.

"I am, Sir Smythe."

"Excellent, Captain. I knew we could count on you." He stood. All, if there is no other business, I recommend we adjourn." All were in agreement. Hudson departed with John, ready to finally prove there was a faster route to the elusive Orient.

*****

The Scrooby congregation smoothly settled into life in Amsterdam. Most of the first arrivals transitioned quickly into work in numerous trades, increasing income and experience. William Bradford was apprenticed to a French silk maker. The international feeling of the Dutch city proved vastly different from the irenic country living back in Nottinghamshire. Tongues of many languages abounded, and the scents and aromas of multi-cultured ethnic foods diffused from the inns, taverns, and open markets surrounding the city's central square.

Bridges linked tree-lined streets busy with lively people inclined to allow others to live their lives as they wished. Bradford quickly comprehended Amsterdam's reputation as a cultural magnet for people fleeing something in search for as much freedom as they wanted. Staring into the beautifully decorated window of a grand chocolatier, Bradford was startled when a young woman he almost bumped into handed him a little yellow flower. Accepting it, Bradford blushed, continuing to the silk maker's shop.

Life quickly altered for the group who moved, a fact made known by Minister Robinson when he wrote to those yet in Scrooby. He wrote, "the freedom with which we practice our Puritan beliefs is in an arena where all religious toleration is the norm, not the exception."

Presently, Dutch autumn was settling on the city. Leaves fell from tress as in England. It was cold, yet dry and sunny. As a unified congregation, the move to Holland was proving to be

200

the promise of a better life for all on many levels, while the plans for the second group's departure were put into action.

*****

If the fully realized presence of true hostility lurked beyond the safe confines of the Jamestown settlement, as proven by the horrific deaths of the entire Wilson family in July, then the unexpected ravaging by an invisible force beyond the reach of piety, prayer, or human understanding presented a newer, more heinous layer of devastation upon the already weary settlers in the Virginia settlement.

Yellow Fever made its unmistakable presence known to the settlement as it swept like a silent debilitating wave over the entire populace of just under a hundred. The losses at sea and the Wilson family deaths originally placed the population slightly over a hundred. No one was free from the illness's opportunistic presence that claimed lives with an unstoppable unknown power.

The illness begins with a rush of a high fever lasting up to ten days. If the stricken person is strong enough, the fevers abate, and the illness completely passes with two weeks of the original onset, leaving the stricken individual alive, and having a complete immunity to the disease. But the old and the very young are never strong enough or immune enough, especially to a disease they had never known in England.

In early August the first indications became apparent. Within a week, everyone was infected, including John Smith. He survived. Bartholomew Gosnold was not as lucky. Just thirty-five, Gosnold's death initiated the mournful tale that would ultimately claim fourteen lives by mid-September, when the final fragments of the deadly disease finally passed. Of the fourteen deaths, thirteen different families suffered losses. Funerals were held every day after Gosnold's death on 22 August. One family lost two children, the only two they had. In all, nine children and five adults succumbed to yellow fever.

*****

The unity that had cemented the settlers in Jamestown following the Wilson tragedy slowly faded, but slowed as yellow fever arrived, once again uniting everyone as the deaths started. The Plascomb family did not escape the disease's death march. Ellen Plascomb, age four, was laid to rest in the recently-begun cemetery where the future church was to be built. No one though the cemetery would be needed so soon for so many at once.

Cecelia was inconsolable, having to be restrained from attempting to jump into the grave with her little girl, one of the last to be stricken. The Plascombs believed they had made it safely; they were wrong. Both Christian and Edmund remained too ill, and several women stayed with them at the small cottage. Ellen died several weeks into September. A steady rain fell on the day of her burial, her light-colored pine coffin growing darker as it absorbed rain water. So many families suffered losses by the sickness no one understood. No post-burial gatherings were held. Mourning and despair could not be lessened with the rapidity and relentless dying in the settlement.

Silently, husbands began blaming themselves for their desires to relocate their families from the safety of England. Outwardly, mothers were too distraught to describe their wretched unhappiness. They had agreed -however reluctantly- to follow their husbands as was their duty, but for this? Had they all traveled thousands of miles, left family, a secure home, and a happy life only to come here to toil daily, and, after it all, sacrifice their children, and for what?

Sickness, violent pagan natives, and hard work was the sole set of earthly rewards. Privately, some wives harbored these feelings, keeping them internalized. Those who did lose children found some solace in one another's company over shared grief. Those who did lose children were quietly shunned for fear of loss by association. A new dividing line slowly drove a new wedge among families, loss against no loss. The sense of separation pushed apart that unity which had so cohesively concentrated lives so parallel in hardship and sorrow.

Cecelia blamed Richard for Ellen's death. It was approaching two months before she spoke to him, while she spoke constantly with her sons, whom she guarded continuously. Their missing daughter haunted her dreams, gave her nightmares. Richard understood his wife would not forget. He felt the visual daggers she cast him, and she remained relentless in her mute attack. He considered another child, but attempt at *that* idea required two people, and in one room. Four weeks after Ellen's burial, when the boys were safely through the worst, Cecelia began sleeping in the boys' room. She had already stopped sex with Richard. At some point in November after summer faded and autumn came cold and fast, Cecelia's first words to Richard surprised him for both their utterance and their message.

It was an early hour on that morning in late November, long after Richard was accustomed to inflexible silence and resilience to any and all of his overtures. The boys slept as Cecelia heated water in the hearth to make oats for breakfast. Richard entered the room, finding a cup of tea at his place. Richard was readying himself to go help build residences for those settlers yet awaiting a place of their own, some families stayed with other families while they waited for a house, and this was unknowingly a direct method of passing yellow fever through the practice of bundling.

Bundling called for families to live together while homes were erected. Living together included sleeping together in one room, at times in one bed. On cold nights, everyone remained dressed while sleeping because it was the only way to provide heat and sleeping quarters for all until a home was finished. For those couples either 'spoken for' or engaged, bundling was no deterrent to procreation. Loving ardor trumps thoughtful logic. Court and church records detailing weddings and infant births clearly show the birth dates prior to marital vows for many. Some couples had several children prior to marriage. Bundling was practiced by families of all religious faiths. But disease transmission was guaranteed when the commonness of bundling was a regular practice when the settlement started.

That November morning, Richard picked up his tea, perfunctorily thanking Cecelia. She addressed him at that moment.

"I want to take the boys and return to England." The harshness of her expressing, coupled with the tone of defiance struck Richard to his core. He convulsed at the table, sobbing.

"Cecelia, I never wanted our daughter to die! You must know that!" he cried loudly. Owl-like, Cecelia turned from the hearth, her unblinking eyes upon her distraught husband.

"Can you not speak her name?" she asked grittily. He shook his head.

"No! it hurts too much! I dream of her. I, too, miss her, but you must forgive me! We know not the scourge that afflicted us and so many families! Forgive me!" he lamented, his tea untouched, his hands buried in his face, hiding his mournful countenance. Cecelia placed her mixing spoon near the hearth.

"Recall, it is God who is all forgiving," she said flatly, moving to the doorway. "Let Him forgive you," she told Richard, passing to the next small room. Richard, suddenly feeling foolish for expressing his emotions, angrily picked up his rifle and pack, wiped his eyes on his sleeve, and wandered into the darkness outside to join Smith and the others for home building.

By early December, quite a few wattle and thatch cottages were completed, reducing the incidence of bundling. The first winter was approaching, and it was proving to be quite different from winter in England. It became quickly clear that although enough firewood was cut, the wood's greenness from being freshly cut resulted in uneven burning, making heating and cooking more difficult than anticipated.

A midday scouting venture, headed by Smith, was in progress. He'd undertaken a significant leadership role since their arrival seven months earlier. At times, Smith thought it felt like an eternity since they arrived. Presently, Smith and his men ventured almost two miles in every direction since they started the scouting sortie. In addition to locating natives' locations, now imperative, the men were also looking for land to expand the settlement. They required good land for farming, verified the endless source of timber for houses, firewood, and, remorsefully, coffins.

Approaching the cold rushing stream they'd previously found almost two hours due west of Jamestown, they stopped to talk over their findings, and decide what to do next. The morning was cold, but dry and sunny beyond the forest. Sounds of the settlement faded some time ago. The sun, its dappled light piercing the dense ceiling of deciduous and evergreen trees above them, signaled the hour. Jerky and roughly baked bread provided nourishment after the walking and hiking, and talk turned to the promise of saleable wood and the need for new provisions.

Smith decided against detailing the need to plan crops the following spring. He'd noticed that when the men had their rifles, they had only hunting or killing on their minds. Smith knew instinctively, and from private talks with the other six councilors, that revenge for the Wilsons lay like a heavy burden on the minds of all scouting parties. Finishing their light meal, the eight men started-off anew, advancing through the forest, searching for any signs of the hidden secretive natives that had not been physically seen, but their presence known because of the Wilson family.

While they walked, Smith considered the problematic nature of many who decided to come to this new place. They were lazy; that he knew. He had to forcefully push his agenda, compelling the men to hard work in order to get things done. At times, some of the men acted as if living quarters would sprout from the ground like crops. One minute they vilified him, calling him 'King Smith', then they would rally 'round him at the first hint of trouble. The only time the men seemed truly happy was when they were in their cups or combing armed through the woods. The focus on settling and building houses meant it was far too late to plant crops for the next year. Food stuffs were yet satisfactory, but water had to be boiled constantly for use since they didn't know if it was safe.

Onset of the mystery disease that claimed so many lives was a serious setback, and the constant threat of violent natives put everyone on high alert. Smith wondered if those natives were watching this party at this very minute. This unknown variable had the force of assuring no one ventured beyond the settlement except for specific reasons. Smith also noticed that in the settlement, the children were being confined to the immediate areas around their thatched cottages, playing only with children who lived nearby.

Looking up, Smith contemplated the sun's position, the men yearning for revenge, and the future of this settlement. Behind Smith, Richard listened to the men behind him talk about problems at the settlement. Ian Johns spit to the ground.

"Charles Ives' wife blames him for their son's death," he said. "She says that if they never came to this forsaken place, she'd yet have a ten-year-old son." Samuel Bendson spoke his peace.

"The women need to keep their mouths closed and legs open to provide new settlers. 'Tis not their place to have a say unless asked." He looked around. "I just want to kill a couple of those savages to make up for what they did to the Wilsons, the bloody bastards!" He spit. Plascomb, Smith, and several others listened yet remained quiet.

"They'll make themselves known sooner or later," said Thomas Risens, who laughed nervously, turning to gaze through the thick woods. Bird calls and the cold air were the only sensations the party heard and felt as they pushed-onward. Risens had more to say on the subject.

"They're probably watching us right now," he said suspiciously, craning his neck to observe all around them. The others did the same, wondering how close to the mark Thomas might actually be. Ian Johns pointed.

"I recommend we start the settlement expansion in this westward direction. The sun comes straight-over, giving excellent crop sunlight most of the day."

"Agreed, Ian," replied Risens, who lost a thirteen-year-old daughter in the 'plague' as the illness had come to be called for lack of complete understanding as to what it was.

"That's strange," Richard said so mysteriously, that everyone stopped walking, turning to him. Smith asked him what he meant. Richard shrugged.

"Well, it's quite strange to hear mourning doves calling so late in the day, that's all." The others immediately looked around.

"Getting squirrely on us, eh, Richard?" asked Ian Charles, hoping for some needed levity. Smith, though, completely understood Richard's cautious meaning.

"There's no telling," he said, looking about. "I suggest we make haste and return to the settlement. We can return in a few days' time."

"Perhaps we could move south next time," Richard said, yet thinking about bird calls typically heard only in the day's early hours. They turned back, instantly spooked when a sudden movement to their immediate right stopped them in their tracks. Three female deer had been moving lazily through the woods but scuttled when the party approached.

"If I only had a shot!" Ian called, but Bendson told him they were all too young. They moved again. Once again, the outing proved uneventful. They marked new sites with red dye for easier tracking on future outings. Now, roughly less than a half-mile from the settlement, sounds of life could be heard again. Laughter, hammering, and people calling were easily heard. It wasn't in sight, but it was hearable out here. Ian Charles was the first to make the sharp right turn to the settlement path, when he stopped so abruptly that Richard ran into him, and Bendson smacked into Plascomb.

"What in the – "someone said, but the remaining words failed him.

Four natives, each holding a taut bow and arrow, blocked the path. To the settlers' right and left, no less than six natives rose from the underbrush, all armed and ready. A noise behind them revealed another group of ready warriors. They all stood immobile, eyes fixed on specific men, covering all of them.

"Don't move," Smith said in almost a whisper. "Nod if you hear me." Heads bobbed the affirmative. "Put your weapons down, slowly, then stand slowly. Do it." He could sense the revenge instinct rear its untimely head. They followed his directions, standing again while the natives watched silently.

"Hands up, palms open," came the newest calmly stated command. "Say nothing." Hands were up chest-high, palms open. The natives wore skins for warmth, strange soft shoes on their feet. They were built much like the settlers. They were tall, short, muscular, slender, but their skin was different. Was it just dark, or was it actually red? Their faces bore red, yellow, and white pigments, running angularly upwards from their chins almost to their ears.

Smith looked to the man he considered the leader because he noticed the braves' eyes shift rapidly shift to him several times, as if awaiting a command. Carefully, slowly, Smith extended his hand to that man, who watched it closely. Smith waited. The next move was his captor's. This much Smith knew as a flashing recall of the slave camp paced through his mind.

The leader suddenly issued an order, making the settlers jump. Arrows were lowered, tips down, hands yet on the quill. The tension, though, greatly -thankfully- reduced. The leader eyed Smith, issuing a second order, at which point several natives stepped forward, separating Smith from the group. Smith now faced his own men, seeing Charles' fingers itching to grab for his rifle. Smith slowly shook his head, a silent yet firm message.

At the third order, the natives retreated several steps, opening the path, the leader made a motion to the men indicating they could go...move on. They looked to Smith, unsure. Smith pointed to the rifles. The native leader nodded, pointing to the weapons, then the men, and made another motion with his hand indicating 'go away', and looked to Smith, repeating the motion. Smith nodded. He looked to his men.

"Pick up your weapon and mine. And go back to the settlement. Say nothing, only nod." They did. They slowly took-up the weapons and reluctantly backed-off, turned, and walked ahead slowly without turning around. Smith looked at the native leader, who now extended his hand. For the first time, Smith firmly shook hands with a native. The leader motioned for Smith to accompany his men to their village. Smith nodded. When the party stopped and turned, the natives and Smith were gone.

"I say we follow them!" suggested Ian Charles. Richard looked to him.

"Where, Ian," he asked skeptically, looking back to where they had been. "On the wind?"

A renewed sense of urgency swept through Jamestown when word of Smith's abduction became common knowledge. The remaining six councilors urged everyone to be calm.

"Captain Smith is a highly experienced military leader who has most likely experienced this type of thing previously," one stated confidently. An extra sentry was placed on the perimeter, and the shared feelings of crisis commonality reunited the settlers once more. Winter was also starting to become harsher.

They had all hoped and prayed for the best. What they were experiencing was in complete contrast to what they expected.

Part One, Chapter Sixteen

December 1607 – September 1608

John Smith had to work to keep pace with his captors, who
remained silent as they crossed streams, rocks, and dense
woods to the village. Keeping an eye on the sun's position,
Smith did his best to remember the directions he was walking.
Lichens on the sides of some trees indicated north, and certain
objects, like streams, brooks, and large rocks offered good land
markers. He was a marvel, a spectacle when the scouting party
arrived in the village. No one had ever been so close to a ghost
man.

In several days of talks using hand signals, drawings in the dirt,
and simple words, Smith learned he'd been brought to the
village of Werowocomoco by Chief Opechancanough, half-
brother to the supreme village chief, Powhatan. He also realized
he was considered a white 'chief'. Smith was always the single
leader to whom all deferred, in a manner similar to the way all
in the village deferred to Powhatan. In two weeks, Smith was
truly living among the natives, having been 'initiated' through
several ceremonies as 'co-chief' to Powhatan himself, and he
intended to learn all he could about native customs.

Powhatan informed Smith that the Wilson family was killed by
a rebel tribe with little contact with the Powhatan Tribe. He
regretted their massacre, but did speak of his concerns about
the increasing number of whites coming to native lands.
Powhatan explained he had seen the white men coming in a
dream that was proving true.

During his time with the natives, Smith was introduced to
Pocahontas, Powhatan's princess daughter. He thought he'd
seen her during what he thought was his trial before the

villagers conducted by Powhatan. Smith guessed Pocahontas to be about ten years. Her straight, shining, black hair fell almost to her waist. Her excellent bone structure highlighted her sharp, almost feline facial features. She was quick to laugh, and spoke some English words with Smith, who promptly capitalized on her language skills to act as a translator. It was a start, Smith thought, working to gain Powhatan's growing confidence.

Upon first arriving, Powhatan wanted to kill the white man, bur Pocahontas chose this opportunity to tell her father that she had been sneaking into the settlement to play with the ghost children, yet untouched by the evils of dislike due to color or ethnicity. Natives doted on their children, showing emotion unfailingly and unquestioningly. After listening to his daughter's stories of being with the whites without harm, he surrendered to his daughter's request to spare Smith. Instead, he accepted the white man as his 'co-chief', treating him accordingly. Therein began the first, if shaky, start at a truce. Yet still living among the Powhatan, the last weeks of December brought the year 1607 to a close.

*****

Daily life in Jamestown continued after Smith's abduction. Nearly a month passed, leading most to believe Smith had been killed like the Wilsons. Contrarily, there were some who were glad he was gone by any means, but his absence created a power vacuum that could not be easily filled by mere strength or force. Leadership, so absent in the new settlement, was more important than force of personality. No one knew of Smith's life experiences, and the question of survival became a heavy burden for everyone. Captain Newport departed Jamestown on 12 June 1607, and should have returned at the latest by September. He had not yet returned. Stores were empty; provisions nearly gone. Nearly one-fifth of the 144 who arrived in April, 1607 had already died, and winter was proving to be harsher than anyone anticipated. The sluggish nature of the settlers in dealing with daily problems required a skillful leader, not a brash loudmouth. Therein, Smith's absence made matters worse. The remaining six councilors decided to have Smith declared "deceased" thirty days after his disappearance without returning. When the councilors met to agree on 2 January 1608, there were only eight days remaining before Smith was declared legally dead, and the official death entry entered into the birth and death log kept by the council.

Beyond the loss of Smith, a general sense of despair gripped the remaining council. In addition to the still-born infant and its mother who died aboard the Sarah Constant in crossing, fourteen died of the summer disease, and four more from winter's severity. Spring was an agonizing ten weeks away. Complicating that fact was that no births occurred in the settlement since arriving nearly a year ago. The cohesiveness of community evaporated again. Food stuffs were devastatingly low. One councilor informed the others that indolence was problematic, and many wives were refusing their husbands their marriage bed claims. A second councilor stated his wife told him that no women were with child. The settlement's success potential for lack of a second generation seemed counterproductive, even dangerous. During the discussion about how to strengthen marriage vows towards being more conciliatory, a loud banging on the council door grabbed the attention of all. Ian Charles burst into the room eyes wide, shouting.

"Drums!" he shouted into the room, announcing the native warning call, the drums. "The savages are coming!" Looking fearfully at one another, the men jumped-up, peppering Charles with questions.

"How near are they?"

"Are you sure, Charles?"

"How many?" They ran outside.

"The drums started ten minutes ago!" Charles told the men. "They're getting closer and louder as well!" Settlers were running to the council office; a panic could spread. Charles had other news.

"There's a young Indian girl among us talking of Captain Smith!"

"Smith?" yelled a councilor as the men turned, heading to the middle of the street they erected at the settlement's center, where the crowd gathered. Moving to the front, they heard calls of, "Smith!", or, "It's him! He's alive!" Before their disbelieving eyes, the native drums beat a rhythmic march-like tune as Captain John Smith entered the settlement, side-by-side, with a tall native, accompanied by several dozen others behind them, dressed like what appeared to be an honor guard. Behind them was a large group of women and children.

  Smith smiled broadly, waving to his incredulous fellow settlers. Suddenly, the native children ran ahead, led by Pocahontas, to see the white children. Instantly the children fell into play and communication as they were able. The drums stopped when greeting party approached, standing a mere ten feet away from the settlers. The councilors stepped forward, unsure of what would happen next. People studied people. Hair, attire, skin features, height, all similarities in one way or another. Only skin color identifiably separated them. Advancing, Smith and the native leader started shaking hands with the councilors, Smith making introductions with Pocahontas' assistance.

"Lord, Captain Smith, we took you for dead, we did!" one councilor declared, thrilled to see Smith.

"I am quite alive," Smith shouted to be heard by all. "This is Powhatan, the supreme leader of the Powhatan Tribe of the Algonquin confederation, here, in Virginia. His men and the women are here to help us. They seek to show us how to grow crops for spring. They are very sorry about the Wilsons. They want us to know they had nothing to do with that event. It was done by a renegade tribe that moves place-to-place, and are not associated with the Powhatan People. I know we can learn from them. They are willing to help us succeed here. We have a truce between us!" Loud applause and cheering erupted among the settlers.

"Please help me welcome them and their help!" Smith called to the crowd. It was later, Smith discovered, the settlers' smiles that assured the Powhatan they were welcome, and intentions were peaceful. Smiles were returned, hands shaken, and a new understanding of Jamestown began.

*****

Problems were equally severe at the colony at Sagadahoc, on the 'maine' coast. Unprepared for the brutality of heavy winter snow and unforgiving weather conditions, nearly half of the original settlers who arrived the previous summer had died. George Popham, the colony's elected governor, died on 5 February 1608, only six months after arriving. His shrouded tied corpse was placed outside the colony in deep snow because the ground was too frozen to dig graves. He and several others would have to wait for a thaw for eternal rest. Raleigh Gilbert was elected to replace Popham.

Some of the colonists started fur trade with the Pemaquid natives, and a fishery was begun. On the whole, though, most colonists refused Pemaquid assistance out of pride or disdain. No one knew about the terrible winters on the northern 'maine' coast. Struggles against climate and adapting, compounded by indolence of some colonist who had been prisoners in England, only worsened the situation. The remaining colonists began to decide what they should do before all provisions were depleted completely.

Men knew a fur trade would provide untold wealth. Fishing was plentiful, but winter on the water was impossible. Women who had not lost their husbands said the colony should be abandoned. Decisions had to be made, but winter would have to pass before anything could be done. This was pointedly true when the colonists had only one ship captain and one pilot. Both had to remain alive if the decision to abandon was made.

*****

In February's final week, Richard Plascomb assisted Ian Charles affix the sign reading, 'Charles-Plascomb Glass Works' above the door of the new glass foundry in Jamestown. Convincing Richard that there was a need for glass in the colony, Richard agreed to invest half his savings in the foundry. Charles discussed how they could make special orders for glass objects, stained-glass windows, special glass, drinking mugs and glasses, and other materials not in existence on the new continent. Besides, Richard thought privately, beyond the investment, the opportunity allowed Richard to escape the confines of the small cottage and Cecelia's daily dose of vilification and ire. He might even make a solid profit as Charles' full partner in the glass business.

Ian showed Richard how to start the furnaces, the glass making process, including using various dyes to make colored glass on their first day at work. Charles also explained how to incorporate lead for heavy stained-glass windows, and also illustrated how to use molds to form special crystal glassware. As busily as they worked to help Richard learn his new craft, they were both surprised when customers began placing orders for items ranging from specially-designed stained-glass windows to beautiful colored glass bowls and ornaments to beautify a home's interior. Richard's learning curve quickly increased.

*****

Hindered by an unexpected snowstorm in late February, the second group departing Scrooby boarded the same boat as the first group a year earlier in the first week of March. Since the new month came in, like one resident said, "like a lamb," the group decided to make haste, using the benevolence of mild weather to make their delayed move to Amsterdam.

Once again, the ample boat proved able to handle forty nine emigrants. Moving smoothly from Lincoln to the Wyeth River's mouth, the group made good time to the waiting ship near The Wash. The second group was decidedly more confident than the first, mostly from learning that the plan had worked already. The hard work was already done. With lodgings and work secured for all, fear of the unknown yielded to the feelings of reunification. Spontaneous bouts of prayers of thanks were shared almost continually. The worst seemed to be over. Only the third, final group remained at Scrooby, where they would suffer the Crown's religious intolerance only one more year. With a bright warm sun, good winds, the group prayed as the larger vessel headed from the Wash to the North Sea.

*****

The same snowstorm that caught the Scrooby group off-guard also forced Henry Hudson to reschedule his meeting with Muscovy Company directors until early March. His son did not attend because he was ill. After general introductions, Sir Smythe asked for Hudson's plan. Hudson tacked several maps to the wall.

"I plan to sail directly to Spitzbergen to locate an opening northward between Spitzbergen and Novaya Zemlya," he stated, pointing to the maps. "Spitzbergen, the largest island of a set of three, known as Svalbard, lay mostly at about eighty degrees north latitude, and between fifteen and thirty degrees longitude, east of the Prime Meridian in the Barents Sea.

"Novaya Zemlya is a scythe-shaped island facing northeast, its hooded tip at the southern end." A director asked Hudson what he would do if the projected plan wasn't possible.

"If that happens, the Hopewell and her able crew will locate a strait taking us to the eastern coast of Novaya Zemlya to the Kara Sea. There, I am positive we will be able to pass to the warmer, clear waters of the North Pole, finally taking us to our objective, Cathay, China, and Japan." Sir Thomas applauded.

"Captain Hudson, that same plan was also our proposal. Spitzbergen is the key, we are firmly in agreement about that." Final details were planned, and e tentative departure date of 22 April 1608 was set.

Hudson had with him a second man he informed the directors he had hired as a second mate. His name was Robert Juet. Superficially welcomed by the directors, Sir Thomas maintained a watchful eye on the man, who appeared, at least to Smythe, to be 'wild-eyed'. He looked to be about thirty, dark-haired. Sir Thomas wondered how Hudson could hire such a scurrilous character. Then again, Smythe knew finances and business. Hudson understood seamen and the sailing.

Hudson was greeted lovingly by his wife, Katherine, and they walked together through the large comfortable home near a park in London in the city's fashionable section. In John's own room, a rarity for most families except those with means, father looked-in on his ill son.

"His cough has stopped, Father," Katherine told her husband as John blew his nose. "It's only the sneezing and runny nose we have to get in control," she added.

"You'll be well, my boy," Hudson said confidently, smiling as John bounded from the bed, arms akimbo.

"I'm fine, father, see?" he declared, offering the best smile he could offer before starting a spam of sneezes, making his father laugh and his mother force him back into bed.

"Rest, John," his mother coaxed gently. "Six weeks will find you fiddle-ready for sailing."

"Your mother's right, my boy!" Hudson barked happily. "We're to be searching again for Cathay in six weeks' time. Get healthy and strong!"

"Alright, you two," mother said, pulling covers up. "Henry, your other four sons are waiting for you in the kitchen. Let's go see them and I'll make tea." In the kitchen, Hudson greeted his sons, enjoying time with his family. He gave Katherine all the money he was paid by the Muscovy Company, a sizeable sum.

*****

The first winter at Jamestown levied a heavy toll on the first settlers. In the seven months since the summer sickness struck unforgivingly, eleven more settlers, six children and five adults, died in the freezing temperatures no one anticipated. By this time almost fifty percent of the original settlers were dead. The newest round of winter deaths began in late December. Once again, The Plascomb family was devastated by Edmund's death in January 1608. The settlement midwife, Mrs. Maude, who doubled as doctor because no children were being born, and no physicians joined the settlers, told the grieving parents it was most likely consumption that claimed their son's life. Edmund was four years. The fact that five additional youngsters died was no comfort to Cecelia, and her husband was unforgivable. Shortly after Edmund was buried next to his sister, Ellen, Cecelia was taken-in by Mrs. Maude, who told Richard she hoped to help her in closer quarters. Dejectedly, Richard accepted her advice.

Christian was almost seven. Once more he experienced sibling loss, but this time he watched all the events, culminating with his brother being lowered into the ground in the place the remaining settler children called the 'cement tree', as opposes to the cemetery. A number of Christian's young friends had gone the same way as his sister and brother. On an early April evening, as daylight increased, Richard and his son sat eating dinner, and Christian broke-down in tears. When he told his father he missed his mother, sister, and brother, his father tried to explain. Christian; however, only shook his head.

"I don't like this place, father. I wish we never came here." Feeling beleaguered and crestfallen, Richard tried to figure out what to do, thinking that his son sounded very much like his mother in this single regard.

*****

221

Hopewell set sail on schedule on 22 April 1608. Hudson, John, the new second mate, Robert Juet, and a new crew made-way into the North Sea on a due north route. Hopewell would sail a continuous north-northeast route, east of the Orkney and Shetland Islands, and west of Norway's coast. Once clear of the northwest European coast and the Norwegian Sea, the ship would head northeast into the Barents Sea above the Arctic Circle, southeast of Spitzbergen, and northwest of Novaya Zemlya. On a section of sailing where little steering was required, Hudson invited his son to pilot the Hopewell northward. John was eager to take the helm.

*****

Settlers at the Sagadahoc colony on the 'maine' coast welcomed spring with an almost gleeful attitude. The decision to obtain every possible benefit from the area and abandon prior to winter was made. Thus, fur trading, fishing, and natural resource collection increased dramatically. Some wanted to remain, but the isolated location and human losses over the previous nine months, not to mention the calamitous winter all etched an undeniable mental image of only sad memories and a less-than-spectacular colonization experience. The best the men could do without wifely support was to fortify the trading posts for future utility. As May approached, the last of the deciduous trees produced their new chartreuse growth, and fishing and fur trading started in earnest with the understanding that this would be the final season for inhabitants to pursue business. The surviving men conducted business; the women began packing to return to England.

*****

On the final day of the first week in June, Captain Hudson made an entry into his log:

7 June 1608 — Northernmost coast of Norway to our starboard side, and has been with us a great time. North Cape is in sight, and the northeast directional shift after passing the Lofoten Islands, in northern Norway, is imminent. John continues to learn navigation splendidly. He also grows taller and stronger, better able to man the great helm with less strenuous effort. Whales abound in these cold waters. The sun is high and warm in daylight. Nights are blistering cold, but hours of darkness are few due to our latitude. Most darkness here is equal to dusk in London on a summer day. The distant view is disappointing — ice sheets may block passage between Spitzbergen and Novaya Zemlya. This, if true, will be a dire disappointment to this second venture. I am hoping this is not the case.

Hudson climbed up to the main deck to lunch with his son, who remained at the helm.

*****

Richard Plascomb began taking Christian to the glass foundry on a daily basis. Christian was learning a reliable valuable trade. On-guard to ensure his son's safety at every moment, Richard offered ample allowance for his son to learn from Ian Charles, who had worked with glass nearly twenty years, starting in Liverpool when he was nine years, taught by his paternal grandfather. Eventually, he made his way to London as a master glass blower. This led to his biggest chance to date, resettling at Jamestown. His wife, Eileen, died the previous winter like so many others, and his young son died a month after his mother. Work helped pass time, keeping the mind occupied and focused, as opposed to grieving and endless sorrow.

Today, Christian was learning to add pigments while spinning molten glass for producing designs on white glass vases and bowls. Plascomb father and son were spinning blue pigment onto white glass when Smith entered the foundry. They hollered greetings over the furnaces, and Smith approached.

Smith's return in January fostered a significant treaty with the Powhatan Tribe. When spring started, village women arrived daily to teach residents how to farm. They planted pumpkins, corn, squash, and several varieties of beans. Former English farmers quickly discovered the richness of Virginia soil, and they were eager to bring forth a bountiful harvest of entirely new vegetables.

On this sunny July morning, Smith had come to speak directly with Richard, who stepped outside, grateful for a break from the intense heat of the foundry furnace.

"How goes thing these days, Richard?" Smith asked seriously.

"Here, John, they go very well, and very busy. We're prepared to hire another hand because orders increase each day."

"That's a good thing, isn't it, eh?" Smith asked, laughing. Richard laughed as well.

"Yes, oh yes, it is. It takes up the day's hours, and the money is really good, too, John. Christian is really taking to making glass. I'll say the money is better than farming." Smith nodded.

"Well, it's farming I came to talk about with you, Richard."

"Farming?"

"Yes, Richard. You know the thousand acres we're clearing at the northwest end of the settlement?"

"You mean the one out towards the falls, right? They stretch westward."

"Same ones," Smith agreed. "Well, the council has been considering designating the land as a huge community farming area to supply food for all to sustain us as we continue to make this colony a success." Richard shook his head.

"Despite the continual setbacks?"

"Correct, Richard."

"We're lucky Captain Newport finally arrived back here in January shortly after your return. We'd have been done-for, I tell you, John."

"I agree, Richard, but that's behind us. I'm here for the future, and your future as well, Sir." Richard asked how.

"Before I describe it, I inquire about Mrs. Plascomb and her health. It's been nearly seven months since..." his voice trailed away, realizing the personal tragedy the family suffered. Richard sighed.

"I understand, John. Cecelia returned to our home three weeks ago. Christian is quite happy, I daresay, as he should be. The situation is as pleasant as can be expected."

"Does she yet blame you?"

"Aye, that she does, but she's widened her wrath to include God, the saints and all the angels in Heaven. Hell itself doesn't contain enough room for us all at once. We take turns being castigated and cast into the eternal flames."

"I am sorry for the home troubles, Richard. If it means anything, there's but one or two families who haven't been scalded by disease or death. If we had a court here, I do think the divorce rate for those surviving marriages would clog the court's log."

"I notice the widow Candler and Roger Wills sharing much time together," Richard said. "They arrived here yesterday together to place an order for some glass."

"Loneliness is a powerful force, Richard, especially in a foreign land."

"I agree, John. One need not be single to be lonely. What of the land?"

"The council seeks to hire you, Richard, to fully manage the crop land we're preparing. We require a man with excellent growing and managing skills. The council nominated you unanimously, you should know. No other man was considered. I am here to offer you the position." Richard was stunned.

"Me?"

"You, Sir," Smith replied. "We need a leader, a strong one. The crop land will become our beacon of salvation and saving grace for plenty of food if nothing else. I'm sure you've noticed how the settlement is split on religion." Richard laughed.

"And just about everything else besides beer," Richard said, and Smith nodded. "I also hear of some aiming to grab land again," Richard added scornfully. "There are those who claim the land can be taken since the Powhatan's continued assistance and friendliness are taken as a sign of weakness by some in the settlement. Knowledge that they didn't kill the Wilsons added to the position they're weak." Smith shook his head.

"That would be a very foolish, very foolish position to hold, and we both know it. Powhatan wanted to kill me, but only for his daughter's pleas, he relented. "But, what of the land management, Richard. We need you, your skills, your insight." Richard saw an opportunity.

"John, the offer is very tempting. Farming is my special area. I must have full management control, including the crops. Those that work, replant after a fallow season. Those that fail, forget them. We have no time for wondering of something will grow. There are mouths to be fed. I also seek that the land be placed in the Plascomb name to establish the Plascomb family as managers over said acreage, and any other land added to the current total acreage. Finally, the land will revert to the Plascomb family as sole owners in twenty-five years -win or lose. The Plascomb family becomes sole owners outright. We absorb all the costs." Smith laughed.

"And the benefits, Richard?" Richard laughed now.

"Yes, those as well, John." Richard shrugged. "Some years good, others not. It's all a gamble, really. Right now, it's growing nothing but some pumpkins, squash, and beans. I think we could have some bumper crops in several years. Talk with the council. Present my offer. I await the reply." Smith nodded.

"I'll try to return with a contract and a deed tomorrow. Is that soon enough?" Both men laughed.

"Tis, John. A day is fine. Harvest is in three months. If accepted, I'll figure what to do with the foundry." They shook hands, and Smith departed.

Richard stood watching his friend walk away, considering he made a solid deal with a guaranteed bargain for his family and Christian in the future. He wondered what crops would grow here. He'd never heard of *pumpkin*! He decided to visit the crop land before the day's end to inspect it. He returned inside to get back to work as several new customers arrived.

*****

Henry Hudson was confounded. Standing at the bow of Hopewell, he searched in vain for a passage into the Kara Sea, north of Russia. Looking through his spyglass, he saw no more than increasing ice sheets. The sun was once more skirting the horizon, and sunlight permeated most hours of the day. There would be several weeks of anything even resembling darkness or night.

Hudson calculated their bearings to close to the Arctic Circle with no possible passage to the Orient. He wanted to proceed, but he had a crew and a ship to consider. After a serious discussion with second mate, Robert Juet, Hudson gave the order to turn back for England, much to his own disappointment. Following an uneventful return sailing, Hopewell and her crew arrived at Gravesend on 26 August 1608.

*****

Richard signed the contract providing he be manager of the crop land on 1 September 1608. All his demands wet met. Also, he signed a deed granting him all one thousand acres, with an additional five hundred each year for five years, a total of 3,500 acres by 1613. The council wanted no part of the land upkeep, particularly if Plascomb was foolish enough to accept the responsibility. The council also agreed to build the Plascomb family a house suitable for a large land manager. Plascomb would grow the colony's crops for sustenance. If the opportunity arose, he could trade the remainder for profit by any means. Yet the council members realized that consideration was folly because the natives had all they needed. In addition, as isolated as Jamestown was, there were no other traders. Besides, what had started-out at just over a hundred people had dwindled to only about fifty. Following application of all signatures, the assembled celebrated with beer, each side convinced it had made a very good deal.

Quite a few tankards were hoisted that afternoon, and Richard walked home feeling grand, heady from robust tasty ale, fully realizing he was now the sole proprietor of the largest land tract in the settlement. His remaining steps home were jaunty, animated. The enormity of the deal -deed in hand-secured the fact that the Plascomb family was the largest land owner in the settlement, and, for that matter, in the whole of North America!

Part One, Chapter Seventeen

September 1608 – March 1609

At his London home, Henry Hudson opened a letter from Amsterdam bearing the name of the East India Company in early September.

2 August 1608

Dear Captain Hudson,

Word has reached us here in Holland that your adept skills at seamanship are legendary. We directors of the East India Company write to you seeking your entry into a contract with us for the purpose of an expedition with great merit. The purpose of the journey is to build upon your most recent venture, searching for a passage around the northern side of the land called Novaya Zemlya. We shall provide you with a new vessel named De Halve Maen, or The Half Moon. She is an 85-foot, square-rigged, three-masted, wooden, sailing vessel. She will carry a crew of 15 to 20 men. The Half Moon bears a shallow draft, a high poop deck and forecastle deck, allowing speedy passage and entry to shallow water. We ask you comprise your crew of half Dutch sailors. A generous contractual agreement shall be proffered to you. We seek your expertise and attendance at a conference in Amsterdam to consult with us in

regard to all terms and agreements between us. Enclosed are documents covering your costs to travel here for you and your family.
Sincerely,

Ernst Veckler
Director, E.I.C., Amsterdam, Holland

Hudson handed the letter to Katherine, who read it, and handed it to their son, John, who entered the room for a break from studying mathematics with his siblings and tutor. He asked if they would go after reading it. His father laughed.

"Your mother and I will talk about it. You return to numbers." Nodding his understanding, John left the room so his parents could talk privately.

*****

Two days later, Hudson received a letter from John Smith. Hudson laughed, not having seen his friend in some time. Hand-drawn maps were included with the letter, and Hudson studied them. He recognized the North American continent's eastern shore, and Smith specifically labeled two locations, 'Virginia' and 'Jamestown'. Hudson turned to the letter.

13 August 1608

My Good Friend Henry,

I trust you are well and returning from somewhere exotic. Whenever you receive this letter, I advise you never undertake colonizing. It is a grueling, thankless, unprofitable business, no matter how good the opportunity sounds. The people here are, in a word, lazy. The men must be pushed and prodded to do most anything, even out of necessity. The women blame the men for dragging them here. They take it out on the men by refusing marital duties, at least those who yet maintain a spouse. Thankfully for me, I have never thought religion too important or women too beneficial. Travel and adventure are good enough companions for me.

We have lost nearly half the 104 settlers since our arrival a year previous. A native raid killed a family of eight, and an unknown sickness ravaged us last summer. If that be not enough, winter proved more severe than anyone expected, claiming more lives. We are at 54 now, and no new children come of remaining marriages that seem to exist only on documents. A third of all spouses were lost to sickness, winter, or the raid. Some children are orphans who have been taken-in by other families to be raised. All is confusion and animosity.

We have devised a truce with the local Powhatan Tribe of natives. They are aiding us greatly in crop growing to feed those of us remaining alive. Tenacity and grit help me muddle through. At times, Henry, the divisions overwhelm the feeling of unity. Only a calamity brings us together, and that togetherness fades with time. Then, a newer calamity returns us to the center together.

Religion is probably the most socially divisive issues. The Puritans among us seek a utopia not attainable by humans on this earth. The Anglicans want to maintain the high church of royalty, free of Rome, led by King

James I. Anglicans see Puritans as holy rollers, while the Puritans view Anglicans as too entrenched in 'popish' ways. They claim there yet remains a direct connection between Canterbury and Rome. You should know that no church has been built here.

Truly, I say to thee that there seems little need for a church here. Those espousing the most pious positions are the same conspiring, back-biting pit vipers upon whom I dare not turn my back. There was a howling pandemonium upon the announcement to my place on the governing council of seven in early September. The majority of those discontent with me are Puritans. They hold that a theocracy works best as government. The fact that their numbers have dwindled so much from hardship and death, as well as their underlying distrust and fear of the natives, being different from themselves, remains the major contributing factor preventing my ouster.

I am sending you the enclosed maps and information about the existence of told channels to the Pacific Ocean across North America. One, reported by George Weymouth in 1602, is said to be at sixty-two north latitude. Another, closer to Virginia, is reported to be at latitude forty north. I am too busy here as a council member to investigate either of these supposed routes. Thus, I send them to you that you might make good use of them if you travel this way. I ask only that you offer me reports of your findings if you make any. I may live-out my days here it seems. I feel the burden of almost sixty people upon my shoulders, but I cannot -will not- surrender my hopes for a better future here. All my

best regards to Katherine and the boys. Have you stated teaching John to sail yet? He must be all of ten if he's a day! He'll be a man in a couple years. Good luck with your travels. Your friend,
Captain John Smith

Having read his friend's letter, Hudson shook his head, looking out the window to a grey London afternoon. His thoughts changed to concerns over which he had no control. Nothing was easy in this life, he thought as Katherine entered carrying tea. Hudson shifted his focus from far-away thoughts of foreign colonies to his domestic sphere, where he had a firmer sense of some tangible control. Together, he, Katherine, and the boys were planning the journey to Amsterdam.

*****

Early in October, a period of hot weather in Jamestown rekindled feelings of summer for the children. Adults knew better. Winter was coming. Leaves fell from trees despite the warm weather. Winter was coming, and they were preparing.

Christian Plascomb climbed a tall pin oak tree on the land Richard told Cecelia belonged to them. She had not believed him at first. Their strained relationship had moved back to center, and they were sleeping in the same room once more. Her doubts ended when he provided her the deed. Now, standing atop a wind-swept knoll overlooking a panorama of hills, dales, and freshly harvested acres of land, Cecelia couldn't believe the reality that had blessed them.

"A thousand acres you say, Richard?" she asked, holding her sun hat against her head to prevent losing it.

"Aye, with five hundred more each year for five years," Richard answered, swelling with pride at their sudden good fortune. Trees vaulted to the bright blue sky. Land undulated endlessly. It was theirs. "This will be Christian's on day," Richard commented as their son, high in the tree, called down.

"Not too high, Christian!" his mother called upward, unable to see her son for the dense foliage. Quickly, she asked Richard to call him down before he fell down. Looking up, he shouted.

With Christian, now seven years, safely grounded, Richard asked Cecelia to select the spot where she wanted the new house built.

"What?" she asked so abruptly, stunned by the statement. Richard told her a grand house was in the contract. Looking about, Cecelia smiled.

"I rather fancy this place, actually. I want these grand old trees to remain as well, and the house among them." Richard agreed, placing his arm about her slender waist. She'd lost a considerable amount of weight, he thought.

"I love you, Cecelia. I always shall." They kissed.

"I like to -no, I must- think the worst is behind us, Richard. It has to be." He nodded.

"Agreed, love. We can't change that which has befallen us, as much as we'd like to do." Cecelia placed her index finger against Richard's lips.

"Speak not of old history, husband. I prefer you don't." Again, he nodded, gazing around.

"What shall you name it?" he asked.

"Name what, Richard?"

"The house, the land...all of it!"

"What of Pineview?" Christian suggested, running past them chasing a rabbit. Cecelia looked at Richard.

"Pineview," she repeated. "I rather like it."

"Pineview it is, thanks to both of you," Richard answered.

"For now, though, land baron," Cecelia said, moving slightly closer to Richard. "Let us go back to our little castle and I can make tea."

"Mother, can we make some of that squash like Pocahontas?"

"You like that squash, Christian?" his mother asked, smiling at her husband.

"Yep."

"Excuse me?" Cecelia asked sternly.

"I mean, yes mother," came the dutiful reply. Climbing into the small wagon borrowed from Ian Charles, they returned to the settlement.

*****

At the end of the first week of October, settlers at the colony of Sagadahoc, on the 'maine' coast, were already almost eleven days into their transatlantic crossing back to England aboard a thirty-ton ship they built themselves, called the Virginia of Sagadahoc, or Virginia for short. The decision to abandon made months earlier was solidified when an English supply vessel arrived with news of the deaths of Sir John Popham, Lord Chief Justice of England, who led the trial of Walter Raleigh, and John

236

Gilbert, Raleigh Gilbert's older brother. Gilbert, half-nephew to Walter Raleigh, now twenty-six, decided to quit the colony to return to England to claim his inheritance of Compton Castle in Devon, on England's southern coast.

Gilbert sent the vessel John and Mary back to England with salted fish, furs, and supplies. The colonists sailed on the Virginia. The 27 September departure offered the benefit of safe sailing prior to winter's arrival. The load of furs and salted fish would prove a reward for those returning home. There were no plans to return to the 'maine' coast.

*****

Henry Hudson relocated his family to Amsterdam in January 1609, taking-up residence in a bright yellow set of apartments on a lively street facing a canal. Katherine was accustomed to moving to suit her husband's demanding yet profitable trade. She was also ready to have Henry gone to sea, out from underfoot after several months at their new home.

While Katherine and the boys familiarized themselves with the new exciting city of Amsterdam, Henry wrote to the directors of the East India Company informing them of his arrival, requesting a date to meet to discuss their mutually beneficial expedition. He also wrote to Robert Juet, directing him to journey to Amsterdam in mid-February.

*****

Sir Ferdinando Georges accepted King James' invitation to present his ideas for a new joint stock company. Georges stood to speak before the king and his privy council, a warming fire burning in the great hearth in mid-January 1609.

"I propose a new stock company to be called the Council for New England. My vision states that the company be chartered

237

by the Crown to colonize and govern any and all new settlements on the North American continent, especially in the northeast section in accordance with the landed gentry class, as opposed to current fashion, which seeks new colonies solely for the benefits of merchants. It is the landed gentry who provide most of the jobs to the masses of unskilled laborers.

"Therefore, Your Majesty, the landed gentry should represent the best our beloved country has to offer for new colonies. To facilitate this new company, a series of fiefdoms may be established under selected gentry families with the financial means to operate a fief. Also, politically selected families with proper connections to introduce new jobs in new colonies should be addressed." Sir Ferdinando seated himself; the council looked to King James, who addressed Sir Georges.

"Sir Georges, under your plan, whose political authority would the newly formed colonies be included and governed?"

"Why, Majesty, the Crowns, of course," Georges replied instantly. The king nodded, glancing to Cecil, who gently nodded.

"This all sounds like an excellent plan for which to allow the Crown to extend its control over new North American colonization. But, in our opinion, we shall table this discussion for now. We are so close to a truce with the Spanish that I want Salisbury focused solely on that truce with Spain. We shall revisit this discussion at a date to be set." The king turned to Calvert.

"Calvert, have you recorded all that has been stated?"

"I have, Your Majesty."

"Good enough, then. Table the present issue until after the truce." All were dismissed as Cecil and the king turned to truce business. Georges quietly decided to sharpen his information for his next opportunity.

*****

On 21 February 1609, George Calvert, now thirty years of age, was relieved of his official secretary duties to Robert Cecil. The purpose for this departure was to take-up his place in Parliament in the House of Commons. His responsibilities were focused on communicating the king's policies to the political body, as well as gathering royal supplies. Calvert's initial reception was well-received, but he also sensed an unspoken level of hostility he could not identify. Shrugging it off, Calvert set to work, deciding time would tell.

*****

John Smith governed Jamestown council with the experience and reliability of a man accustomed to adversity and an understanding of economic and social demands. His first priority was colony discipline. Survival depended on those able to provide strength and foresight. The indolent would be jailed. The colony's immediate future, as well as the remaining lives, depended upon everyone, especially the men. Days of laziness were passed.

The crop lands, under Richard Plascomb's leadership, was producing pumpkins, squash, corn, and beans. The natives, led by Powhatan, had worked tirelessly to help the struggling settlement ground itself before everyone died. The first harvest was approaching. The truce was absolutely required to continue, regardless of the unspoken undercurrent of residual dislike of the 'red man' harbored by some in the settlement. Smith had openly stated that refusing to allow one's children to

239

play with Pocahontas and other native children only because their skin color was different went against the ideas of new world thinking.

"This is not the old world," he scolded. "We left that word behind," he added, pointedly blaming the guilty parties.

Agriculture was his next path to colony survival and success. Everyone took turns working the fields at the crop lands. Try as Richard did to call it Pineview, the name Croplands became synonymous with the Plascomb family. Richard started trading with the Powhatan, trading food for land, in addition to land contracted by the council. Land obtained through dealings with the natives stretched southward, away from the colony. In only five months, Plascomb gained nearly four thousand acres from the Powhatan. Croplands was the largest business in the colony, and the large home under construction atop the knoll was testament to the success of the Plascomb family.

Additionally, the glass business continued to grow monthly. Demand for beautifully stained glass and objects for home décor were desired and prized as status. The severity of difficult living conditions resulted in the colonists attempting to bring a sense of beauty into their thatch-roofed dwellings. In addition to ornamentation, those who sought such works desired something different, thereby making their home individualized, a reflection of who they were.

Establishing a colony required an unprecedented amount of conformity; therefore, individualism sprouted through home beautification. The Charles-Plascomb Glass Works benefitted directly from the desire for the new, colorful, fresh. Richard divided his time between the glass foundry and Croplands, maintaining a very busy daily schedule. The foundry had hired a dozen men and eight boy apprentices.

Out of necessity or the sheer power of will, Smith's commanding leadership forced a resurgence of the unity that typically resulted from calamity. People pulled together. New crops were planted. Homes were repaired or replaced. Timber started to replace wattle and thatch houses. Those who worked and could afford them were the first to obtain timber houses. By mid-April, a sense of true cohesiveness, orchestrated by Smith, Plascomb, Charles, and other newly-prominent men of the community were slowly driving forth a semi-successful colony that held promise of emerging from the desolate ashes of intense isolation and numbing personal losses.

*****

Executive changes reorganized the Virginia Company at Plymouth, London. Sir Thomas Smythe assumed his new duties as treasurer on 1 March 1609. A more influential and organized group of strong Puritan faith took direct command of the company, which had experienced a sharp decline in investments in the Jamestown colony. Bad news travels fast, and its negative effects multiply across the miles. In a closed meeting, the new leaders decided a new influx of capital was required to ensure Jamestown's success. The quickly hoped-for return on investment capital saw great losses instead. A new royal patent would be sought from the king, and a new scheme to draw new emigrants to Jamestown would be devised. Following those agreements, the board invited three Puritan ministers into the open portion of the meeting.

The ministers entered in grim, sullen, Puritan fashion. Simple welcomes were offered. Minister Fenwick Finster, a plain bespectacled man of sixty-eight who never smiled, opened his address by ceremoniously dumping a sack of letters onto the directors' table, the multiple letters spilling across the table, and several to the floor.

"Gentlemen, I shall be direct. Your company is losing money because your settlement is beset by savage native pagans. Not only that, but this man Smith is a godless leader who is no better than the pagans he has befriended, and who killed innocent women and children. It is no wonder your investments have fallen. What you need to do is install a governing body that will establish a colony of God and Godliness in that tree-shrouded forsaken wilderness, that land of rampant native fornication and death.

"Before long, we shall receive word of one of our own living among *them*, the heathen pagans, and where will marriages of white women, lured by the undulating pagan flesh, to natives, lead us?" Finster waved his hand.

"I'll tell you where it will lead us, gentlemen. Race mixing will take us directly down the road to perdition, that's where. And *please* do not introduce the thought of a white man mating with one of those animals! Can you see it? Mixed-race offspring, the spawn of Satan himself! Such a thought is an abomination too evil to consider!" he hissed contemptuously.

"Not even God Himself would accept such a degradation of that half-human form," he declared, looking at the men around the table. "There is enough fornication in *this* country that results in street urchins everywhere in our midst. One only need to walk the London streets to see them grasping, grabbing, dirty faces, barefoot, rags, to understand the base humanity that live here. Let us not export fornication as our main commodity. We are a noble people -God's *select* nation- and above the base, vile, and common earthly pleasures that produce the urchins.

"Install the God-like presence in government. Cast-out the pagans and their heathen friend, Smith. I am informed he considers himself the king of Jamestown. Invest with God, and your returns shall multiply. That is all we have to say." The other

242

two ministers scooped-up the pile of letters while Finley studied the directors.

"You may keep the letters as evidence, should you decide to file criminal charges against the pagan Smith for *any* reason you see fit," Finster stated quietly, smiling churlishly. One director stood.

"Minister Finster, thank you for your time and presence today. That will not be necessary for the time being. If you maintain the letters, we shall request them from you when needed." A second director stood.

"On account, Mr. Plumb, I recommend we maintain the letters here for safe-keeping. This way, we will have them to read them, categorize them, and store them for future use. The Minister is correct." A vote decided to keep the letters. Finster was pleased.

"We shall go, gentlemen. God will do the rest. Do not allow the corruption of the races by mixing, for God will smite thee." The first director stood again.

"Gentlemen, your message reinforces our determination and clarifies our mission. It is the time for renewal at Jamestown. Thank you for visiting us." The ministers departed as sullenly as they had arrived.

Following a discussion about the new patent, the directors departed to their business. The second director, falling behind, stopped to talk with the apprentice at the door. Removing several coins, he handed them to the apprentice.

"Thomas, do you see that sack on the table?"

"Aye, Sir John." The director nodded.

"Good, Thomas. Take that sack at this moment and heave it into one of the furnaces below, sack and all. If anyone ever asks you about them, and they shan't, you direct the individual to me." Two pairs of eyes, one knowing, the other learning, locked briefly.

"Aye, Sir John," was the unquestioning reply. The director departed; the apprentice grabbed the sack.

Part One, Chapter Eighteen

May 1609 – July 1609

Blue sky and calm water held promise for a successful supply run for the Jamestown colonists as a nine-ship fleet of supply ships, led by the Virginia Company of Jamestown's newest flagship, Sea Venture, built specifically for delivering supplies to the fledgling colony, departed from Plymouth on a brilliant sunny morning on 23 May 1609. Sea Venture was the largest, fastest, and best-armed vessel of the fleet. Her guns were placed on her main deck, rather than below decks as was typical for the time. This meant that the ship did not need double-timbering, and Sea Venture may have been the first single-timbered, armed merchant ship built in England. The hold was sheathed and furnished for passengers. She was armed with eight, nine-pounder demi-culverins, eight, five-pounder sakers, a medium-sized cannon, four, three-pounder falcons, also called light cannons, and four arquebuses, or long guns, like rifles.

Commanded by now Vice-admiral Christopher Newport, Sea Venture led the additional eight vessels to open water. Aboard Sea Venture was John Rolfe, now twenty-three years, and his wife of nearly a year, Sarah Hacker.

Company Treasurer, Sir Thomas Smythe, amassed the most significant oceanic supply fleet to-date. Not only were regular supplies included, but almost six hundred interested new settlers that included whole families, answered pamphlets seeking new residents at Jamestown. Also, all manner of livestock was included to bolster the colony and the people living in it. Pigs, cows, chickens, geese, and tons of provisions to supply the colonists were packed aboard the nine vessels.

Sea Venture was joined in the monumental sailing by Blessing, with Captain Gabriel Archer and Captain Adams, Catch, a pinnace, or a lightly built, single-decked, square-sterned vessel suitable for exploring, trading, and light naval duties, and lead by Master Matthew Fitch, Diamond, the second largest vessel, captained by John Ratcliffe and Captain King, Falcon the third largest, with Captain John Martin and Master Francis Nelson, Lion with Captain Webb, Swallow, with Captain Moone and Master Matthew Somers, a nephew of Sir George, Unitie with Captain Wood and Master Robert Pitt, and Virginia, another pinnace, headed by Captain James Davis and Master Davis. The fleet represented the Virginia Company's most determined effort yet to salvage Jamestown. Aboard Sea Venture, Rolfe and Sarah talked excitedly with other passengers eager to start a new life in a new world offering land, opportunity, and a chance at a promising future. Also aboard Sea Venture was Sir Thomas Gates, the first appointed governor of the Jamestown settlement.

*****

Henry Hudson firmly determined his new ship to be sea worthy according to his demanding specifications, especially for a northern voyage around Novaya Zemlya. Smaller, yet more nimble than Hopewell, the Half Moon, provided and paid for by the Dutch East India Company, was completely filled with excellent and abundant provisions for the journey. Directed by Hudson to select able English deckhands, Robert Juet appeared with a handful of rough-looking men, all eager to earn a wage. Following introductions between the English and Dutch crewmen, final preparations were made.

Hudson, his son, John, Juet, and the crew of eighteen sailed from Gravesend on 1 April, 1609, setting a familiar course for the western coast of Norway. Once again, John, now nearly twelve years, was growing into a superb navigator and ship's pilot. The crew found him to be a very reputable source for information about the Norwegian coast. To aid the Captain, Juet volunteered to keep the ship's log. The bright canvas sails whipped in the wind as Half Moon sailed from Gravesend. The expedition was beginning superbly.

*****

The New Virginia Company at London, the proposed name for the open investment company proposed by the governors of the Virginia Company at Plymouth, sat in conference with King James, proposing their ideas for obtaining a second royal patent. Sir Thomas Smythe, the treasurer, declared that the purpose of the new company was to increase potential profits by inviting all investors seeking to join the company, including those of the merchant class. Sir Thomas addressed the gathering.

"The first Plymouth colony, as we know, was a failure. The Popham Colony, or Sagadahoc, only lasted a year due to abandonment. We also know at this time that The Virginia Company at Plymouth has folded. As a result, this leaves the Virginia Company at London with multiple opportunities to obtain new colonies by having more territory available."

The king scrutinized the maps lining the table, listening keenly to proposals as he questioned directors about reports of serious troubles at Jamestown. Directors responded by explaining the difficulties of starting settlements in previously unsettled territories. King James nodded.

"Nothing is as perfect as a splendid idea gone bad," he commented, picking up a map of North America. Directors were unsure of the king's meaning by his comment, but they were very relieved when he spoke again.

"It is imperative that I justify this much-increased investment. Thus, it shall be recorded here, 23 May 1609, that a second royal patent is granted for the Virginia Company of London. Said patent pertains solely to the new company and no other. Further, I decree that the land grant for said patent is granted to all points two hundred miles north and south of Old Point Comfort, the location where Captain Newport and the first Jamestown settlers landed. Further, this tract of land shall extend also, and fully, without opposition, to the entire west and northwest to the Pacific Ocean." King James looked to his scribe, who already understood what the king wanted to know.

"I have it all, Your Majesty."

"Good. Prepare the correct number of documents for Crown and the Company." He turned to the directors. "Congratulations, gentlemen, you have a new company. Gather your investors with care. Nothing succeeds like success."

*****

Richard and Cecelia Plascomb officially moved into their new residence at Croplands in mid-May. The immense stone house dwarfed the little family as they stood before its twin front doors made of Virginia oak trees.

Inside, a massive cooking and eating area with a stone hearth large enough to roast a suckling pig and chickens at the same time commanded the entirety of the north wall. A grand parlor, a large study lined with bookshelves, six bedrooms, and several sitting rooms on each of the two floors left Cecelia perplexed as to what to do with them.

"Maybe we can fill them with children," Richard said, the words tumbling from his mouth before considering more

248

pragmatically. To his surprise, Cecelia looked at him, smiled, and wrapped her arm in his.

"Would you like to, Richard?" she asked softly. "You're nearly thirty-five, you know. Your middle-aged." He guffawed.

"Wife, some snow may be on the roof, but the hearth does yet burn." Laughing, Cecelia led her husband to a sunny window seat looking down the knoll to farm land below.

"Besides, you're twenty-four yourself, Cecelia. You're catching-up fast."

"Maybe one more, Richard, but I'm not so sure I'm up to it," Cecelia said, sighing deeply. "I so do miss our Ellen and Edmund, our babies, ourselves, forever gone, and by no fault of their own." Richard studied the panoramic view.

"I miss them too, and I know Christian does as well," Richard lamented.

"Well," Cecelia quietly said. "Perhaps after we are settled here, maybe we could try," she almost whispered, her voice filled with hesitation.

"We've come a long way, Cecelia," Richard told her, staring at the endless expanse of land and forest and hills.

"Aye, we have, Richard. We've seen the worst. Maybe the better is here for a change." Sitting in the sunlit window seat in what would be the eating area, they kissed just as Christian ran from upstairs.

"Ich," he said, screwing-up his youthful face, his mother pulling him into herself, kissing him with motherly affection.

"I kiss you all the time, Christian Plascomb," she teased, while he squirmed to escape, yet enjoying the attention all the same.

"That's different," he replied, settling as his mother embraced him. Cecelia looked to Richard.

"I wonder what they would have looked like," she said, staring vacantly ahead. Richard's smile faded to a look of remorse. He chose to leave the past in the past, yet had also considered the same question.

"They would be so beautiful, that's what I say," he said evenly. Cecelia only nodded.

*****

Henry Hudson again sighted North Cape on 5 May, but self-doubt had crept into his mind, and there were other new problems. In addition to his inner turmoil, verbal disagreements had started escalating to physical altercations between the English and Dutch crewmen. With a fortnight, Hudson listened to arguments, including his lack of success on two previous expeditions in this same region. With veiled threats of mutiny multiplying daily, Hudson decided to try a completely different plan designed to erase self-doubt and quell crew troubles.

Producing the maps made by the Virginia Company of London, Captain Hudson proposed that the crew find a pathway to the Pacific Ocean. With the crew's overwhelming support, Hudson ordered the Half Moon to change direction. John Hudson successfully steered the Half Moon into eastern winds, making way 180 degrees in the opposite direction they had been sailing. Very soon, the Faroe Islands lay to the ship's port side. The Half Moon's crew were sailing to the New World. Robert Juet made the entry into the ship's log.

Captain Samuel Argall listened to Sir Edwin Sandys describe the Virginia Company's desire to determine a faster, more northerly sailing route to North America, particularly a route to the fledgling Jamestown settlement.

"In addition to this faster route, Captain, particularly for supply and emigration purposes, we seek that we may prevent our vessels from falling prey to Spanish interests, including privateering and outright piracy. Do you have some insight to this route?" Argall, self-assured and confident, studied the many maps strewn across the long wooden table. Never short of his opinions regarding his abilities, Argall methodically stroked his beard, responding to Sir Edwin.

"The typical sailing route takes English vessels southward along the Spanish and African coasts below Morocco, and into the tropics, finally turning westward on the trade winds. I propose sailing completely away from the Spanish coast, aiming instead for the Azores, turning to Somers Island, also called Bermuda, and, finally, due west to the mouth of the James River." Argall let the map fall to the table.

"Is it doable, Captain?"

"Sir Edwin, you hired me to do a job. I assure you I will attest to giving you my best effort to be successful. I do believe it to be, as you say, doable." Sandys considered.

"Very well, Captain, assemble your crew. You will sail in four weeks. Your ship will be fully supplied with provisions and whatever you require. Give us a faster route." The men shook hands, and Argall departed to prepare to be successful.

A truce between England and Spain ended the war coming to be called the Thirty Years War. It was finally over. In Holland, troops started disbanding as units were released from fighting. Men were ready to return home, many having fought for years.

Relieved of his duties as an army captain, Miles Standish walked the Amsterdam streets, searching for lodgings and work. The self-proclaimed professional soldier had to make changes since the war was over. He thought the goodness of war would never end, but here he stood, looking across the line of bridges over the canals, wondering where he could find another war. At twenty-five, the thrill of fighting was an exhilarating tonic. Standish's attention was caught by the sight of a man he was sure was a Puritan minister. He moved to catch-up, some three bridges away.

The man wore a simple black shirt and white collar. His gaze was forward, turning in neither direction, focused. Standish quickly grew closer to the man, whom he could tell was older than himself. He called-out.

"Minister!" he called, repeating it to slow or stop the man. Turning, the man waited for the stranger with dark hair and beard approach him on the bridge. A few feet away, Standish spoke.

"Good day, Sir. I'm sure you're a Puritan minister." The minister, if he was one, looked to be in his forties. "I'm Miles Standish. I'm a Puritan. I was born in Lancashire, 1584. I be twenty-five. I've been a captain in the army fighting against the Spanish in aid to the Dutch a few years. With the new truce, I seek lodgings and work. I've not seen any Puritan congregations, but I spotted you a few bridges away. I would be very happy in a Puritan congregation." The older man smiled thinly, extending his hand.

"I am a Puritan minister. My name is William Brewster. I was returning to my congregation. We came from Scrooby, Nottinghamshire, to escape religious persecution under King James I. I understand your desire to be enclosed in God's house. We have been very happy in Amsterdam, but we are having some internal problems. As a result, a group of us are readying to move to Leiden tomorrow. I was making some final arrangements.

"I tell you what to do. Join us in Leiden in Eldenstrasse in three days' time. There, we shall be better ready to assist you. Now, I must be going." They shook hands.

"Thank you, Minister. I shall be in Eldenstrasse waiting for you." They parted. Standish, noticing the early hour of the day, decided to travel to Leiden, not far from Amsterdam. There, he would be sure to find lodgings for several days, more if needed. He might even find employment.

*****

In July 1609, Henry, Prince of Wales, son of King James I, and heir to the English throne, ventured with his retinue to the Tower of London specifically to visit Walter Raleigh.

Imprisoned in the Tower since 1603, Raleigh and his family were appointed well-furnished apartments, where Raleigh spent his time writing and performing scientific experiments. Life was quite lonely at times for the family, especially for sixteen-year-old Walter Raleigh. Carew, his brother, was born four years earlier in the Tower, and had no idea of any other life. Damerei, his eldest brother, had died when he was only a few months old in 1591. Raleigh worked to engage his sons in his experiments. Walter also learned numbers, Latin, played musical instruments, and painted.

Prince Henry, now fifteen and an excellent student himself, had an assignment he thought only Raleigh capable of doing, and doing correctly. With the proper introductions performed, the teenage prince sat with Raleigh, now fifty-nine years, and as surprised as his family to be visited by the Prince of Wales.

"Mr. Raleigh, I come with a special request of you."

"Anything, Prince Henry. But how may I be of service to you in the Tower?" The prince smiled.

"Raleigh, your travels have afforded you a perspective on the world known only by very few men. I believe you have a duty to educate everyone about that which you have seen, heard, and learned. Basically, I want you to write a history of the world." Raleigh was stunned.

"A world history?" he asked incredulously. "What of resources? I have none that would benefit me in such a work." The prince nodded.

"Make a list. It will be retrieved in four days. Ask for anything you require," said the Prince, standing. "Thank you for accepting this most wonderful endeavor on my behalf." Turning, the prince departed, followed by his entourage. Raleigh's family rushed into the room.

"What was that all about?" Bess asked breathlessly. "Are we to be freed?"

"Alas, no, Bess. The prince wants me to wrote a history of the world." His wife scoffed, seating herself.

"I don't know, Walter, but I'd much rather *live* in it instead of simply *writing* about it." Raleigh sighed deeply.

"We do as we are able, my dear. We can do no more," Raleigh said disappointedly, seating himself to start his list of reference materials.

*****

Captain Samuel Argall sailed from Gravesend, London, determined to find a faster route to North America. His ship, the Mary and John, sailed into strong winds and good weather, the crew unfurling all sails as the big vessel made way to open waters.

*****

The nine-vessel fleet heading to Jamestown with new colonists, food, provisions, livestock, and high hopes was at sea nearly six weeks, with an additional five or six to go before they arrived. Weather and seas had been favorable, but both were quickly changing badly in early July.

Unknown to anyone aboard the nine ships, a storm that started by blowing five days ago, moving westward across Bechar, Algeria, to Marrakech, in Morocco, passed forcefully out across the Atlantic Ocean gathering strength as it passed over the Canary Islands. Gathering severity as it passed over open warm water, the storm continued its westward trajectory.

The typical sailing route to North America takes English vessels southward along the Spanish and African coasts below Morocco, and into the tropics, near Somers Island, or Bermuda, finally turning westward on the trade winds. The path was no different on this journey. As the crews began initiating the final trajectory to Virginia, passengers and crew alike were completely horrified as the black clouds that had been so distant appeared to be bearing-down on the fleet. Winds suddenly increased sharply. Passengers were immediately ordered below decks as crews scrambled to avert a calamity as a heavy rain started falling in torrents. Into the captain's log aboard Sea Venture was entered, 'the day of the tempest arrived', as 25July 1609, also known as St. James Day. The calamity had come.

*****

Captain Samuel Argall proved there was a faster route to North America and Jamestown. The successful voyage took nine weeks and six days, slicing almost three weeks off the usual route. Argall maneuvered the Mary and John to the mouth of the Chesapeake, continuing up the James River to Jamestown. Anticipating a hearty reception after his successful sailing, Argall was taken aback when he arrived and discovered sickness and scant resources.

*****

Admiral George Somers, having shared the helm with Vice-Admiral Newport throughout the tempest, decided they had no choice but to purposely ground Sea Venture in a bay he spotted after the storm passed. Water bailing by all healthy passengers proved futile after the storm, proving that no vessel, no matter how majestic, how military-capable, or sea worthy, could hold together if the timbers had not set, leading all calking to fail, as happened on Sea Venture. The fleet was separated during the tempest. Sea Venture was alone in the tropics, and none of the other ships were in sight all the way to the horizon. Somers decided he had to force the three-hundred-ton vessel aground. His only, other, more dire option was loss of crew and 150 passengers. The order to ground upon the reefs was issued, and passengers braced for the worst on the open main deck since it was too dangerous to be below decks for a grounding on a reef. Newport, standing mid-ship, then ordered all starboard side guns be tossed to remain afloat. George Somers, Admiral of the

256

Company, remained at the helm. Children and women cried; men did too. The crew, working furiously, pushed guns over the side as fast as possible.

 John Rolfe grabbed Sarah, retreating in preparation for a hard landing near Somers Island. Rolfe also knew Sarah was carrying their first child; they had to survive. The tropical sun was extremely hot. Captain Newport, shouting continual orders, watched as Somers steered the great ship directly into the sharp reefs off the eastern shore of Bermuda as his crew scrambled to salvage as much of the ship as possible. Newport also considered the fates of the other eight ships of the supply fleet.

*****

"We've no supplies, Captain Argall, and no rain for almost six weeks!" exclaimed John Smith to Argall, currently sitting in Smith's cottage. "Our winter food supply at Croplands fails every day!" Argall ordered all provisions aboard the Mary and John be distributed among the residents immediately.

"We've not much ourselves, Captain Smith," Argall said. "We've been at sea nearly ten weeks." Smith said he understood, having been at sea. Argall inquired about the lack of settlers, appalled by Smith's articulation of deaths due to a strange summer sickness, a frigid winter, and lack of supply ships from England. Smith also told Argall he would talk with the Powhatan for supplies for Argall's return trip to England.

"In the meantime, Captain Smith, I suggest we tend to getting things in order," Argall suggested firmly. The men shook hands, understanding the dire straits the settlement faced with winter only two or three months hence. The crew of Mary and John joined with the remaining settlers at Jamestown to assist as they could.

257

Towards the end of July, a scouting party led by Richard Plascomb returned to the colony with news of a foreign ship sailing along the coast, and possibly into the James River. Argall prepared his vessel to search.

"Most likely Spanish," Argall said as his crew quickly readied the Mary and John. "They've colonies in Florida, south of here. They're most likely trying to spy on the settlement. If they are aware you are struggling, they'll kill all and claim it for Spain. Any men who wish to join us are welcome. Plascomb and a few others, including Ian Charles, boarded.

The Mary and John sailed to the river's mouth to open waters of the Chesapeake. Immediately, calls and yelling of, "port side!" rang-out. Extending his spyglass, Argall determined the ship to be of Spanish origin.

"Yes, it's the La Asuncion de Christo. She's captained by Francisco Fernández de Écija. She's most likely out of St. Augustine, their main colony." Argall gave the order to chase the vessel.

"She's turning westward, Captain!" a sailor called from the crow's nest.

"They see us," Argall told the men, ordering all to, "hold steady, men!" he ordered, watching the vessel that almost entered the Chesapeake, but was now turning away. "Stay to!" came the Captain's order. "She's departing!" Within a half-hour, the Spanish vessel distanced itself from the Chesapeake, sailing southward. Argall changed the order to return to Jamestown.

*****

The date in the captain's log was recorded as 2 August 1609. Henry Hudson was positive he was sailing along the coastal

258

waters of the location John Smith detailed in his recent letter and maps. The successful Atlantic crossing reinforced Hudson's determination to find the waterway leading to the Pacific Ocean. Deciding he was at thirty-eight north latitude, Hudson brought the Half Moon about, starting a northeastern run along the North American coast, searching for the wide opening to the westward passage.

Studying a small inlet unknown to him, Hudson decided the opening was too small for such an important passageway. What he didn't know was that he was looking at the mouth of the James River, where Jamestown lay only thirty miles upriver. A second waterway also appeared too small for such an important connection, so he continued sailing.

*****

Calls rang through Jamestown about the approach of four vessels sailing upriver. Once docked, the captains explained the fleet and its mission, detailing the tempest at sea, and how all the vessels became separated over three days. Blessing, Falcon, Lion, and Unitie carried mostly passengers but few supplies.

"The majority of supplies were aboard our flagship vessel, the Sea Venture," Captain Gabriel Archer told Argall and the settlers. "We've not seen her or the other four ships since the tempest," he added somberly. When Argall asked how many passengers they had, Archer said there were almost three hundred among the four arriving vessels.

"Maybe another three hundred on the others, minus those who died."

"Died?" Charles asked.

"Yes," Gabriel answered. "Yellow fever broke out on two of these four vessels. We buried thirty-two at sea. Some remain sick. We have no idea about what may have happened aboard the others." Argall shook his head.

"More mouths to feed, some sick, no supplies, and little food. Gentlemen, we have some work to do."

Three days later the Diamond appeared, followed by the Swallow. Captain Ratcliffe of the Diamond reported London plague broke out on his vessel. They were buried at sea. When counting new arrivals was finished, Jamestown grew by nearly three hundred new settlers. No one had word of Sea Venture, but Captain John Martin of the Falcon reported he saw Catch sinking with all aboard.

"She is lost," he said quietly.

"Well, rest their souls, all of them," Argall said, looking about the dock teeming with new people. "Well, men, we better get to work."

*****

On 2 September, Henry Hudson found what he was sure was the waterway across America to the Pacific Ocean. The sizable width of the waterway appeared worthy of representing such a respectable waterway. This waterway also matched the approximate forty-degree north latitude described by Smith. The Half Moon entered the river known as Manna-hatar.

The journey up the broad river was as rich in resources as it was for the hope as the westward passage. Keeping the log, Juet noted the many resources the areas offered, including an abundance of fresh fish, corn, copper, and lumber in the forms of oak, chestnut, and walnut trees, to name a few. The sight of

260

natives standing along the banks of the wide river astounded everyone, especially young John. From the deck, the crew could see the natives and their village behind them. In the village, it was easy to see crops growing. Corn and beans grew in amounts Juet described as, "enough to load three ships besides what was growing in the fields." Hudson and Juet discussed the strong probability that the palisades along the river contained valuable minerals. Hudson also noted that the further north they sailed, the shallower the water was becoming.

The journey upriver lasted three weeks until the Half Moon's draft was too much and was forced to turn around. The crew weighed anchor and went ashore for rest and exploring. They spent almost a full week camping, hunting, exploring, and discussing a return expedition. Satisfied with all his crew accomplished, Hudson journeyed back down the expansive river to its mouth. Passing from it, Hudson declared the river be named the Hudson River. Hudson was also proud that he was only the second European to visit this area since Verrazano, in 1524, almost eighty-five years earlier.

As Half Moon passed the small island at the river's mouth, Juet described a tall cliff he observed as one, "of a color of a white-green as though it was copper or silver." Moving out to catch the westerly winds at open sea, Juet recorded Hudson's words describing the expedition. "We weighed and came out of the river into which we had run so fare." Half Moon and her crew made way for home on 4 October 1609.

*****

The 150 aboard Sea Venture swam or walked ashore the island to relative safety. All survived the reef grounding. Immediate needs had to be met. Men began erecting shelters, while women, men, and colder children searched for food stuffs. Sir Thomas Gates disagreed with Admiral George Somers about whom should be the leader. Gates believed he should be because they were now on land. Contrarily, Somers saw himself as leader because the land was not Jamestown, and, as a shipwrecked vessel's leader, they were yet considered at sea until rescued or found a way to escape the island. For the sake of the survivors, they elected to co-serve. The Sea Venture's long boat was salvaged, fitted with a mast and sails, and eight men, led by Henry Ravens, were to sail to Virginia and Jamestown to report on the grounding after some rest and food.

The decision to reuse as much as possible of the Sea Venture to build a new vessel was put into action. Crew started by salvaging all the sails and rigging. No one had any idea how long they would be on the island. Rolfe and Sarah now understood their child would be born on this island.

Part One, Chapter Nineteen

October 1609 – January 1610

The Governor and directors of the Virginia Company at London met in October with several items of new business. Treasurer, Sir Thomas Smythe, opened the meeting with a terse rebuke of Henry Hudson.

"Gentlemen, it is a fact that Captain Hudson, whom we have dutifully employed in our graces, is reported to be in the employ of a competitive Dutch company, the East India Company, seeking to locate the northwest passage to the Orient. Thus, he has undertaken an enterprise that can only be viewed as detrimental to his own country. We can only deduce he is at sea since no word has come from any of the usual ports where ships heading to the Netherlands may stop, including Cornwall, Dartmouth, or Gravesend. We have alerted all port masters to report if a ship called the Half Moon makes port." Smythe seated himself as a director stood to address the group.

"Gentlemen, our attention has been drawn to the apparent issue of Godless guidance in our Virginia colony. This is in addition to a number of hardships befalling the settlers, many of us here believe, stems from the complete, unquestionable, and very real impact of God's wrath upon the people at Jamestown specifically due to their heathen ways.

"The directors of this Company are actively taking measures to offset this pagan culture with God's directives. As I speak, Sir Thomas Gates is probably taking his place as the first Governor of the Jamestown colony. Sir Thomas sailed aboard the Sea Venture. By now, he is in the colony establishing God's order among the native-loving pagan elements there, particularly John Smith, who will be removed from the council.

"Sir Thomas' arrival with the fleet will replenish supplies to the settlers, along with a soothing settling feeling of God's laws upon the people there. Sir Thomas asked that I extend his firm desire to help Company profits by helping those at Jamestown find success through God. Thank you."

With the opening comments completed, the men turned to other business.

*****

Miles Standish was welcomed in Leiden by the members of the Scrooby group who, following disagreements with other Scrooby members from upholding their strictly Calvinist views of man's predestination, broke away and moved to Leiden. Among those who moved were William Brewster and John Robinson. William Bradford, now nineteen, also moved to Leiden, and was proving to be more of a church leader as time passed.

Standish was hired by the group as a military advisor. Bradford and several other men in the group easily found work as fustians, men who worked making products from linen and cotton. Once more, the group realigned itself in its continuing efforts to adhere to its religious fervor despite the odds against them.

*****

John Smith completed a walk-about of the Jamestown settlement with the men assigned to accompany him. Upon meeting briefly with the replacement scouts, all working to ensure the settlement's safety around the perimeter, Smith returned to his residence. He was truly disappointed by the Croplands' failed harvest, but lack of rain over several months, paired with summer's heat, dried and cracked the land. Smith feared another dire winter, especially after three hundred new emigrants arrived several months earlier. Another severe winter would devastate the tottering colony. Pouring some ale into a tall mug, Smith enjoyed a long drink before cleaning his gun, preparing it for use if needed.

After cleaning the weapon, Smith placed his gunpowder holder on a shelf, when it fell, striking a spark, causing a small explosion, burning Smith on his arm and legs. The sound of the explosion, despite its small size, caught peoples' attention. Men ran to Smith's cottage, finding him writhing in agonizing pain. Some worked to put out the fire that started, and others aided Smith carrying him to his bed where the women quickly went to work with the midwife's help to settle the burns.

Captain Argall was preparing a return journey to England for badly needed supplies, and took Smith aboard to obtain medical attention in London. Inwardly, Smith already knew his decision had been made. He'd done all he could for the settlement, but now he had to seek attention for his wounds. Argall sailed on 14 October 1609, and John Smith would never return to Virginia.

*****

Henry Hudson docked Half Moon in the southwestern port town of Dartmouth, east of Plymouth, England for rest and resupply before the final journey through the English Channel and the North Sea to Holland. His arrival was discreetly noticed by a member of the Virginia Company at London, who was checking on vessel arrivals in Dartmouth and Plymouth. The envoy quickly sent word to the local Dartmouth magistrate. In the span of several hours, the magistrate arrived with a sheriff and a small entourage of men, confronting Hudson and his crew at a harbor tavern.

"You have involved yourself in an enterprise against your country in the service of another," the magistrate stated firmly. "Neither you nor your crew may leave England. You are not under arrest, but must remain in Dartmouth until additional orders arrive." The rough seamen, unaccustomed to taking orders from someone other than a sea captain, merely shrugged their shoulders, continuing to enjoy their pints.

"One port in the storm is same as another," one said to his mates.

"Right that, mate," the other sailor replied. "Even a political port."

Several days later, Hudson and his son were summoned to London. Before departing, though, Hudson covertly gathered the complete set of charts, maps, and logs, shipping them to the East India Company directors in Amsterdam, believing that they deserved the very information they paid to obtain. A day later after a search of the Half Moon, Hudson claimed the information was lost at sea in a storm. His crew agreed fully. Hudson and his son were going to London.

*****

In Amsterdam, the excited East India Company directors poured over the treasure-trove of maps, logs, charts, diagrams, and descriptions submitted by Hudson. Rich mineral deposits were supposed, as were valuable and plentiful timber, fertile soil, friendly people called natives and their abundant crops.

Also, having been advised of the discrepancy of Hudson's employment and the seizure of their ship and its crew, the directors lodged a protest for return of their vessel, its crew and her captain, demanding all be rightfully returned since no laws were broken.

The directors also began devising a systematic plan to exploit the region they had financially underwritten for exploration, thereby establishing their rightful claim to the territory to colonize as they deemed conducive to Dutch colonization. Lastly, the directors also initiated plans for a more diversified portfolio with the formation of the Dutch West India Company.

*****

Beachside bonfires, grilled wild boar, fish, and vegetables quickly became a way of life for the survivors of Sea Venture on the uninhabited island of Bermuda, now also being called Somers Isle after George Somers, Admiral of the fleet provided by the Virginia Company at London. In mid-November, a group of leading men of the island inhabitants gathered on the beach discussing plans for their escape vessel called Deliverance, currently under construction.

Sir Thomas Gates, Admiral George Somers, Christopher Newport, Stephen Hopkins, secretary William Strachey, and John Rolfe stood watching the new vessel being constructed by men and older boys. Somers, knowledgeable in ship-building, had concerns about the ship's carrying capacity. Though all salvageable materials from Sea Venture were used in the new ship's construction, the builders quickly discovered the excellent wood provided by Bermuda cedar trees. The trees were equal in strength to oak, but were lighter in weight, allowing for faster sailing and the ability to carry extra materials due to the reduced mass of the vessel. Use of the trees also enhanced maneuverability. All work to construct Deliverance was unimpeded due to the superb weather conditions on the island.

Sunshine and warm weather were a blessing, even in mid-November. Somers had an idea he sought to share.

"Men, she's going to be superb on the water, but Deliverance shan't carry all of us and foodstuffs and supplies." The men looked at the ship being built. Sit Thomas guessed what Somers was thinking.

"Are you saying, George, we require a second vessel?" Somers nodded.

"Aye, Thomas, that is my idea. The sooner we begin, the sooner we may evade this glorious paradise and make way to Jamestown." Some scratched their heads. Rolfe volunteered.

"I'll get a group together to start felling more trees. Like Sir Thomas said so correctly, the sooner we start, the sooner we depart." Rolfe left to gather more men. The others returned to assist with shipbuilding.

*****

Richard Plascomb sat watching the growing snow drifts outside the window at Croplands. Inside the large home, the great hearth easily burned seasoned hickory wood, providing ample warmth and the scent of woods in the eating room. Across from Richard sat Christian, now eight years, reading from the Book of Psalms in The Bible. Richard and Cecelia both taught Christian how to read and his numbers, partly from reading The Bible and working numbers by calculating crop yields measured in bushels. Addition and subtraction formed the bedrock of Christian's number learning. Books were rare in Jamestown. Even if someone wanted to bring them, little opportunity could be afforded on the restrictive quarters aboard a crowded vessel.

Thus, The Bible afforded the most advantageous method for reading.

The winter of 1609 was becoming the most disastrous yet. Lower-than-expected crop yields added to the suffering. Little food could be found, and the supply ship that sailed in October would only now be arriving in England. Time would be needed to restock and prepare for the return voyage, and that was if Argall was successful at arriving in England. There were other signs that the winter would be disastrous. In fall, an infestation of rats in the corn was discovered, and mold destroyed the remaining corn stores. For some unknown reason, the Powhatan stopped trading with the settlers. Those who ventured beyond the settlement to hunt for food would be killed.

Before the cold weather arrived, several hundred extra graves were dug to prepare for the deaths that would start after the ground became too frozen to dig the graves. The sight of all those open graves, gaping like groaning stalls awaiting filling was too difficult to comprehend. Yet they were being filled daily. When the previous new settlers arrived, Jamestown's population increased to almost five hundred. At the present time, late December, over a hundred had already perished. Age was no protection; Death claimed in equal proportions. Rumors swirled that some families purposely drank arsenic to be free of the winter and the misery. Some were using their own homes for firewood. Considering all this, Richard shuddered, realizing that there were at least twelve additional weeks of inhospitable weather.

The Plascombs were faring better than others. They had enough food stores preserved to see them through the winter, but only if they were very frugal. Nothing could be wasted. A tentative dubious alliance loosely tethered the tottering settlement run by the feeble council, a hollow body after John

Smith's departure in October. His absent leadership, liked or not, respected or not, produced a leadership vacuum seeking an able replacement. There seemed to be no one since the populace was striving to survive, let alone govern. People hid in their homes. But, not far from Croplands, desperate times were leading to very desperate measures. Everyone was calling this winter, "the starving times."

In early dreary January 1610, Richard sat at the eating room window eating a bowl of squash soup. Cecelia baked some bread. It all was better than nothing, Richard told himself, refusing a second bowl to save it for another meal. Christian enjoyed a second bowl. Looking through the window down the knoll, Richard often wondered why Cecelia selected this spot for the house. The cemetery was distant, but slightly visible only in winter due to the loss of leaves from deciduous trees. He often found his wife sitting at this same window, obviously lost in her thoughts. One day in fall, Cecelia explained her position.

"I can see the children from here," she announced plainly, sighing. Surprised by her admission, Richard viewed down, left, where he could see the once-small cemetery where Edmund and Ellen lay sleeping in eternity's indiscriminate embrace. Now, on this late January afternoon, Richard stood, staring outward to the little cemetery that had grown faster than the Jamestown population. So much death in so little time, he thought.

Death, in its harshest manner, swept continuously into Jamestown, unquenched in its lust for dominance and power over the reason that rules men. Only hopelessness competed with death, its fanatical grip of the populace due to lack of food and supplies. Richard heard the stories of those boiling leather goods to make soup. Many of the settlement's dogs and cats had disappeared mysteriously. Rats were even spoken of as meat. Stories were rampant, as was fear and despair. Something caught Richard's eyes, a movement in the cemetery

270

on this late afternoon hour. Was it a lamp? Deciding it was another hasty burial, Richard was turning away when he noticed a second lamp. Yes, there two lamps now. He watched.

The lamps were stationary, unmoving at first. Instead, the glowing lamps moved up and down, sideways, to-and-fro, as if whomever carried those lamps was looking for something among the dead. Richard thought the lamps had been there too long, even for a fast burial. Cecelia entered the room.

"See anything, Mr. Plascomb?" she asked quietly, kissing Christian's head.

"Oh, I'm looking at the children." Cecelia gave a little laugh.

"And, how are they?"

"Shh, they're sleeping," Richard answered, yet observing.

"I'm ready to read, Mother," Christian said. "Tonight, I shall read from Kings." His mother said that was a good choice as she sat next to him on the bench, placing a lamp nearby. Richard had an idea.

"Cecelia, I'm going to get more firewood." Cecelia nodded as their son started reading.

Richard moved quickly to the front hall, dressing warmly. Putting on his hat, he stepped out to the frigid afternoon air. The sky, which remained a slate colored layer of stratus clouds for several days, began to darken quickly. Moving down the knoll toward the settlement as fast as he could maneuver in deep snow, Richard cut-off the main path into the woods, completely masking his approach to the cemetery.

Plascomb slowed as he neared the tree-line leading into the clear where the graves lay. Male voices, heavily muted by the cold dense air, reached his ears, but he was unable to understand what was being said. He moved forward to the tree-line. Leaning against the thick trunk of a great elm tree, Richard braced himself, peering into the cemetery clearing where all those open graves awaited occupants. He scanned to where the voices had come. The snow-covered landscape, capped with makeshift markers, offered an eerie otherworldliness as Richard scanned for the voices in the available late afternoon light. Ahead in his direct line of vision, Richard saw the two figures when lamps were lifted again. Roughly about seventy feet away, they were dressed in dark robes, the cowls pulled over their heads. Able to observe them, Plascomb thought it odd that they would be burying someone so late in the day and with no family members. Maybe there were none.

Those imaginings had just formed in Richard's mind when what happened next seized him with the most visceral reaction, realizing that they were not burying someone. Instead, they were stealing a body! Richard moved closer into the cemetery, one marker at a time for a better sight.

The wrapping around the body was unwound, starting at the head, revealing, to Plascomb's horror, the face of Holly Hascomb, the fourteen-year-old daughter of Hiram Hascomb. The family was an August arrival, and Holly had only died two days ago. As if in slow-motion, Richard watched as one man forced the dead girl's body into a semi-sitting position, hold it in-place, while the second man raised an iron and forcibly slammed it into the skull several times. The sickening sound of metal striking bone jolted Plascomb when the third strike resulted in the unmistakable sound of a great "crack!" in the cold dense air.

272

"One more ought to do it," one voice said loud enough for Richard to hear clearly. The bar was raised again.

"That's it!" one cried so loudly the sound seemed to echo a little in the air. They laid the body down and hovered over it, doing something Plascomb couldn't see. He moved.

Running through the snow as best he could, Richard felt his heart banging in his chest. He couldn't run fast enough through the deep snow, but he tried. He started yelling as loudly as he could while he trudged sloppily in the snow drifts. The men shot up, seeing him approaching. Within three feet of them he lunged at them since they hadn't time to stand. His forward momentum knocked them forward over the dead girl's body. The second man screamed in reaction to Plascomb's appearance and attack, like an apparition from Hades. The second individual fell into the shallow grave, but scrambled out, grasping for the shovel.

Richard and the other hooded person fought in the snow, rolling over the corpse several times while the second person aimed his blow with the shovel in the gathering darkness. Staggering to his feet, Plascomb maintained a hold of the man's cowl, shaking it wildly, punching at the hidden face. The second man dropped the shovel and ran-off, leaving the other to fend for himself. In the split-second Richard saw the one man running away, the man in the cowl freed himself, flinging his robe over Richard's head and shoulders. A sharp punch struck Plascomb in the stomach, followed instantly by another forceful blow. He doubled-over, feeling the vomit coming.

The shovel struck him in the back, and a determined push by a man's boot shoved him falling, tumbling into the grave where Holly lay until recently. The wind knocked out of him, Richard lay unable to move. He had to catch his breath, and he feared

273

his arm was broken. Sounds of crunching snow faded as Richard gathered himself. His arm wasn't broken; it simply hurt. The danger evaporated, but the wrenching horror did not. Standing slowly to brace himself, Plascomb threw the robe to the ground as he climbed out of the grave, where the world looked vastly different.

The robbers and the body were gone. Matter on the ground, a mix of some blood and dirt, also contained what Richard understood to be parts of skull, brain, and hair. He vomited heavily as he felt another shudder. Forcing himself up, Richard plodded wearily but determinedly to where his children lay sleeping in forever. To his somber pleasure, a thick blanket of untouched snow lay like a beneficent mound of white warmth. Richard thanked God and started his way back home.

"Dear Lord above, Richard Plascomb!" Cecelia screamed when Richard stepped inside. "What happened? You look as if you've been set-upon by wild animals!" she cried, applying some fabric to Richard's face, directing Christian to fetch water. Richard explained everything. Aghast, Cecelia backed away from her husband, her hand clutching her chest.

"Dear God in Heaven!" she exclaimed. "Have we come to this?" Richard blotted his bleeding nose.

"Obviously." Cecelia began crying. "I have proof," Richard said, pointing to the front door. "I have the robe worn by one of them. I'll got to the council tomorrow."

Part One, Chapter Twenty

January 1610 – June 1610

Plascomb quietly sat across form the council members who stared at him in mute disbelief until he placed the robe upon the table, opening it to reveal its contents. He was neither comforted nor dissuaded from his revelation of incomprehensible descent into the dreaded world of cannibalism. On the robe, or more stuck to it, honey-colored hair rendered a silent testament to its origin.

"Go look in her grave," Richard added somberly for emphasis. "Tis empty, it is. The cloak belonged to one of the two who stole her. I came upon them suddenly. We fought. I lost." Richard's black eye also served as proof of a tussle. Quietly, Richard departed the council office.

Word of the story spread with the ferocity and intensity of a great storm as a new wave of panic and disgust gripped the starving dying people of Jamestown. More had died since Christmas. Men began organizing grave watches, setting pairs of sentries with a fire for warmth in the cemetery.

As January harkened the most brutal cold, the worst possible actions created a new collective fear. A man, whose wife was not seen by their neighbor for some time, was found dead in their home. The husband had killed her, and had been carving flesh from the body to boil for food. He was hanged. A sudden sense of agreement was found at the imminent decision to abandon Jamestown with the next supply ship's arrival.

*****

It was early February, 1610 in London as directors and officers of the Virginia Company at London, supplied with new hefty stock investments for the Virginia colony, introduced Thomas West, 12th Baron De La Warr, as the new leader of the next venture to Jamestown. Lord De La Warr assured the dinner crowd that his plans for the Virginia settlement included three ships filled to capacity with supplies, and two hundred new settlers currently preparing for the journey. De La Warr was buoyant and confident in his address to the businessmen who had come to listen to the man selected to organize the colony properly, thereby producing a swift, profitable return on investors' equity.

De La Warr's background impressed the dinner guests. He'd fought valiantly in Ireland under the command of the late Robert Devereux, as well as the Netherlands. He was officially appointed to be both Governor of Jamestown, and its Captain-General, a lifetime appointment. The affable forty-two-year old told the crowd, eager for business success, that he held a sharp skillset for proven leadership in both his military and business experience. The crowd applauded its support. Lord De La Warr stated that his three ships, new colonists, and his own deputies, would sail to Jamestown in March, barely over one month in the future.

*****

On the ever-sunny island of Bermuda, Deliverance was completed and ocean-tested. She was a remarkable success. Several wild boars were killed for cooking over an open pit to celebrate. With enough cedar trees felled for the second ship to be called Patience, work began in earnest to finish the second vessel.

Sarah Hacker Rolfe gave birth to a daughter in the second week of February, but the child died several hours later. Sarah, too, died within an hour after their daughter. Grief-stricken, Rolfe named the daughter Bermuda, and burial plans were made.

*****

The Marshall family increased by one in early March 1610. Andrew and Elaine Marshall were one of the last couples to emigrate to Holland from Scrooby the previous year, joining the group in Leiden. They were the parents of the first Scrooby child to be born in Holland. Mrs. Marshall fared well during her delivery, and the Dutch midwife offered her most serious assessment of mother and child, saying, "a great effort for a wonderful boy child."

Pleased with the old woman's knowledge and compassion, and careful care for her two patients, the women of the Scrooby group, fast calling themselves the Leiden group, promised the midwife, Mrs. Krebs, a plump, jolly, Dutch woman who lived in Leiden her entire forty-three years, a growing business as the Leiden women settled-in, and got down to the, "business of babies and families." The other women who aided the midwife laughed with her until Mr. Marshall entered, having been summoned from the local tavern with the men.

The stern Andrew Marshall entered abruptly, eyeing the company, saying, "I see the hens are gathered." The women quietly exited the room, leaving the family and midwife in the small room. Marshall approached his wife, studying the feeding infant.

"I approve of the masculine child," he said, touching the infant's face with his index finger.

"What shall he be named, husband?"

"We shall name him Israel, for he is born in the promised land."

"I like it, husband," Elaine said peacefully, looking down at their son. "The name is soft on the ear."

"I am glad, wife."

Mrs. Krebs broke away from her thoughts and silent observations, beginning her final cleaning for these new people whose men always seemed so somber. Mr. Marshall returned to the tavern.

*****

On the same day Israel Marshall was born in Holland, Henry Hudson sat across from Sir Thomas Smythe, Sir Dudley Diggs, and Sir John Wolstenholme at the Company headquarters in London. All Members of Parliament, these were men whom Hudson knew focused on the singular objective of profit and its motivators. Two months earlier, Hudson had met with Smythe to be debriefed about his Dutch 'misadventure', as Smythe called Hudson's working with the Dutch. Since the desired water route to Cathay and the Orient remained elusive, the situation seemed inconsequential. Initial overreaction by Virginia Company directors resulted from patriotic feelings, and now the entire episode was anticlimactic.

Hudson countered by establishing that colonies would be formed by those who could afford them, as opposed to those who merely wished for them. The three men agreed, and were willing to pay, as Hudson soon discovered.

"We, the three of us," Smythe said, glancing to his two partners, are personally funding this expedition. The Muscovy Company shall finance the remainder. We are supplying you with a newly constructed three-masted, fifty-five-ton bark called Discovery. Your objective is to reach Iceland and locate the waterway passage across North America to the Pacific Ocean.

"The Cathay passage is on hold until we discover the waterway across the new continent. We are certain that if the passageway exists, we can move quickly across North America to the Orient and maybe Japan. The sail date is planned for 16 April 1610."

Agreeing with the terms, Hudson was informed he was free to select a crew totaling nineteen, including his son. His request for Robert Juet to be brought to London was approved. In response to Hudson's inquiry about the Half Moon and her crew, Hudson was told the ship and crew would be released and the Dutch sailors and the ship returned to Holland by summer.

*****

Admiral Thomas West, Lord De La Warr, in command of the vessel De La Warr, sailed from London on 12 March 1610, starting the fourth supply run to the Jamestown colony. His vessel was accompanied by the Blessing of Plymouth and the Hercules of Rye. Aboard De La Warr's vessel was Samuel Argall. Passing from the River Thames, the three supply vessels passed into the English Channel to open water.

This supply mission was well-planned and organized. A doctor was aboard the De La Warr, and additional new colonists were joined by a contingent of 150 armed men paid for by De La Warr for colonial protection after Argall's stories from his visit. Blue sky and billowing, white, cumulus clouds held the portent of a safe and successful journey.

*****

Robert Juet arrived in London on 24 March 1610, enjoying a reunion meal and stout ales with Hudson at a London tavern. Past journeys were relived, and talk quickly turned to the newest adventure, discovering the northern waterway passage across North America. As first mate, Juet was directed to hire sixteen able seamen for the expedition. To assist his first mate with the task, Hudson gave him enough funds for room and board, and front-money to attract worthy sailors.

Instead, Juet began living richly with a woman he met at a tavern along the docks. Lulling him with her favors, Juet lavished her with Hudson's money, spending a sizable portion on good wines, ale, foods, and fancy. He saved a significant portion by living with her in her quarters at the inn a few doors from the tavern.

It was during one evening of usual frivolity that Juet realized there were only eight days remaining before the sail date, so he started surveying the crowds for sailors. Unfortunately, the majority of truly worthy sailors and seamen were already selected, or won-away by captains willing to pay for the best men. Locating a bawdy group at a table across from his own, Juet briefly observed them before he approached them. He attracted the serving girl's attention as he stood at the men's table.

"Fresh ales all around for these good men!" Juet barked sportingly, gesturing to the group. Calling to a second serving girl for help carrying the heavy tankards, she went to retrieve the drinks. Meanwhile, the men looked from each other to Juet, smiling magnanimously as the tankards were set upon the already crowded wooden table.

"I'm Abacuck Prickett," one man stated firmly, lifting his new tankard, his fourth. "For what do you owe us for the pleasure of our company?" The others laughed over their hefty tankards at the twisted joke. Prickett appeared as disheveled in manners as he was in hygiene. His graying beard was long and unkempt. His voice, raspy from years of pipe smoking, was loud, feral. Gesturing to his right around the table, he offered names.

"That there's John King, a right quartermaster."

"Yea," one man called loudly. "When he's standin' up!" More ribald laughter went around the table as Prickett continued.

"Eh, don't let Mr. King's dour looks deceive you. He's on the mark on the water." The second voice sounded again.

"Yeah, when he's not in the sauce!" A new source of howls responded to the comment. Prickett pointed to the commenter.

"That's our smart-mouth, Philip Staffe, a first-rate ship's carpenter." Staffe raised his tankard to Prickett as the next man introduced himself.

"John Williams, ship's gunner," he announced, wiping his mouth with his sleeve. Juet looked to the last man at the table.

"Henry Greene," he said, looking as shifty-eyed as the others. "What can we do for you, your lordship?" Laughing riotously seemed to be a regular character aspect of this group. They waited to hear what the stranger had to say.

"I am Robert Juet, and I have need for a crew to sail in a week's time. It's the king's business." This pronouncement made them all sit up as Prickett spoke.

"Aye, the king himself, you say? Are you the captain, Mr. Juet?"

"No, I am the first mate. The captain is Henry Hudson, a sea master if you will. We sail to find the northern water passageway across North America to the Pacific Ocean. The ship is a newly constructed bark, the work hard, but the rewards good for those willing to work." Prickett shoved a chair with his foot, inviting Juet to sit for the first time.

"Have yourself a seat, Mr. Juet," he said, looking around at his mates, all who leaned into Juet as he ordered another round and began detailing his needs.

*****

Richard Plascomb continued working in the fields at Croplands despite the council's vote to abandon the settlement when the next supply shipment arrived.

"If it *ever* arrives," one councilman offered fitfully at a recent meeting. It was the first week in April, and winter was slowly releasing its deathly grip of the settlement. The council stated that the population was at a new low of under two hundred. More than three hundred deaths occurred over the winter, and they continued in spite of the warming weather. A second decision to attempt crops until departure for food on the return trip was also made, so Richard had his job set for him. The council did state that those who wished to remain could do so, but at their own peril. No further supplies would arrive, the natives were restless for unknown reasons, and all knew the endless grief and unspeakable calamities that befell the settlement.

Richard talked himself into remaining, but he knew well that Cecelia would seek -demand- a return to safe England, but for what? Richard rejected the idea of returning to a life of scraping-by hopelessly, never sure of what was to come. Hard times happened no matter where one lived. Here, he and Cecelia owned the largest home in North America, a residence so much larger than either of them had ever known. The amount of land alone boggled the mind, and this didn't account for the land to be awarded for the next five years. How could Cecelia leave all this behind?

Gazing across the seemingly endless field, Richard could see his wife talking with a group of women, obviously discussing the return when it occurred. He'd have to talk with her sooner than later, and he could hear it all now. What of Christian? How could they take him back to a life of agrarian loneliness? Disheartened, Richard returned to his planting.

*****

Discovery approached the Icelandic coast on 11 May, almost three weeks after departing England. Juet entered weather conditions into the ship's log, and Hudson maintained as close an eye on the crew as he did the jagged coastline.

He regretted his decision to run the ship as a democracy because it fell far from his intent of captaining the most superlative expedition yet. He had severe reservations the day he met Juet's selected crew, but with three days before sailing, he was out of options. His initial doubts changed to tangible fact when he discovered the cask of rum secretly stored among the ship's provisions. He and John dumped the cask overboard one night as Discovery sailed on a moonless night on the vast Atlantic Ocean. There was no place for rum on a seafaring vessel. The crew was angered when their subsequent findings were made, and Hudson confirmed he did dump the cask, and he began to sense an overwhelming dread at the hands of this

283

unfit motley crew. Using Juet as his go-between, Hudson gave his orders through Juet while he focused on discovering the waterway to the Pacific.

An unsettling unholy alliance settled over the entire crew, and Hudson maintained a silent yet observant eye on his son, whose approaching thirteenth year formulated his striking good-looks. He was tall, slender, with long, dark, brown hair, possessing a sensitive disposition and piercing ice-blue eyes. Time at sea only increased ardor. Juet, Hudson decided quickly, had made the worst possible crew selections, so diligence and fierce attention were required. John pointed northwest, shouting.

"Fog coming in from the northwest!" Every head turned or looked, as even the worst crewman knows the possible death knell from being lost in fog.

"To shore! Bring her about!" Hudson roared at Juet, presently at the helm. Turning the great wheel as fast as possible, Juet's face held the look of terror. The fog was dense and moving quickly across the water's surface. Crewmen scrambled up ropes to trim sails to the prevailing winds. Nearing the coast as close as possible, crew weighed anchor, moving to shore in several longboats. They were setting camp, tents, and a fire when the fog overtook them in the early afternoon. Hudson flatly denied John to tent with John Cay, who had suggested he and the boy tent together. Shrugging, John, also called Jack, said he would advise Cay. Meanwhile, a plentiful meal was prepared as the crew settled for however long the fog might remain.

Two weeks passed before the crew was able to return to Discovery and set sail. Rested and seemingly less contentious, Discovery headed southwest to Cape Farewell, located on the southern-most tip of Greenland. His plan, discussed with John and Juet, was to sail just around the sixty-degree north latitude

284

line, hoping to locate the passage. Juet entered, 'fog gone after two full weeks. Weather favorable, ice intermittent' into the log.

The crew assumed duties while Hudson maintained his bearings on the ocean and his lackluster ominous crew. John King turned out to be dour and sullen most of the time, while Henry Greene openly boasted that his experience should make him second mate after Juet. Privately, Greene also believed that young John Hudson, despite his stories of previous expeditions, and smart for his age, wasn't ready to be a grown man at sea. Greene, thinking himself smarter than John and Juet combined, used every opportunity to illustrate that opinion.

If all these issues weren't enough to weaken the required cohesiveness among a crew, the incident surrounding the lost rum was not forgotten. Hudson, keeping a silent confident control over his son's personal safety, knew for sure he had his hands full in more ways than he cared to possess. They were entering the month of May.

*****

Patience was declared water-ready in the first week of May 1610. A great surge of pride in excellent workmanship in building two ships from local materials bolstered desire to continue to Jamestown. The order to gather supplies and food was given. The stranded settlers had been at Bermuda Island, now being called Somers Island, for ten months. They would finally arrive in Jamestown and the five hundred colonists already there. With Captain Christopher Newport at the helm of Deliverance, and Somers captaining Patience, departed Bermuda, sailing for Jamestown on 11 May. In his small number of belongings, John Rolfe discovered the large violet pouch containing the seeds he was given when he departed Tangiers

285

several years earlier. Having an idea, he wondered if the seeds would grow in Virginia soil. The seeds were tobacco seeds. He was surprised and glad to have found them.

*****

Aboard Discovery, Henry Hudson approached a massive body of water on the same day Deliverance and Patience sailed from Bermuda. The waterway, located between two significant land masses, was the largest body of water Hudson encountered other than the ocean. The first problem he had upon approach were massive ice sheets, and was icebound for two days before being able to continue. When Discovery did move ahead to the great body of water, Juet approached Hudson, gingerly steering the ship around additional ice sheets in the limpid blue water.

"Captain, the men want to return to England," Juet said flatly, waiting for Hudson's response. Maintaining his forward focus, Hudson realized all his consternations about this crew were becoming dangerously real.

"I hear you, Mr. Juet, but all men signed-on to do a job. We all have come too far," Hudson replied quietly, firmly, rolling the wheel hard left, aiming for placid iceless water. Juet, knowing Hudson as he did, understood the Captain's decision was made, final.

"Is there anything else, Mr. Juet?" The first mate shook his head.

"Good, then. We shall keep it that way, Mr. Juet." Juet had to assuage the crew's growing hostility to Hudson.

Hudson entered the massive body of water. The great width between the granitic palisades, topped by dense woodlands,

286

was significant enough to support an oceanic pathway across North America. John stood quietly at the foredeck in the sun using the sextant. Hudson, increasingly concerned about the immediate success of this problematic expedition, sensed a growing concern for the safety of his son and himself. His worries subsided when cheers went up by the crew upon thinking they had discovered the elusive waterway leading to the Pacific Ocean.

*****

Two weeks after sailing from Bermuda, Deliverance and Patience caused a stir when they arrived in Jamestown on 23 May. Cheering from the decks helped those on land briefly forget their troubles as new faces and hopes for food replaced the winter's starving times. Captain Newport was stunned to see so few people. He learned the grave news in a meeting with the council, Sir Thomas Gates, Admiral George Somers, and several others, including John Rolfe.

The newly-arrived Governor, officers, and Rolfe learned Jamestown had lost eighty percent of its population during what was now remembered as the starving times. They were told, "we couldn't bury them fast enough" by one councilman. Another reported that, "one-in-five died, and they've not stopped. There are about sixty of us left out of almost five hundred. Please, do you have food?"

Additional discussions after a tour of the dilapidated fort James, crumbling housing, failed crops, lack of food, shortage of safety due to hostile natives' beliefs that the settlers were asking for too much food, as well as their stated position that their true friend, John Smith, had gone, and had no need for the settlers.

287

"It's been said that after Smith departed, the Powhatan decided to starve us out of Virginia," one councilman told the men. Considering all he saw, heard, sensed, combined with the possibility of new sickness, and the shocking details of survival cannibalism led Governor Gates to declare the settlement had to be abandoned forever. Having been informed some were choosing to remain, Gates flatly and immediately rejected the notion outright.

"I am the *Governor* of this settlement at this moment. My word has the effect of law. *None* shall remain; *all* will depart in short time. Those who do otherwise shall be returned to London in chains, tried for treason, and hanged. Pass the word instantly, and start the evacuation to depart in roughly a week. The crews require some rest."

When Gates inquired about Henry Ravens and the seven other men sent to Jamestown from Bermuda to tell of the Sea Venture, he was informed they never arrived. Gates shook his head, looking at the decrepit settlement and its few rag-tag inhabitants.

"We have obviously attempted to do something we know nothing about in this desolate unforgiving place called North America." Plans for sailing to England were readied, and the word about leaving went-out to all. When Richard Plascomb received word, he was incredulous, defiant, but began preparing to return to England, but to what?

Part One, Chapter Twenty-One

June 1610 – December 1610

In the late morning hours of 9 June, Powhatan and a group of braves stood atop a bluff silently watching three English ships sailing downstream from Jamestown. Pondering the departure, Powhatan told his braves he wanted them to reclaim all the land of the abandoned settlement after the ships were out of sight for three days. Everything was to be destroyed as if the ghost men had never come. As the Powhatan stood thankfully watching the ships in the distance, a brave ran to Powhatan, hurriedly informing him of a new fleet of three approaching ghost ships.

Deliverance and Patience sailed nearly thirteen miles, approaching Mulberry Island, when calls of an approaching fleet of three ships were shouted from the crows' nests. Surprised by the news for fear of a Spanish attack, spyglasses were rapidly employed.

"They're English ships!" Newport called as uproarious shouts and cheers sounded from the pair of departing vessels. A longboat from De La Warr, the largest of the arriving fleet, met with a longboat from each of the two departing vessels, where much talk and greetings occurred. When the longboats parted, Captain Newport returned to Deliverance to report the news to eager passengers and crew. Gathering everyone closely, Newport stood on the ship's railing as to be heard clearly.

"The fleet is from England! The mission's leader is Thomas West, 12th Baron De La Warr, who has been appointed Governor and Captain-General of Jamestown for life! As such, his decisions have the force of English law. He has ordered that we return to Jamestown!"

Loud anguished cries were heard from one ship, soon followed by the second. Newport understood.

"We must comply with the order! The fleet bears food, livestock, tools! We must return, and you must return to your own homes!" Newport called, turning to his first mate at the helm. "Turn her around! We must return!"

Aboard Patience, Richard Plascomb cheered inwardly as the five vessels began the return journey to Jamestown. Perhaps, he thought, with new supplies and food, maybe it would work after all.

When the renewed fleet returned to the settlement, De La Warr immediately began issuing orders. He wanted a head-count of people, names of all families, and number of children, their names and ages. He wanted to know who had lost spouses and children, and whom had remarried since the last religious figure died in the previous winter. He directed Captain Robert Tyndall to take Blessing out to the large bay for catching fish.

"Take some of the men with you," he added, turning his attention to other matters.

Ten days later, Admiral George Somers, yet fuming for being considered second to Gates, and not wanting to have to report to West, recommended he sail with his nephew, Matthew Somers, and a crew for Bermuda to gather additional food, including would boar, fish, sweet potatoes, and other animals. West agreed. Somers, captaining Patience, was joined by Argall in command of a second vessel for a larger haul. The two vessels departed Jamestown on 19 June.

*****

290

John Rolfe and Richard Plascomb were introduced in De La Warr's small office, where Richard listened as Rolfe explained his idea of growing tobacco in the colony.

"If it will work at all," Rolf added with a shrug. "I don't know if the climate here is suitable."

Then, we are in the same position, Mr. Rolfe. Before last summer's drought, we did well with beans, squash, pumpkin, and maize, but I'm not sure bout tobacco." Richard shrugged. "Also, we don't even have a currency here. I don't know how I'd pay for the crop if it did grow." Rolfe suggested he pay with the crop itself.

"There are locations where tobacco is used as currency." They looked to De La Warr, who threw his hands in the air.

"Gentlemen, I leave the remainder to you. My objective was to introduce you. That is done. Anything to help this fledgling colony is welcome -demanded- to help it survive and flourish. To-date, it has been an absolute failure, I am sorry to say." He stood.

"I share with you the fact I shall be governing this colony along with Sir Thomas Dale. I have already submitted my first colony report to him. I anticipate his arrival within a year, and his methods are significantly different from mine. I recommend you establish a firm plan before his arrival. Be sure to have a set of rules determining how Croplands is run, Richard, as Sir Dale is of the most pernicious beliefs." Richard had something to say.

"All respect, Governor, but religion has no place in business. That's why it's called business, not religion."

"Respect taken, Richard, but if we Puritans had our way, we'd have one of our own on the throne if we could. Presently in England, their clamoring grows, and the king has ritually forced all those deficient of the Anglican religion underground." The Governor opened the door.

"I have another meeting, gentlemen. Keep me informed of your decisions." They shook hands and departed. Outside, Richard turned to Rolfe.

"Come to Croplands, Mr. Rolfe. Look at the grounds. I am confident we can arrange a mutually beneficial arrangement."

"Call me John, please. I fully agree with you."

"Very well, and I, Richard." They walked towards Croplands as Plascomb described life in Jamestown since his arrival three years earlier.

*****

Captains Argall and Somers were separated in a storm followed by thick fog lasting several days. When conditions improved, Somers' vessel was unseen to the horizon. Argall decided to weigh anchor, start fishing, and establish his bearings. All his crew could do was catch fish and return to Jamestown. Unknown to Argall, Admiral Somers had better weather luck and continued to Bermuda.

In the last week of July, De La Warr directed Captain Adams to return to England for additional supplies aboard Hercules. Adams departed on 25 July 1610, vowing to return as soon as possible.

*****

Pointing to the vast horizon, Robert Juet hollered, "this must be the water passage to the Pacific!" to Hudson. Standing next to Juet, John Hudson leaped with excitement as his father steered Discovery slightly more westward. A huge water passage loomed ahead of the three-masted vessel. Hudson, joyful to have evaded the ice sheets that seemed odd at this low latitude, eagerly turned the wheel while the crew scrambled up and across the rigging and netting like adroit crabs to catch the prevailing winds propelling the ship ahead. Cheers echoed down from the crow's nest and the tall rigging, from where shouts telling Hudson of a huge body of water ahead with no land in sight.

Juet rushed to collect the log to enter the newest findings in the first week of August 1610. Four months had passed since their departure, and Juet suddenly believed this would be the most successful expedition yet. John took the helm while his father and Juet studied the vast watery horizon ahead of them though spyglasses, discussing the great mysteries that lay ahead.

*****

"I am not John Smith," Governor De La Warr stated unquestioningly, sitting with men from Jamestown mulling his next action. "I do not operate with diplomacy. I demand action. Last December, the Pamunkey natives, an off-shoot of the Powhatan, killed Captain John Ratcliffe." The Governor gave a raw laugh. "Killed? I meant mutilated him by tying him to a stake in front of a fire while native women removed the skin from his body with mussel shells and tossed the pieces into the flame as he watched. They skinned his face last and finally burned him at the stake, a gruesome ending for an honorable English Captain offered corn, but, instead, found an ambush. Ratcliffe's death shall be avenged.

293

"Then the Powhatan strive to starve us out of Virginia, allowing some five hundred to die needlessly. Then, Powhatan dares to tell us to either stay in our fort or leave this place? If that's not enough, I order the hand of a native to be severed and delivered to Powhatan with an ultimatum, and he responds not? The time for Captain Smith diplomacy is over." De La Warr looked to George Percy, the colony's leader after John Smith until De La Warr's arrival.

"Take seventy men and attack the Paspahegh capital. Destroy everything. Depart as soon as your brigade is ready. Report directly upon your successful return. Go." Percy almost ran from the office.

"The quiet time is done. Time for action has arrived," the Governor said, ending the discussion. Others departed to join Percy.

*****

At the Virginia Company's main office in London, Sir Thomas Dale sat grimly reading the Jamestown report submitted by De La Warr. Company directors sat talking, awaiting Dale's comments, and discussing their own ideas about the colony's success. Several books published about the colony by Captain John Smith did have the effect of renewed excitement about the colony. This was proved true because new investors were eager to be part of the winning hand when it came.

Outside, a steady rain ran in rivulets down the windows in mid-August as Dale finished, laying the document on the table, tapping it.

"Gentlemen, I advise you up-front that I take a particularly Puritan position on this entire situation. You have assigned me as assistant Governor and Marshall of the colony, and you expect a return on investments." He nodded. "You shall have it.

"It is obvious Governor De La Warr is doing all he can, faced with the drastic odds he and his deputies must adress. Lord De La Warr fought with his first cousin, Robert Devereux in battle, so he is not a stranger to hostility. I tell you as I sit here that the colonists remain a lax, lazy, and slovenly lot. Their numbers are greatly diminished since their first arrival. The suffering and deaths are God's hand controlling the outcome of the results due to laziness and errant ways.

"As I prepare to go to Jamestown, I carry with me all the laws divine, moral, and martial, with which I shall rule the colony. Leadership shall be provided through steady, constant, and unwavering discipline. The Bible shall be our covenant with God. Responsibility must be shared among all the citizenry in the colony, including children, who can reason." Directors nodded at Dale's position regarding the unyielding authority and discipline he intended to apply to the godless colonists at Jamestown.

*****

George Percy stood before Governor De La Warr.

"The village is destroyed, Governor. Homes burned, crops destroyed or looted, most, about sixty or more, killed. We took the chief's wife and many children, including her own. As we sailed back, we threw all the children overboard and shot their brains out in the water."

"What of the chief's wife?" the Governor asked.

295

"She is here, Sir, in Jamestown, in the stockade." Nodding, De La Warr looked out the window to the stockade.

"Put her to the sword. We have no use for her. Do it now." He leaned back. "Let us see if Powhatan responds now." Percy departed to fulfill his newest mission.

*****

Captain Argall returned to the Chesapeake, aiming for the James River, where he returned to Jamestown on the thirty-first of August. While salted and freshly caught fish were unloaded, Argall explained his separation from Admiral Somers in the thick fog, additionally detailing he did not see him when the weather cleared.

"I decided to begin fishing. Admiral Somers will return, I'm sure. He's a professional man of the seas." Agreeing with the seasoned captain, De La Warr welcomed Argall back safely, turning his attention to administrative matters.

But Admiral Somers was not faring well in Bermuda. When the fog cleared, he and his nephew, Matthew Somers, and their crew continued to the island they had known so well. Beyond his determination not to play second-place to Gates, Somers planned to remain in Bermuda to consider his options. He did; however, become ill on the voyage, but remained determined to continue to Bermuda. With no doctor on the island, Somers remained bed-ridden while the needed supplies were collected for the return voyage by Matthew and the crew.

*****

Hudson realized he had not found the water passage to the Pacific by mid-September. Instead, he understood he had sailed

296

into the largest bay he had ever encountered. They sailed continuously with the shore on the starboard side of Discovery. Hudson and Juet maintained detailed logs describing the natural resources, geography, and abundant fish and wildlife.

Discovery finally reached the southern-most region of the in late September, Hudson naming it James Bay. For rest and good food, the crew went ashore to set camp.

In the same month at Jamestown, De La Warr and Argall watched as the Blessing of Plymouth and Hercules of Rye departed Jamestown, sailing for England. Several ill colonists were aboard the two vessels, joining Captain Newport and Sir Thomas Gates.

*****

Folding his letter dated 2 November 1610 to King James, Richard Bancroft, Archbishop of Canterbury, affixed his gold wax seal of his holy office to the document. The letter contained the most recent news regarding discoveries, reprimands, and low-level arrests designed to frighten more than persecute. Bancroft, like the king and others, was increasingly concerned over the quiet growing Puritan presence in Parliament, universities, and London businesses. Pressure upon non-Anglican religious groups was intensifying, further driving Separatist groups underground in attempts to evade royal officials.

Handing the letter to his secretary, a vicar from Kent, Bancroft thanked the priest and stood, looking out across the rainy wind-swept gardens beyond his sumptuous office.

"The rain coals for a sherry," Bancroft said, crossing the large office to an ornate table containing glasses and decanters. "Come in," he called to a knock at his door.

297

Mrs. Thortonfer, the Archbishop's chief cook, poked her head in the door. Mrs. Thortonfer was plump, jovial, and always in good humor.

"My dear Archbishop, will you be entertaining tonight for dinner? Kitchen staff has no visitors scheduled this evening, but I want to double-check with you before we start the afternoon's meal." The Archbishop sipped.

"No, Mrs. Thortonfer, I shall be dining alone this evening for a change. The quiet will actually be a welcome respite, but don't quote me on that," he replied jovially, the head cook laughing with him. Thanking him, she departed to plan the evening's meals.

Studying the place where his chief cook had stood, Bancroft sipped his sherry again, crossing to his desk to address his next matter of church business, when he was abruptly seized by a sudden overwhelming pain. His glass dropped, shattering on the floor. He lunged at his desk for support, but he was propelled backwards by the same riveting pain that gripped him moments ago. The Archbishop grabbed-hold of a high-backed chair briefly before collapsing grotesquely to the thickly carpeted floor. Richard Bancroft, Archbishop of Canterbury, moved no more.

*****

Hours behind Canterbury, England, on the same day as the Archbishop died, on the sun-drenched island of Bermuda, Matthew Somers oversaw the wrapping of his uncle's dead body. Admiral George Somers died early in the day on 2 November 1610. Matthew Somers was faced with a decision.

"Shall we set sail to Jamestown with all these provisions, Sir?" asked a crewman of the young Somers, now Captain of the Patience. Somers, realizing he was his uncle's sole heir, Somers

298

looked to the sea and the endless blue-green waves crashing ashore. He decided.

"No, Ridley, we sail to England." The seaman was stunned.

"*England*, you say, Sir?" Somers nodded; thought quickly.

"Yes, Ridley, I say England because my uncle, the Admiral George Somers, should only have a proper English burial in his homeland." The young Somers observed Ridley, who nodded at last.

"Yes, Captain, you are correct, Sir. A proper burial 'tis only fitting a man like your uncle."

"Thank you, Ridley. Prepare the crew. We sail immediately." The seaman saluted.

"Aye, Captain." When Ridley started calling to the crew to set sail immediately, Matthew Somers looked again to the sea, talking as if to the water itself.

"Return to that waste-water settlement full of sickness and death, no. This Matthew Somers has a hefty inheritance to claim, and my uncle's body will prove my case." Patience sailed for England within the hour. Though not in Bermuda, winter weather was beginning to settle across North America.

In James Bay, far north of Bermuda, Henry Hudson realized he had waited too long to sail from the massive bay he found and studied for several months. Discovery was besieged by expanding ice sheets and inhospitable winter weather. There was no choice but to move ashore, seat camp again, and ready for a winter stay at the southern section of James Bay. When a crewman asked how long the stay would be, Hudson said he guessed about four months.

John Rolfe visited Richard Plascomb at Croplands in early December after accompanying Captain Argall on a trading mission north of the Chesapeake for winter furs and maize with Iopassus, Chief of the Patawomeck natives, and half-brother to Powhatan. Iopassus remained on friendly terms with the settlers. No new supply ships had come, and winter's arrival usually indicated none would arrive until early spring. The supplies brought by De La Warr's fleet satisfied the settlement's needs, but winter always calls for additional resources. Rolfe had come to discuss tobacco with Richard.

The pair enjoyed ales sitting before a warming fire discussing the seeds Rolfe planted at Croplands the previous summer to discover what they might do in Virginia soil. After the seeds did produce some growth by regular harvest time, Rolfe deduced the soil would support tobacco growth. A fresh planting of the remaining seeds in spring would be the true test. Richard originally set aside five hundred acres for tobacco plants. Of course, some seeds wouldn't fill that much land, but a successful harvest would need additional land the following season. Unfamiliar with growing tobacco, Richard asked Rolfe to explain it.

"Tobacco is an annual crop, like most of the vegetables you grow, Richard. It's grown for its leaves. They're wide and oval in shape. A single plant can grow up to ten feet tall before harvesting. In the West Indies, one mature plant at harvest produced over two hundred square-feet of leaves! I think the best time to plant here is early May, and harvest in the fall when pink flowers appear as clusters at the top of the plant.

"We harvest first by topping, or removing the flower cluster. This increases the leaf's weight and enhances aroma in the growth process. We then stalk-cut the plant, removing the leaves. Then, we cure the leaves by spearing them onto lathes, also called a tobacco stick, and hang them in a curing barn."

"A curing barn?" Richard asked as Cecelia entered with more ale.

"Yes, a curing barn is roughly twenty-feet-cubed. We hang the leaves in the curing barn with hardwood fires -small ones, of course- and the tobacco is surrounded by the smoke in the tightly-closed barn. This is called fire curing. Smoke permeates the leaves and exits through eaves higher-up in the barn. Lastly, we allow the leaves to age and ferment. This brings the tobacco flavor to its height, increasing aroma and reducing bitterness. We can add flavors if we want during the curing process to enhance flavor. At this point, the leaves are ready to sell." Richard commented that it sounded rather labor intensive.

"That it is, Richard. In Trinidad, I watched the entire process, and calculated between two or three hundred man-hours of labor for each acre." Richard's eyes widened.

"Acre?" Rolfe nodded, and Richard asked where they'd sell the tobacco. Rolfe laughed.

"Why, Richard, we sell it to England!"

"England?" Richard echoed, looking to Cecelia, who laughed.

"Aye, Richard, England, do you remember the place?"

"Aye, Cecelia, I do, but, I never considered the thought of actually selling to England." Rolfe lifted his tankard.

"Richard, with your land and my tobacco seeds, we are going to be very rich men!" Tankards touched.

"The biggest problem with growing tobacco, other than the intense labor, is land. Tobacco demands a significantly large crop area and a fallow season to replenish soil because tobacco is a heavy feeder of soil nutrients. If you grow a hundred acres this season, you need two hundred the next season."

"One active and one fallow, correct, John?"

"Aye, Richard. You've got the idea. Imagine a very successful harvest over several years." Richard nodded.

"I am. Well, John, land I have. Do we have enough seeds?"

"For a starter crop, yes. We'll get new seeds from the flower clusters when we collect them. We plant them shallowly in late April or early May. The plant produces its seeds and we harvest them for the next season."

"And, I suppose we must also start building curing barns," Richard said. Rolfe agreed.

"Yes, and I'd say four or five for starters, increasing them each year if harvests are good." Richard suggested selecting barn sites the next day.

"I agree, Richard. The sooner we plan for growth space and barn construction, the more ahead of the game we'll be." At Cecelia's call, the pair joined her and Christian at the meal table for stew. Christian said grace. They ate, planned, and talked, enjoying the fire and the communion of people joining in a meal. Maybe the worst was behind all in Jamestown as December progressed and winter arrived.

Part One, Chapter Twenty-Two

February 1611 – June 1611

The King James Bible was released in early February 1611 to the absolute enjoyment of all who could afford to purchase it and could read. Its publication was an instant marvel. Seven years of intense translations by forty-seven theological scholars working in six groups from three different sites across England culminated in the singular-most comprehensive and expansive version of the Latin Bible. Its poetic prose and easy readability made the King James Bible the most sought-after book in publishing. Theological and secular scholars alike raved about the most superb English translation.

In London, King James was securely confident that something positive had finally come from the highly contentious and disagreeable Hampton Conference in 1604.

When John Robinson obtained his copy in Leiden, he, too, was struck by the simple majesty of beautiful language that invited the reader to embellish himself in the great story. Brewster, Bradford, and the others in the congregation admitted the king, despite his Anglican orthodoxy, had truly done the Bible its greatest service. The name the King James version became the name all called the new Bible. As word of the King James version of the Bible widened, King James selected George Abbott to replace the late Richard Bancroft as Archbishop of Canterbury.

*****

The absence of all-out war between the colonists and the Powhatan that began the previous summer with De La Warr's decision to attack the Paspahegh capital, resulting in the deaths of almost eighty natives, and the sword death of the wife of the native leader, Wowinchopunk, did not diminish the intermittent skirmishes that occurred as winter's grip slowly abated in the new year.

In mid-February, De La Warr accepted a report from a military scouting group who reported the Paspahegh village was abandoned, and the chief, Wowinchopunk, had been killed by the scouts near the village. De La Warr stated that better fortifications were necessary, but he would await the arrival of Sir Thomas Dale and the supply fleets to bolster existing fortifications. De La Warr was also widening his battles against natives.

In late September the previous year, he sent a second scouting party, led by Captain Argall, to attack the Warraskoyaks village, but native scouts alerted the villagers, and all fled before the scouting party arrived. Nonetheless, despite the desertion by all, the party burned the village and destroyed all the crops before harvest.

Three days after De La Warr accepted the scouting report in February, a group of three settlers was killed near the Jamestown fort in retaliation for Wowinchopunk's killing. De La Warr decided the settlers and the natives were at war. New security measures were announced to prevent colonists from leaving the settlement. De La Warr eagerly awaited the supply ship's arrival.

*****

Spring renewed safer ocean travel, and multiple supply ships were departing England for Jamestown. John Smith's books about the settlement and North America sharpened the public's interest in the colony, and financial investment increased in the

304

Virginia Company at London. In early March, Captain Adams, who departed from Jamestown the previous September, departed Gravesend for the colony. Soon after his departure, a fleet of three ships, the Elizabeth, Prosperous, and Starr, commanded by now Vice Admiral Christopher Newport, also sailed from England carrying three hundred new colonists, horses, livestock, and a multitude of supplies.

In London, Sir Thomas Dale, appointed Lieutenant-General of Virginia, began his preparations to sail to Jamestown in May. His plans included establishing an authoritarian government over the colony because he believed only strict, unyielding and pitiless discipline would solve the colony's problems.

*****

The land-locked, unhappy, and near-rebellious crew of Discovery existed discontentedly at James Bay through the Arctic-like winter into spring 1611. Yet the calendar did not match the ice thaw. In late March, Discovery remained ice-bound, actually raised from the water like a rising mountain, held in-place, her hull encased in a wall of thick ice.

Long dark periods of frigid temperatures and relentless winds, accompanied by frequent snow squalls, forced the disgruntled men to remain bound in their tents to stay as warm as possible. Endless darkness and the strange dancing green, blue, and red lights in the sky made for discontentedness. Quarrels arose out of absolute boredom and rapidly dwindling food supplies.

Hudson assured the unhappy men that they would sail for England as soon as the ice released the ship. Yet, individual oddities and strange behaviors among the men began to occur across the long winter in the absolute silence and dominant whiteness of snow and ice.

At some point, Hudson gave Henry Greene a coveted green cloak, which Juet wanted as first mate. Then, following an argument about the ice between Hudson and Greene, Hudson demanded the cloak be given back. When he received it, Hudson instantly gave it to Juet, angering Greene more, intensifying his dislike of the captain, and leading Greene to talk more of mutiny with those who agreed with him. They had to wait because they had nowhere to go if they did overtake the indecisive captain, who, increasingly, appeared to forget something he had said only minutes ago.

As freezing Arctic winds bore-down on the stranded seamen, arguments increased daily, an no one was spared the verbal abuse, including John Hudson, now almost thirteen, and wizened to the adult world. All eagerly awaited the great thaw and a return to England.

*****

Despite the coldness, Rolfe and Plascomb, along with Christian, started constructing curing barns for the crop of tobacco they'd plant in several months. As they sawed, cut, and hammered, Rolfe explained he learned about tobacco in Bermuda and Trinidad.

"Spanish soldiers introduced the crop to Spain upon returning from New World expeditions, as did the Portuguese, around 1550."

"That's only about sixty years ago," Christian said, swinging his hammer, just missing his thumb.

"Careful, boy," Rolfe warned. "That would really hurt."

"Yes Sir," came the sheepish reply as Rolfe smiled.

"Very good with your numbers, Christian," he praised, hammering his portion of the newest barn.

"Yes, it's rather a new crop. Tobacco reached England about fifteen years later, about 1565, by Sir John Hawkins, a navel hero. Twenty years later Sir Richard Greenville, the naval commander, reintroduced it. One year after that, a colonial administrator, Captain Richard Lane, returned with tobacco and pipes. That actually started pipe-smoking in England." Rolfe explained that the Virginia tobacco that grew wild was too harsh. But he also said he had a secret weapon against that problem. He suggested a break to reveal the secret.

In the warmth of the Croplands kitchen over tea and scones, Rolfe revealed a large emerald green pouch from which he poured some seeds onto the wooden table. Oddly, Rolfe looked around, seeming to be sure no unwanted eyes watched.

"It's just us, Uncle John," Christian said, himself casting a quick glance about. Rolfe leaned closer to the pair.

"Truth be known, any man not of the Spanish Court specifically assigned to possess or work with these seeds is under threat of death." Christian's blue eyes widened.

"Truth, Uncle John?" Rolfe nodded.

"Aye, lad, death by order of the Spanish Crown." Rolfe pointed to the seeds. These are Orinoco seeds. They have a much better, sweeter taste than the native plants here." He looked to Richard.

"If we care for this crop, and we are successful, there's no telling how big the demand will be. Plascomb father and son picked up a seed, studied it, smelled it.

"They're tiny," Christian noted.

"Aye, again, lad, but the wealth from them could be enormous."

"What I think so interesting is that something so small could have such a large effect on us all," Christian said, much to the praise of his father and Uncle John, who tussled Christian's near-white blond hair.

"Aye, you are as intelligent as you look, Christian Plascomb," he said, scooping the seeds back into the pouch.

"Richard, these Orinoco seeds from Trinidad we shall plant in only a few weeks. If we succeed, we will be the wealthiest men in the colony. With hot tea finished, the trio returned to building curing barns.

*****

Commanding the Hercules of Rye, Captain Adams docked in Jamestown on 7 April 1611, and learned that the De La Warr sailed to the island of Nevis for additional supplies a few days earlier. New supplies were eagerly welcomed as the unloading started.

About six weeks later in London, late in the month of May, Sir Thomas Gates was in command of a three-ship fleet departing for Jamestown. The Sara, Swain, and Trial carried another almost three hundred men, twenty women, more than two hundred head of cattle, pigs, dogs, and enough new supplies and provisions to carry the colony. Traveling on Gate's vessel was Sir Thomas Dale, lieutenant Governor of Virginia Colony, ready to instill his authoritarian control over the colony.

*****

The cracking sound began with a short loud creak, followed by what was like an explosion, the sound reverberating across the barren landscape. Subsequent similar sounds shook the ground, awakening all of the crew.

Hudson was up instantly, throwing-off skins to peer from his tent shared with his son. His long grey hair hung over one eye while he poked his head from the tent to look at his ship. He looked a second time to confirm his sighting. The ship was free! Other shaggy heads looked from tents, surveying the obvious. Cries of joy sounded as loudly as the cracking ice.

Camp was disassembled in rapid time and the crew boarded Discovery, floating freely in azure water, free of the ice that bound her to this blinding-white hell. Sails were unfolded, billowing in the strong spring winds, cascading like giant folds of white hope.

"To sea!" Hudson yelled. "Pull anchor! All hands-on deck!" Men scattered to perform their duties one last time. Juet announced it was, by his calculations, June 15, 1611, surprising even Hudson. They were marooned nearly eight months. Discovery began moving across the water, and the crew never wanted to see James Bay again.

Hudson headed northwest instead of southeast. The men, too busy working to notice they were heading the wrong way, continued their tasks. Robert Juet noticed, but remained silent. The others would realize very quickly.

Three days later on 24 June, Juet and Hudson engaged in a stormy argument. Juet, representing the crew, argued that food stores were dangerously low. Further, he claimed they were sailing in circles, and not making headway home. He also stated that the crew didn't want to die at sea since a new expedition would surely be underwritten.

But Hudson had grown strange in the course of the previous eight months. Juet was positive Hudson was sailing in wide circles, and no passage was to be found here. Hudson appeared to hear Juet's side of the argument, but he wasn't really sure if the Captain was actually listening. Hudson simply looked ahead, steering calmly, as if the objective he sought was in sight. Disgusted, Juet departed the helm to below decks, where the crew awaited.

"He's lost his mind," Juet said, shaking his head.

"He's incapable of command," Prickett said, looking up to the opening to the main deck. Juet nodded.

"Right, then, men. If you are in, we take over tomorrow like we planned back on the ice."

"Agreed," came the response from most of the men present. They dispersed to make their plan ready.

*****

New tobacco plants were growing rapidly at Croplands in the June sun. Planted in March and transplanted in May, the plants were responding as if they were indigenous to the area. Rolfe inspected new leaves that were spreading quickly. Rolfe told Plascomb they would be excellent plants; a superb crop.

Richard divided his time between Croplands and the glass foundry, and Christian was learning two valuable trades in between reading and number learning. Now ten years, Christian was growing taller, eating more, and his mother complained that he grew out of clothes in a day. Richard laughed, saying it had to start one day. He returned to the fields to work with Rolfe and his son.

That same afternoon, the fleet of three ships under the command of Vice Admiral Newport arrived in Jamestown. Elizabeth, Prosperous, and Starr, captained by Newport, quickly began unloading much-awaited supplies, foods, livestock, including cows, and other provisions to a needy population.

*****

Sun crested the horizon while the crew, both faithful and mutinous, went about their daily chores with little conversing. Early morning banter stopped long ago for this tired, angry, uncertain crew, now fully and secretly divided in their alliances to the captain or the crew. Those involved in the mutiny warily eyed the stairway leading form below, aware that every man must emerge from that opening. One man was working on a net located above the portal from below. Everyone was in place; they only required Hudson to emerge. Footsteps sounded on the stairway. The net man readied but stopped in time. It was the boy with his sextant, running above to take measurements. The Captain would appear soon. He did.

As Hudson ascended the stairs, the net man timed his single toss. There would only be one chance. The captain was on deck. The net man tossed, catching Hudson completely in the net, which was grabbed by several mutineers who held Hudson captive aboard his own vessel. He yelled, but the grips of many overpowered him. John's sextant fell to the deck, breaking, as he was seized and dragged to his father.

"Mutiny!" someone shouted. Heads turned in shock or anticipation. Knives or sharpened tools were offered as

311

warnings of the seriousness of this mutiny. A longboat was lowered to the water while the war of eyes raged on deck.

"Aye, all you listen good," Juet ordered. "This ship is now under the control of myself and Mr. Greene. We are sailing to England this day! Man the helm, Mr. Greene. Take us southeast to freedom and home."

"Aye, Captain," Greene replied, moving to the vacant wheel, turning the vessel until the morning sun was directly in front of them. Juet spoke again.

"Those of you with us, gather on my left. The others on the right. Move now or I'll make the choice for you." All remaining seventeen moved to one side or the other. To Juet's left stood ten men; nine stood to the right. He ordered them into the longboat, ordering they be given tools and several weapons, but only when they were all in the longboat. Knives, food, gunpowder, shot, blankets, two skillet pots, spikes, and two oars were unceremoniously dropped or tossed into the longboat.

"We'll tow you!" a mutineer hollered as the small craft lurched forward, pulled by the might of Discovery. A few minutes passed before Greene appeared with a knife.

"We said we'd tow you, but not for too long!" he called loudly, laughing madly. Applying his knife, he cut the rope, and the rope fell limply. As if in slow-motion, Discovery started pulling away from the longboat, quickly distancing itself from the abandoned crew.

One man started to pray aloud; John cried into his father's shoulder. Two others began to row toward shore. Hudson, realizing the end had come, watched mutely as his ship shrank to a mere pinpoint on the southeastern horizon. The end was truly upon them all, and he wanted to make it as comfortable for his son as possible.

Part One, Chapter Twenty-Three

August 1611 – November 1613

Thomas West, 12th Baron De La Warr, returned to Jamestown from Nevis in mid-August aboard his ship, De La Warr, carrying new supplies and information about the islands in the Caribbean. Two weeks later, on 30 August, the fleet of three ships under the command of Sir Thomas Gates, Lieutenant-General of Virginia, arrived in Jamestown to a flurry of excitement surrounding the supplies, including horses, all manner of livestock, tools, cookware, and other important daily needs for improving the colony. Sir Thomas Dale was also aboard, and was quickly disgusted by what he saw of Jamestown.

Dale, as Governor, called a meeting of the council several days after his arrival, and quickly established his law-and-order methods of governing, "this lackluster indolent crowd of heathens." The council was stunned by Dale's forthright bitterness. If his general demeanor seemed less than hospitable, then his planned application of the set of new laws governing the colony, what Dale referred to as Articles, Laws, and Orders Divine, Moral, and Martial, sounded unduly harsh in every aspect.

"The word martial refers to soldiers and their actions, responsibilities, and punishments for not performing said duties. Divine and moral refer to crimes and punishments of civilians. Death is mandatory for most offenses after public humiliation, then public whipping, and death for a repeat offender. Puritan authority shall not be usurped.

"I expect each of you shall read the laws so you maintain an understanding of them, and I intend carrying them out to the letter of law," Dale forcefully informed council members. "I want the settlement rebuilt. It is in disarray, decrepit, and unseemly for a settlement carrying the king's name." By the time the meeting was ended by Dale, the council members were ready to spread the word.

*****

The mutinous crew of Discovery knew they had to stop for supplies before making open water. Supplies were already quite low, and a two-moth journey to England would prove disastrous without replenished supplies. They elected to stop at Digges Island, an arm of the large bay where they were marooned, when it came into view.

Henry Greene, Robert Bylot, William Wilson, and John Thomas moved ashore in a dingy to trade with some Eskimos who waved them over, holding up blubber and furs. The Eskimos waved until the four were close enough to attack with harpoons and other weapons. Henry Greene fell dead instantly, run-through by a harpoon lance. The others fled back to the dingy. Wilson and Thomas were struck by the same harpoon lances, falling to the ice, but stumbling up, reaching the dingy, where they rowed as fast as possible while trying to remove the lances at the same time. Back aboard the death vessel, the scant crew of twelve, now reduced by one, made way without supplies in order to save their lives as lances, thrown by additional Eskimos in small crafts, whizzed by their heads. They'd have to take their chances.

By September, with westerly winds blowing strongly over the Atlantic Ocean, the weary, ragged, beaten mutineers sailed into the first English port town they could reach. Passing the Isle of Sicily, off the English southwest coast, the sickly remaining men took turns piloting Discovery past Lizard Point, finally docking in Falmouth, in southwest England, near Cornwall.

315

They were surprised they made it at all. Robert Juet died of starvation and was thrown overboard. Both Thomas and Wilson died of their wounds and were handled in the same manner as Juet. The remaining men suffered from severe scurvy, a lack of vitamin C. The sickening disease loosened teeth, making chewing anything painful or nearly impossible. It also stiffened joints, making the simplest movements difficult. They were also dehydrated and starving. Many on the dock took interest because they looked like dead men on a ship. They babbled about Eskimos, ice, ice, and more ice. They were raggedy, scruffy, almost dead. They were taken for being mad. Most had to be carried into the tavern, and the great commotion they caused captured the attention of the port authority.

The agent on the dock that afternoon saw the men from the strange ship. He knew of Prickett because there was rumor that he was a Virginia Company spy put aboard Discovery to watch Hudson's activities. This wasn't proved, but the agent studied the vessel. Men of the sea remember currents like lovers, the good, the bad. This port agent recalled stopping Hudson several years earlier in his Dutch expedition. The agent knew two additional pieces to the puzzle. The vessel belonged to the Virginia Company at London, and, second, neither Hudson nor his young son were carried into the tavern. Where were the Hudsons? The ship's name? *Discovery*. The agent quickly moved to have the vessel seized and alert full port authorities to certain irregularities leading to possible foul play. The crew was placed under arrest after a quick initial investigation.

*****

In early October, Plascomb and Rolfe studied the protruding flower clusters atop their tall tobacco plants at Croplands. Their immediate satisfaction with successful yields turned to considerations for harvesting. Rolfe bent a shorter plant so Richard could study the clusters of light-pink flowers forming a

316

funnel-shaped cluster atop every plant. Each flower held five stamens and a pistil, which, according to Rolfe, were quite hardy at self-propagation. In addition to the reproductive parts, a two-compartment seed pod held many tiny seeds, all to be collected and stored for the next season's new crop.

Richard was amazed by the volume of leaves a single plant produced. On one plant he counted twenty-eight, giant, oval-shaped leaves, all colored in varying shades of light-to-dark green. Rolfe illustrated how to 'top' the plant simply by cutting-off the mature pink flowers. He explained that by doing this, they could force additional plant growth since the plant's energy was put to producing the flower cluster. Richard understood this from his farming days harkening back to his father's farm in England. That all seemed like such a long time ago.

Spreading-out, they started topping the clusters from plants for seeds. While topping, Richard mentally planned the land for the new season's crop in 1612 since this acreage would remain fallow one season. He also considered what Rolfe's comment, "that if Richard thought planting and replanting were hard work, then harvesting would introduce him to an entirely new level of energy demand." Leaves had to be collected, separated, speared, cured, recollected, fermented, and aged. Curing fires were started as harvesting began.

By early January, 1612 the trio of Richard, John, and Christian moved every leaf to the docks to ship product to England. At this point, all they could do was be thankful for rest until the anticipated positive response came from the merchant in London. But there was no rest for Richard or Christian.

They returned to work at the glass foundry. The new responsibilities of growing tobacco demanded almost fourteen hours of work every day except the Sunday, where Dale's Codes made it illegal to miss a church service.

Richard sold his share of the foundry to his partner, Ian Charles, who thoroughly enjoyed his new-found trade, and took over the business in his own name. As for the London response about tobacco, Rolfe had shrugged, saying he thought it might be June before they heard.

"By that time, Richards said, "the second crop will already be growing if it's as good as this one was." Rolfe agreed, asking Richard about his opinion of the new Governor. Richard shook his head.

"I don't care for him or his laws. They're too harsh. There's a whipping for everything, a bodkin through the tongue, public humiliation, or death for many offenses," Richard noted. Rolfe agreed. Though critical of the Governor, Rolfe and Plascomb remained at Croplands unless a need to go the settlement presented itself, though It rarely did.

Richard held that his dislike of Dale stemmed from his continual injection of Puritan religious beliefs into every aspect of daily settlement life, including its governing. This was mostly due to Richard's Anglican beliefs, which differed greatly from the Puritan perspective. But, contrarily, Plascomb had to agree with Rolfe that because of Dale's Code, any laziness that existed in the settlement had rapidly disappeared as the result of one young man's plight.

Hanson Barringer was sent away on the same ship carrying the first lot of tobacco. He rebelled against the Governor's decrees. He was bound neck-to-ankles for one night in the public square, publicly whipped the second time, and upon disobeying a third time, was sentenced by Dale to one year in the galley aboard a convict ship leaving England. Only being fifteen, Barringer's

318

mother cried for mercy and forgiveness, but Dale was resolute, unforgiving, and outwardly used Barringer as an example to anyone who considered breaking his codes. Master Barringer was sent away in cuffs. One quick result of this caused people to lose their original good-natured spirit that returned with the continued return of supply ships. They remained indoors, out of sight of authorities. Some looked upon others as a source for being Dale's informants, so settlers spoke little to others, especially the newest arrivals. Children didn't play because Puritans did not believe in child's play. Children were to be inside reading the Bible. Life had, indeed, changed in Jamestown across the previous five months.

*****

John Cotton was now twenty-seven-years-old when he accepted the position as vicar of the Anglican parish church of St. Boltoph's Church, Boston, in Lincolnshire, in England's northeastern section. Cotton, a Puritan in an Anglican church, was eager to establish himself as a profound man of religion. As such, he accepted the position, engaging himself in administering to his parishioners. An unannounced visit by royal commissioners for religious affairs surprised the new vicar, but his firm position of Anglican worship, "to the letter," neither bothered him nor openly gave the commissioners any reasons for concern. Yet the Crown's obvious interest, perhaps considering him untrustworthy, gave Cotton, at the very least, reason to consider, to think about his new position. His thoughts were interrupted when a parishioner approached, carrying a basket of baked bread, welcoming him to the parish church.

*****

Life continued in London as the wayward Discovery crew was returned to London for legal proceedings. Meanwhile, fully

319

recuperated from his gunpowder accident, Captain John Smith continued to publish books and articles about Jamestown, fueling interest in the colony. Although the Virginia Company sought to commission Smith as a spokesman for the colony, directors finally decided against this idea due to Smith's uncompromising positions against Company policies, coupled with his high asking price. The Company did; however, initiate negotiations with Smith developed around the idea of his leading a new expedition to the Cape Cod region of North America. Smith agreed to the negotiations. On this day in late April, 1612 Smith stood ready to address the House of Commons about devising a policy of properly establishing colonies in North America.

*****

John Rolfe hurried to Croplands in early May after receiving a letter from the London tobacco merchant. Out of breath but too involved to care, Rolfe waved the letter excitedly in the air as Cecelia admitted him into the house. Greeting Cecelia, John called to his two partners when they entered the front hall.

"By Jove, we've got word! We've done it!"

"Done what?" Richard asked, trying to see what Rolfe was waving about.

"Why, we've sold all the tobacco! All of it!" Rolfe stopped to catch his breath. "They want more as well! Twice as much next harvest!" Richard was stunned.

"Yes, Richard, the aroma, taste, fragrance, they're all there! We did it!" Cecelia broke-in.

"You two, come sit and read the letter to us all," she invited, leading the happy group to the kitchen's eating table.

"Christian, fetch some tankards, my boy."

"Right, father." They sat as Cecelia retrieved ale for all of them, and Rolfe opened the nearly crumpled letter. The three gathered close as Rolfe unfolded the one-page letter.

London, the Market
4 March 1612

My Dear Mr. Rolfe & Mr. Plascomb,

I write first to congratulate you on your highly successful crop of New Virginia tobacco, which we received on the 2nd February 1612. The entire parcel of 600 pounds was sold in two hours, a time frame we never anticipated.

The product's aroma, flavor, texture, and high degree of success garnered the highest price paid to date here at the Market. Your payment, along with that of your partner, Richard Plascomb, is a total of £4,568. Said funds shall be deposited in London under the control of Edward Ramplay, Esq., your personal account manager. Mr. Ramplay shall be contacting you in a subsequent letter.

At this time, the London Market is well prepared to pay a premium price for your fine product, granted its quality continues in the manner of this first crop. We seek at least twice the volume of this yield at the 1612 harvest period, so we ask you plan and plant accordingly.

Please write with any inquiries. Mr. Ramplay's contact information is included. With all success in the new season, I am,

Yours truly,
Lord Essel Wyleslow
Director-General
The Market, London

"Almost five-thousand Pounds!" Richard yelled exuberantly, startling Cecelia, who also was profoundly amazed. Tankards were raised, toasts made.

"'Tis a far good thing we planted almost three times as much this season, John," Richard declared, drinking happily.

"We'll need more curing barns," Rolfe said seriously. Richard studied Rolfe's face.

"John, perhaps we can hire some men and boys to help, you know, lighten the load on us."

"And me," Christian said, making everyone laugh.

"You're one of us, son. Don't you fear." Christian smiled, nodded, drank.

"You're right, Richard. We can't do it alone anymore. We should begin hiring tomorrow. But, how will we pay? We have no currency here." This stumped Richard until Rolfe said, "Richard, we'll pay in tobacco, or we'll think of something." Cecelia retrieved more ale as the men started planning how best to hire the best men and boys for the crop.

*****

King James was in the royal garden on 24 May when he was informed by special messenger about the death of his loyal advisor, Robert Cecil, Earl of Salisbury, at forty-nine years. Cecil died at his estate at Marlborough, Wiltshire, in the central-southern region of England.

As Cecil's funeral was planned, King James named his favorite, Robert Carr, who was made a member of the privy council a month earlier, as the Earl of Salisbury's replacement as secretary of state and the king's closest advisor.

*****

Life's perpetuation continues in equal proportion to its termination. On the same day King James learned of Robert Cecil's death, the Fauseth family in Leiden grew by one. Miller Fauseth was born to William and Mary Fauseth, one of the couples who made the move from Scrooby to Leiden with the Puritan congregation. The baby boy was very healthy, cried loudly, and fed hungrily when introduced to the tit. When the midwife, Mrs. Krebs, was satisfied, she admitted the father into the room to see his strapping son.

The couple named the infant Miller because that was his father's trade in Holland. William worked at the Leiden flour mill, producing flour for bakeries and private bakers. Both parents wanted their son to know his beginnings and his father's honest trade.

*****

George Calvert was surprised to discover he was one of four executors of the late Robert Cecil's vast estate and holdings. Calvert's expert diplomatic abilities under pressures, associated with the incredible holdings of the late Cecil, his manager for many years, illustrated Calvert's people managing skills. Robert Carr, now on the privy council, selected Calvert, whom he had known when Cecil managed him, as his own secretary in foreign policy matters.

Sharing a meal and wine with Carr one afternoon at Hampton Court, Carr informed Calvert that, "part of this assignment originates from your adroitness with diplomats during the coronation of France's new king, Louis XIII, two years ago,

323

George," Carr explained. "Reports came back to his majesty regarding the great contentment of your discreet conversational abilities." This subtly informed Calvert he was being told he held a very successful future.

*****

A dozen men and older boys were hired at Croplands to build curing barns, and they worked steadily for the several hundred acres of tobacco already proving to be a successful crop. By the middle of June there were almost forty new barns ready for use at harvest. The plan was to build ahead to be ready for continued growth. With necessary acres divided into manageable sections, the new barns were placed in close proximity in a central location for easy mobility and maximum crop development. Fires were planned for the new barns in August to season the interiors, switching from construction to utilization. Richard suggested pre-cured wood might help quicken the cure or offer enhanced flavor.

In addition to working at Croplands, Rolfe had taken a portion of his profit sent from London to build his own estate along the James River, planning to call it Varina Farms, a reference to the mild Spanish tobacco. It was located about forty miles upriver of Jamestown, and it was coming along superbly. Rolfe informed Richard he planned to grow tobacco at his estate to keep up with demand before any competitors could catch-up in similar production. This made Plascomb think.

"So, what you're telling me, John, is that you want us to have a monopoly on tobacco." Rolfe nodded.

"Right, Richard, before the rich guys in England figure out our plans, and start coming here to obtain great land tracts for themselves." Rolfe stood. "I'm off to Varina Farms to see how far construction has gotten. I'll be back tomorrow." Shaking hands, the pair walked around to the Croplands docks, where Rolfe tied his boat.

"Tomorrow, Richard," Rolfe called, casting away from land for the ride upstream. The boat proved much faster than on horseback.

*****

Sir Thomas Smythe addressed the meeting of Virginia Company directors regarding the return of Discovery, the mutinous remaining crew, and the new, third, royal patent for a new expedition to discover the northwest passage.

"Gentlemen, as you know, my news today surrounds the most recent, third, royal patent for our newest expedition yet to discover the northwest passage to the Orient. Two ships have already sailed to what we are calling Hudson Bay to continue searching for the elusive passage. The ships are Resolution and Discovery, the same vessel Henry Hudson sailed.

"We have hired a new captain, Sir Francis Button, a Welsh office of the Royal Navy who shall see us to our objective. We have been joined in this newest expedition with financial underwriting by none other than George Abbot, Archbishop of Canterbury, as well as Sir Francis Bacon, our solicitor general, geographer Richard Hakluyt, and mathematician Henry Briggs. I would say Captain Button has assembled a sterling group of backers." One director had a direct question he testily asked.

"What about that roustabout mutinous crew of blackguards from Discovery who killed the captain, his son, and the others?" Smythe nodded.

"Director Richards, we only have the Prickett story to go by. All the remaining crewmen agreed with Prickett, stating there came a severe storm over the Atlantic that washed the men overboard." Richards wasn't satisfied.

"I don't believe them, not one disgusting word of it. What absolute rubbish, I say! What about their trials for mutiny on the high seas?" Sir Edwin Sandys addressed that question.

"Director Richards, in view of our significant economic resources being applied to this project, which failed under Captain Hudson, members have considered that the remaining crew, some who have already been tried for mutiny, but pardoned, based on their firsthand knowledge about the geographic region, landmarks, sailing routes, and important expedition benchmarks of what we are calling Hudson Bay. This information will give the Company a decided business edge over competitors in future sailings.

"Therefore, the Company has approached the judges in this case, requesting pardons for those crewmembers. In fact, Robert Bylot, the navigator aboard Discovery during the mutiny, is currently sailing with Captain Button to Hudson Bay. They sailed about three weeks ago, late in May." A second director addressed Sandys.

"Are you saying that a man's life is less important than financial gain?"

"I wouldn't put it quite that way, Director Edwards."

"Then how exactly would you put it, Sir Edwin?" Edwards asked gruffly. Sandys pondered a moment.

"Director Edwards, one man's life is merely a measure of meeting our requirements. We have investor equity at stake. Captain Hudson was, at that time, our most valuable resource, and what does a business do with its resources?"

"We use them," Richards answered.

"Exactly," Sandys declared easily. "We must utilize our resources as they become available. When the time comes, we seek new resources, all in the guarantee of return on investor equity." Director Edwards stood.

"I've heard enough. If this is the sort of business model we pursue, it shall be the ruin of mankind. I would have voted against it. I am in the minority, and I know it." Sandys smiled.

"Perhaps, but you won't feel too badly when your investments double or triple," Mr. Edwards.

"But, how many lives will that doubling require? It's blood money," Edwards declared forcefully, departing the meeting. "Carry-on without me. You know where I may be reached," he added, shutting the door behind himself.

"He'll be back," one director said. "Sir Edwards has a soft heart for humanity."

"Not a good business model to adhere to," Sir Edwin commented, bringing laughter around the table as the meeting moved to its conclusion.

****

Anne Marbury was almost twenty-one as she approached her August wedding day. Daughter of Reverend Francis Marbury, who was reputed to be of strong Puritan leanings, Anne married William Hutchinson, becoming Mrs. Ann Hutchinson. Mr. Hutchinson was a wealthy London garment merchant, and he looked forward to a large family. Anne, too, was equally enthusiastic about her desire to, "have a brood about her." The couple planned to live in London until final residency plans were decided.

*****

Eleven-year-old Prince Charles, second son of King James I, was awoken by his man servant, Peers, in the darkest hours of night. The prince asked if it was already time for breakfast, but then realized darkness ruled the hour.

"Whatever is…is happ…happening, Peers?" he asked, standing, so Peers could drape a robe about him. "This is most un… unusual," Prince Charles added. Peers wasn't saying much, and he, like all at court, were used to the prince's stammering.

"Sire, your father has sent for you and your sister, Elizabeth. I think it best I leave news for him to share with you. Come, he awaits. Quickly."

Making their way to the king's personal apartments, Prince Charles discovered the most unusual assemblage of people at this dark hour. Most were in night clothes like himself, and all were strangely, eerily silent and somber. They also had the most perplexed looks on their faces when Charles entered his father's room. Only his father spoke quietly with John Carr and several other advisors at a table littered with documents. His older sister, Elizabeth, now sixteen, entered the room with her attendants. Elizabeth joined her brother.

"Charles, where is our brother, Henry?" she asked in a whisper. Charles looked about the crowded, candle-lit room, shaking his head in response, heightening his adolescent curiosity. Elizabeth called to their father, who turned to them, standing.

"My children, God has called my son, your brother, Henry, to Heaven above. Henry has died." Elizabeth broke-down, and was quickly aided by her assistants. Charles' eyes widened at the words, and he felt his heart start racing as their father addressed them again.

"His illness took him an hour ago; it was worse than the doctors thought." Charles understood that Henry was only eighteen, but, as Prince of Wales, he was next in-line for the English throne. Charles' heart raced more because he suddenly understood what this congregation meant.

There is a moment in the life of each boy and girl when, in a brief spec of time, he or she realizes childhood has ended; however abruptly, and that youthful life has entered the adult world. This was Charles' moment. He was to be advised of the official notice. He was correct.

John Carr, his father's most influential advisor, turned from the documents on the table, stood, instructing an attendant to prepare the royal wax seal, and addressed those in attendance while Elizabeth cried woefully in a corner, surrounded by her ladies.

"In accordance with divine right of kings," Carr began clearly, strongly, demandingly, fracturing the somber silence beyond his sister's lamentations.

"Every prince who shall ascend to the English throne shall cast his lot before God and those earthly men responsible for his advisement. Therein, upon the dearth of Henry, Prince of Wales, at the premature age of eighteen years, it is heretofore declared that Charles, currently Duke of York, as is customary as the sovereign's second son, and Knight of Bath, Prince Charles is now heir apparent, as he cannot be displaced from his rightful claim to the throne upon his father's death. Also, be it now known that Prince Charles, eldest surviving on of the King, is forthwith declared Duke of Cornwall and Duke of Rothesay.

"Further, it is declared that Charles, second son of King James VI of Scotland and James I of England, shall ascend to the throne of England and Scotland upon the death of his natural father, and shall be called King Charles I of England and Scotland." Carr looked to the trembling prince, requesting his presence at the table, offering him a quill.

"Prince Charles, your signature on these documents signifies your understanding of all that has been decreed. You shall begin preparations, as did your late brother, to accept the crown as King at the time of your father's death.

"Also, your applied signature establishes that you shall work tirelessly to provide for, protect, and remain loyal to your subjects, so help you, God." Carr looked around.

"Where's the vicar?" Charles' hand shook as he reached for the quill. He would be twelve in two weeks. His father nodded quietly when Charles looked at him. A servant rushed into the room.

"The vicar is here, Majesty," he called, followed by the vicar rushing to apply his collar. Charles thought he might vomit as quill approached parchment. Where was Henry, the brother he sought to emulate, the brother he loved so much?

"Not yet, Charles," his father said calmly. "The vicar must pray first." Charles nodded, waited as the vicar opened the Book of Common Prayer, reciting an official prayer. Carr's finger pointed to the lines to which Charles had to apply his signature. He signed one document after another as prayers were recited.

When he was finished, the wax seal was applied to each document as the vicar first blessed the new heir apparent, followed by the king, then all in attendance. A servant shook powder over the signatures, blowing-off the excess.

"It is done," Carr announced loudly, calling for Peers, Charles' man servant. The man approached.

"Peers," Carr said, "Prince Charles shall be tended to by Mr. Pyres, his late brother's man servant. Your duties will be shifted." Peers nodded as the young prince was shunted over to Pyres, whom Carr addressed.

"Pyres, return the prince to bed forthwith. He must be awakened and refreshed no later than eight o'clock. His first instructions in state matters begins at nine, followed by royal treasury instruction at ten. Good night, Prince Charles. May God be with you always," Carr said with finality. All bowed as Pyres led the heir apparent from the room.

  Alone in his bed, Charles lay thinking about all that had just happened. Where was Henry? What had happened? He was awoken a boy, returning to bed as the next king of England. That night, Charles prayed his father ruled for a long, long time.

Part One, Chapter Twenty-Four

January 1613 – March 1614

The Croplands tobacco harvest produced a bumper crop. The men hired worked to work at Croplands were, "mighty grateful" for the work, and Richard was completely educated in large-scale tobacco production. He and Rolfe began long-term planning for additional acreage dedicated to tobacco after an inspection the previous October by the Governor, Sir Thomas Dale. The successful management at Croplands had not evaded his domineering scrutiny. During his visit, Dale informed both Plascomb and Rolfe that he planned to do away with the communal planting at Croplands. Dale had taken over for De La Warr, who had become quite ill, forcing his return to England almost two years earlier.

"It is my belief that every man be responsible for his own standing in the settlement. Therefore, I am changing land distribution. Every man here now, whom I refer to as ancient planters, shall receive three acres of land to settle for himself and his family. Smaller plots will be allotted to those who arrive later. Each man will grow his own food. A Puritan must pull himself up by his own means, as opposed to anticipating a hand-out. The plan will go into effect later this year, but I have not a date at this time. Plan your land use as you wish since there will be no further communal plantings." Based on Dale's information, Rolfe and Plascomb started planning for additional tobacco.

Half the yield was shipped in late December to Mr. Ramplay, the account manager in London. By the end of January 1613, the remainder was shipped to London, permitting a brief period of rest, repairs, and planning. During this time, Richard added an addition to the house, a large sewing room for Cecelia, where she could sew, store fabric bolts, and enjoy a quiet seating area for conversation. When it was complete, Cecelia anticipated ordering fabrics from London.

"It is surely a grand room, Richard. Thank you," she said, kissing him. He thanked her, thinking how she retained her youthful graceful appearance.

"I've been thinking about how far we've come since the dark days, Cecelia." She laughed a little, agreeing. "Do you know I'll be thirty-nine this year?" he asked, making her laugh outright.

"I never thought I'd be married to an old man," she teased.

"But I'm a gentleman now," he countered.

"I love thee, Richard Plascomb. If we have survived those events I once thought insurmountable, then we shall remain bound all the days of our lives."

"I agree with you, and I believe what you say," he replied, sitting at the table in the seating area. Cecelia stroked his hair, seeing flecks of grey among the dark brown. She didn't mention them, but she smiled all the same.

"This room is grand, Richard. Will you be teaching Christian to ride in spring?" He nodded.

"Aye, I shall that," he said excitedly. "He shall pick his pony today, bearing the responsibility for caring for it. The work must be in equal measure to the enjoyment."

"Just like marriage, right, Richard?" He laughed.

"Like life!" he exclaimed, pulling Cecelia to the bench with him. "Let me take you on the table. You shall be my breakfast," he said, caressing her as their son entered the room, making Cecelia laugh as she stood, seeing the funny look on Christian's face.

"Ah, too late, Mr. Plascomb. You will have to be content with some oats for breakfast," she commented, kissing her son's flaxen head. "Come, oats and tea for breakfast, men. Richard, tell Christian of his new pony." Christian's eyes opened widely at the announcement.

"My own horse?" he asked excitedly as the family sat at the kitchen table.

"Aye, son," his father told him as bowls of hot oats were eaten.

*****

The loneliness that beset Prince Charles after the death of his brother almost a year ago intensified in February, 1613 on the day his sister, Elizabeth, now seventeen years, wed Frederick V, the Elector Palatine of the Rhine in the Holy Roman Empire, and who would be seventeen in August.

Now twelve, Charles observed the royal wedding unfolding, meaning he would inescapably alone, plodding through endless hours of discussions about diplomacy, royal finances, the treasury, and listen to others eventually planning his own marriage to the best suitable princess to guarantee political alliances and the proper redistribution of wealth between families.

Charles, small for his age, continued to stutter, but was learning to control it. He was most happy with his horses, about which Henry had taught him much, and hunting, a favorite Stuart family tradition. Charles missed Henry immensely, and his sister would now be out of his life for the foreseeable future, possibly for the duration of his own.

Yet Charles' initial resistance to being forced to grow so fast started to fade as he began to understand that he was more than merely a boy living in a palace. He was next in-line to be King of England. Elizabeth smiled at hm as she passed him after the ceremony was finished. He smiled and nodded in return.

*****

Samuel Argall sailed up the North American coast in late February, 1613 to execute his newest orders from the Virginia Company at London, expel any French settlements reported to exist or under construction on English land. Argall was Born in Bristol, a seaport town on the eastern shore of the Bristol Channel across from Cardiff, Wales, in 1572. As early as 1601, Argall was hired by the Company to find a shorter route to Virginia to fish for sturgeon. Nine years later, he was named Admiral of Virginia, and he was to expel any French settlements to prevent reported expansionist plans by French King Louis XIII.

The Company wanted a man capable, willing, and forceful enough to carry-out their demands. Argall was a mean-spirited vindictive man. He'd made a name for himself through ruthless military matters. Hence, his assignment was to seek and destroy. He was firm in his dedicated effort to eradicate all non-English settlements where he discovered them. Now forty years, Argall quietly observed the coastline as his ship sailed toward Acadia, near the 'maine' coast.

*****

John Rolfe made his residence at Varina Farms while Argall sailed to Acadia when construction was finished in early March 1613. On a pleasant spring morning the same month, Rolfe sat on the riverbank drawing a design for his new dock. The sun had risen to a high point in the late morning sky, and the day was warm and bright as Rolfe caught sight of something that flashed to his left.

Eight native canoes glided effortlessly along the James River. He considered waving, but stopped when he saw Pocahontas in the lead canoe with her father, Powhatan. Rolfe stood, offering respect, despite the sour relations between the natives and settlers. As the flotilla passed directly before Rolfe, he waved to Pocahontas, and looked directly to her father, nodding. In return, Powhatan looked from Rolfe to his daughter, who was gently waving back at Rolfe, smiling. Powhatan, noticing the shared greetings, nodded in return.

The feelings Rolfe experienced for the raven-haired, beguiling, native princess were equal in ardor to those he had felt for his late wife, Sarah. Rolfe silently watched the canoes until they rounded a bend, deciding he loved the princess, and would marry her, despite their ethnic and cultural differences.

*****

John and Mary Winthrop continued living at the Forth Estate, home to Mary's parents, at Great Stembridge, in Essex, in proximity to London. Together, husband and wife, and their three children, spent most of their time at the estate. John studied law, while Mary tended to the children and gardened with her mother.

In spring, 1613, John received word from his father, Adam Winthrop, director at Trinity College, Cambridge University, that he had decided to transfer the family holdings, including Groton Manor, over to John, now twenty-six years. Groton Manor was the family's five-hundred-acre estate originally purchased from King Henry VIII during the Reformation. This was being done because John had remained married to Mary and illustrated his unwavering religious piousness. As a result of his father's decision, the family made arrangements to live at Groton Manor.

John also took control of his father's lands in Suffolk, in eastern-central England, as well as properties his wealthy mother's family owned in Suffolk and Essex. John was now Lord of the Manor at Groton. Simultaneously, John took a position of practicing law in London, following his father's example. He enrolled at Gray's Inn, reading the law.

Mary Winthrop respected her husband's apparently extreme piousness, yet she never shared his resolute religious perspectives. His positions gave their children a firm, if somewhat authoritarian knowledge of faith, but Mary maintained her calm demeanor upon the children, lending them some untold freedoms to offset their father's religious intensity.

One previous winter evening, John told his wife that, "I want that God would give me a new heart, joy in His spirit; that He should dwell within me." Mary had been knitting; John reading the Bible. Mary nodded while continuing to knit.

"Well, John, the kingdom already abides within thee." Understanding his wife never shared his degree of religious beliefs, John returned to Bible reading, enjoying the new King James version.

*****

Edward Hutchinson was born the first child to William and Anne Hutchinson in Alford, Lincoln, England on 28 May 1613. He was healthy, and both infant and mother fared well with the midwife's help.

*****

At Croplands, the season's new growth for tobacco and vegetables was producing superb crops, including the most abundant tobacco crop to-date. With newly hired workers, Richard and Rolfe planted eight hundred acres of tobacco, and Mr. Ramplay wrote to say the Market already claimed all yields at harvest! In addition to the Croplands acreage, Rolfe planted seventy acres at Varina Farms.

Unknown to either Rolfe or Plascomb was that their efforts were having a decidedly positive economic effect on the settlement and its population. Men and boys were working. London merchants were spreading the word about the new tobacco from Jamestown.

Contrarily, news of harsh living conditions under Dale and Argall also circulated in London, even after the king granted the third patent giving governing rights of the colony to the Company. Negative information about bad relations with the natives had the effect of lowering numbers of prospective new colonists.

Many natives lived in one winter location, moving to a different village in spring and summer for fishing and planting. Increasingly, native scouts were forced to patrol lands not is use because settlers took it upon themselves to attempt to claim the land since no one was using it. This was a gross illustration of English insolence and disrespect for the native culture. As land poaching increased, good relations quickly decreased.

In late April, it happened that a rogue band of one of Powhatan's many federation tribes had taken seven Jamestown men hostage for land poaching. No one knew where them men were, but were thought to be alive because no blood or bodies were found. Immediately, the men of Jamestown began organizing a plan to rescue the men. Many of them had traveled with Argall to find French settlements, and they hadn't yet returned. Argall said he would develop a plan on the trip.

*****

King James spoke clearly and with conviction in his discussion with the men at the table.

"Your mission, Calvert, along with Sir Humphrey Winch, Sir Charles Cornwallis, and Sir Roger Wilbraham, is to fully investigate Catholic grievances in Ireland. Your commission, gentlemen, will permit you, on my authority, to remain in Ireland so long as is required in effort to determine the legitimacy of said grievances." The king was referring to riots in northern areas of Ireland against Catholic suppression. The four men at the table commissioned to do the king's work were fully informed of their responsibilities. They departed for Liverpool, where they would sail to Dublin.

*****

Adriaen Block accepted the documents from the States General, the Dutch governing body, directors of the Netherlands, granting him and three associates exclusive rights to trade as official Dutch representatives in the New World. Block, an able sea captain and explorer, was no stranger to North America. Following Henry Hudson's Dutch expedition in 1609, Block made four subsequent trips to the area Hudson explored for the Dutch East India Company.

339

Descriptions of friendly natives eager to trade, abundant natural resources, an endless supply of beaver pelts, and unclaimed lands stirred the visionary, intrepid, and entrepreneurial Dutch to begin the chase for the unclaimed region in the northeast for new markets promising a bounty of desired raw materials. The end of the Dutch-Spanish War allowed the Dutch to focus all energies on their plans for colonization in North America.

Block was directed to assemble his crew and be ready to sail aboard the Tyger to the new locations the Dutch were tentatively calling New Amsterdam. Signing his documents, Block thanked the States General representatives, and departed to make his final departure plans to sail in two weeks before the start of April.

*****

The Powhatan Federation extended for several thousand square miles in every direction from the center of the main village. One late spring morning after returning from Acadia, Argall and his armed men paddled silently up the Delaware River in a flotilla of twenty-two canoes and several sturdy rafts, searching for encroaching French settlements on English Puritan lands, in violation of property rights claimed by the Virginia Company. Argall's instructions to his men included his claim of a search and destroy mission, as were all his missions.

In addition to looking for French settlements, the men also sought to locate the seven missing colonists taken by Powhatan's braves. Lastly, they were working to ensure they weren't the newest to be taken hostages. Danger lurked everywhere, and random raids and deaths were a constant in daily settlement life. Rounding a bend to the right, Argall noticed movement, realizing he was correct when a young

340

native girl stood-up, having been bent to pick wildflowers. One of his men whispered to him.

"That's Pocahontas, Powhatan's princess daughter," Argall was told, instantly capturing Argall's attention. The girl, about sixteen, was obviously unaware of the canoes. Argall motioned for the crafts to the banks, where he and ten men jumped to shore, hiding themselves in the dense woods. This was an excellent strategy to regain the seven men. Argall would take Powhatan's daughter as hostage, and they could trade captives. Argall made hand motions to inform his men what to do, and they quietly surrounded Pocahontas in an enclosing circle.

Three of Argall's men suddenly jumped from the woods, causing Pocahontas to throw her flowers to the ground, turning to run. When she did this, she ran smack into Argall, who quickly muffled her screams, and was assisted in carrying the flailing girl to the canoes where her hands and feet were bound with rope.

Argall motioned for the flotilla to quickly move-out while he studied the beautiful girl with the black shining hair and wild eyes. He could tell she was quite angry, yet she held herself regally for one so young. He asked the men if she spoke English.

"Aye, Captain, she's been around the colony since it started some six years ago. Argall studied the girl.

"We will not harm you. Do not fear us." Rage filled the girl's face as she inhaled deeply.

"I do not fear you; I despise you, especially you. You are a mean brutal man!" she hissed angrily. Argall laughed aloud.

"And how do you know that, young lady? You know me not."
Pocahontas studied Argall a few moments before replying, as if
she was looking into his soul.

"Your being is written in your eyes, and nothing can mask the
dislike you feel for anyone different than yourself." Pocahontas
turned her back on Argall, looking silently ahead. Looking away
himself, Argall noticed more movement – a settlement! He
motioned the flotilla to the banks again. All but two men
guarding the native princess moved ashore.

When they were about thirty yards from the settlement,
Pocahontas shouted a native warning, briefly stopping both
French and English in their tracks before the French started
running in every direction. One man slapped Pocahontas,
silencing her. Shots were fired onto the air as thirty settlers, all
men and boys, were rounded-up and brought to the center of
the settlement's clearing.

"What is this?" Argall barked to an older bearded man.

"It is Saveur," the man replied with a distinct French accent.

"it is French, yes?" Argall asked, and the man nodded.

"Oui."

"You are informed you are squatting on land owned by the
Virginia Company at London, Sir. All lands below the Forty-sixth
parallel belongs to said Company. You shall be removed." Argall
ordered all hands bound and all taken to the flotilla. The man
asked about the settlement. Momentarily, Argall observed the
solid construction, water wheels, beginnings of a garden.

"Destroy it all," Argall ordered. "Destroy every stick of it." He turned back to the canoes as his men carried-out his orders. When they were done, the flotilla returned to Jamestown where all the captives were put in the fort's prison.

*****

The English countryside is breathtaking in summer. The more northern latitudes help maintain a comfortable union of low humidity and pleasant temperatures. Combined with blue sky and low-hanging billowing cumulus clouds, St. Boltoph's Minister John Cotton was married to Elizabeth Horrocks in Balsham, Cambridgeshire, on the third day of July, 1613.

In keeping with his strict Puritan beliefs, Cotton and his new wife quietly returned to their home to begin their marriage.

*****

The Commission sent to Ireland to investigate Catholic grievances and religious persecution returned to London in late August after almost five months in Ireland. George Calvert took it upon himself to write the majority of the report of findings to be submitted to the king for a determination of subsequent actions.

The Commission determined that religious conformity to Anglicanism in Ireland should be enforced with increased pressure and determination. In addition, suppression of Catholic schools should be pursued, along with the removal and punishment of bad priests.

Calvert, aware of the report's negative effects on Irish Catholics, especially in consideration of his own unspoken Catholic faith, troubled him greatly, but he forced himself to put aside his personal beliefs and positions partly because the solution to immense problems with the Catholic-Protestant question was beyond the abilities of only one man.

*****

Argall's plan was simple in theory; trade the men for Pocahontas. It's actuality, though, was proving to be more difficult. It was early September, and no word had come from the Powhatan Federation. No settlers were permitted beyond the colony's boundary for fear of retribution. Any good relations that might have existed previously were gone. By now the entire colony knew Pocahontas was captive. Some didn't know who she was, but they learned quickly from the few original colonists who knew her when she was a child in the settlement.

Political solutions never occur in a vacuum. As surprised as Dale was when the French captives came to Jamestown, he was stunned to discover the native princess. Argall and Governor Dale talked of brokering a peace deal. The Frenchmen captured at the squatting settlement were sent back to France. Pocahontas was the focus of a peace settlement.

Dale had taken Pocahontas under his custody. He took her into his residence, treating her as a true princess. After several months, he recommended she learn English ways of living, and she agreed, having little choice or options, remained living at the Governor's residence.

By October, 1613 Pocahontas had been at Dale's residence more than six months, learning English quite proficiently. Across that span of time, she was formally introduced to John Rolfe by way of Richard Plascomb, whom she knew from playing with his son years ago. Plascomb was aware that Rolfe loved Pocahontas, but had to devise a way to tell her if he wanted to

344

marry her. Richard suggested he write the Governor a letter, arranging to talk with Powhatan in the process.

"It's the only way, John," Richard said during harvesting. Rolfe nodded, considering the many variables in this equation, including the reality that the Federation could descend upon the colony with all its thousands of people, destroying it and everyone. Rolfe was as unhappy with Dale and Argall as the next man, but he had to make a decision as he turned attention to curing tobacco.

*****

Twenty-three-year-old William Bradford married Dorothy May, the daughter of a wealthy English couple living in Leiden with the Separatist Scrooby group. The couple was married in a civil service since they could find no example of a religious service in the Scriptures. The couple wed on 10 December 1613.

*****

That same December, Pocahontas decided to convert to Christianity. Reverend Alexander Whittaker officiated her baptism, and she chose the Christian name Rebecca. She was called Lady Rebecca.

In January, 1614, Lady Rebecca remained living at the governor's home, and his concern changed to worry as time moved forward without word from Powhatan. Was he amassing an army to attack? The answer to all Dale's concerns, and a chance at peace, came in a letter from John Rolfe. Opening the letter, Dale read with surprise, then sincere hope.

4 January 1614

Dear Governor Dale,

   I am writing to you believing our Lord God has you in His firm grasp. Another successful crop of tobacco is on its way to London Market. There are times when Richard Plascomb and I are of the opinion we cannot grow enough tobacco to meet the demands of the English market. However, I am writing with a different concern and request of you.

   I have come to sincerely and truly love the Lady Rebecca, to whom I was introduced as Pocahontas. By the time you receive this letter, I will have already spoken personally to Powhatan, obtaining his permission to marry his daughter. I am writing to you after his permission was granted to me. Therefore, I am requesting that you also grant your permission for the marriage to happen since, in addition to our joint Christian life here in Jamestown, we could possibly make a treaty with the Federation for peace and stability.

   My heart is filled with the desire to marry Lady Rebecca and have peace among us.

Sincerely,

John Rolfe

   Dale sat studying the unexpected letter, surprised by its content, and pleased at its timing. He considered the possible finality of a fully compelling peace with Powhatan, but his thoughts abruptly shifted. He also had to consider the diluting effects of a white man marrying a native. Children would be half-breeds, he thought. Which world would accept them, reject them? If Rolfe was not so important financially for his tobacco production, Dale could run him off, but not now. The product was having a firm stabilizing effect on the colony. Lastly, Dale

346

pondered the political necessity outweighed the personal fallout from this marriage union.

Perhaps he could use the marriage as propaganda for the colony. He decided to grant permission and send emissaries to Powhatan, including Rolfe and Plascomb. He moved across the room to his desk to reply to Rolfe. Maybe this dubious union would help the colony after all.

*****

John Davenport entered his first year at Oxford University in the spring of 1614. Born to wealthy parents in Coventry, Warwickshire, southeast of Birmingham near the River Avon, John, born in 1597, and now sixteen years, crossed under the full front gates of the university to study theology.

His father strongly advised him to be studious and remain apart from all Puritan influences at university. Meanwhile, his childhood friend, Theophilus Eaton, was already a wealthy London merchant, and, much to John's bewilderment, had turned his religious convictions to the Puritan manner of thought.

*****

Severe winds blew stinging snow into the face as it accumulated on river banks and the forest floor. Tisquantum, or Squanto, of the Pawtuxet Tribe, decided frozen water hurt no matter how it struck the face as he and a group of braves hunted for deer for the village. Now a man in the village, Squanto held the gift of language abilities. Dealings with wandering English and French trappers and traders developed Squanto's communication abilities, and though not fully fluent, he remained adept at conversing in French and English. Villagers believed this gift was given to Squanto by the sky spirits as a sing of his future as a sachem, or village leader. On this frigid morning the deer were not to be found, so fishing would provide food for the village.

Standing on a palisade near the area of the Massachusett Tribes, fishing proved successful. Tall raking whitecaps underscored the fury of the open water, but at least the snow stopped. Squanto, looking out across the water, suddenly called-out, pointing to the unmistakable great white sails of two ghost ships sailing very close to the coast where he and the others stood. Certain the white men were looking through their magic glasses, Squanto called for all to fade into the trees.

Word from Powhatan spoke of trouble that follows the white men. They were mean-spirited, and were made crazy by thoughts of the yellow metal they sought to much. The ship swayed and rose, fell from the great waves and swells, like a watery ballet. Squanto and the others watched the white men scramble, crab-like, up ropes. They watched others move like busy ants doing whatever the ships required on rough seas.

Squanto ordered two braces to return to the village and report the ship, telling his men they soon would be in Mohegan territory if they continued sailing up the coast.

"The water spirits do not favor them," he told the others, who agreed with him. "Look how the spirits shake the boat on the water." The ship passed directly before them, continuing its northward path.

Aboard the vessel, Captain John Smith commanded a crack crew of able knowledgeable seamen who worked tirelessly. Smith sailed from Gravesend in early January. He'd considered stopping at Jamestown when he began moving along the coastline, but decided against it. He never wanted to return after the reports he'd gotten. Smith was sailing again, working for the Virginia Company at London after a sixteen-month negotiation process. His responsibility was to map the northeastern coast of North America.

Moving carefully along the area his late friend, Bartholomew Gosnold, named Cape Cod, Smith thought about his friend who died of fever that first summer at Jamestown in August, 1607. Had seven years passed already? Smith laughed at himself. Gosnold didn't like Jamestown, thinking it unsanitary. Smith handed the helm to his mate because he had an idea after viewing the natural beauty of what Gosnold had seen so long ago. He called for the ship's scribe.

"The name of Cape Cod shall forever remain," Smith told the young scribe, marveling at all he observed. "Record that on this day I am naming this entire area that forever shall be known as New England," Smith announced, repeating it. "New England, yes, I like it. Record it, scribe, for posterity."

"Done, Captain."

"Very good, and that shall be all for now, lad," Smith said, studying the coast again, calling for his crew to begin looking for a suitable landing site.

By the time a longboat was released for landing, the Mohegan tribes were fully aware of the ship's presence, and a Wampanoag greeting party formed on shore as Smith's landing party approached. A peaceful people, the Wampanoag waved in a friendly manner as Smith and his party landed, stepping ashore. Unseen, though, a small yet heavily-armed group of braves remained out of sight.

Part One, Chapter Twenty-Five

April 1614 – December 1615

The ice broke in late March for Captain Button and his crew aboard Discovery in the same unforgiving waters in the western-most section of James Bay in the larger Hudson Bay. By April, the ice sheets were melting and sailing resumed. In an estuary where Button believed the northwest passage led to the Pacific, and led there by none other than Robert Bylot, the same man promoted to be Henry Hudson's first mate almost three years earlier. The site was mapped in significant detail. As Sir Sandys had said, the crew had first-hand knowledge of the area, and their deaths after their mutiny would stifle the existing information about the region.

Nosing through the breaking ice, Button and the crew, including Bylot, who privately scanned for ghosts, moved gingerly along the southern end of Southampton Island in the extreme northwest portion of Hudson Bay before sailing through Hudson Strait, and out to the Labrador Sea to the Atlantic Ocean, completely free of treacherous ice.

In his log, Button, not giving a care to whatever dealings Bylot had with his former captain, surely now dead, along with his son and small party, entered his belief that there is a passage, as is like the one between Calais and Dover. Sailing beyond the ice at Killiniq Island, Discovery moved into the safer Atlantic, bound for England. As Button sailed home, Jamestown was preparing for a celebration.

*****

The pending marriage between Pocahontas and John Rolfe produced gossip, back-biting, stories of naked, half-breed, red-and-white, heathen offspring behind closed doors. Publicly, though, the colony presented its best social behavior for what many could not believe, a white man marrying a native woman. Following Dale's announcement of the marriage in early March, opinions ranged a spectrum from blessings to blasphemy, rallying to raging, support to segregation, and everyone seemed to have an opinion as the date approached.

Prior to the wedding, Rolfe acted as intermediary between Powhatan and Dale. The union of Rolfe and Pocahontas officially sealed the guarantee of peace between the English and natives of the Federation. Powhatan gave his word that the attacking, rogue, native bands would cease their actions. In return, Dale promised to ease-off from acquiring native land. The seven settlers taken hostage were safely returned the day Rolfe, accompanied by Richard, spoke with Powhatan.

On 5 April 1614, the wedding was set to start at noon. To the Powhatan, the Great Father in the Sky was blessing the marriage with fabulous blue sky and warm temperatures. The English, Anglian and Puritan, thanked God in heaven for the same after another difficult winter and survival. The path to thankfulness led to the same place, regardless of the religious road taken in belief of getting there. Excited crowds formed as the noon hour approached. Natives and colonists mingled, talked, laughed, and anticipated the exciting event. Reverend Richard Burke prepared his sermon and his Bible. Meanwhile, Pocahontas accepted blessings from a Powhatan medicine man in a tent erected for her.

Pocahontas, also called the Lady Rebecca, had a place in two distinct worlds, one as a Powhatan princess and, in the other, a lady in the burgeoning English ruling class in Jamestown. Rolfe, one of the wealthiest men in the colony, stayed at Croplands the previous night to save the journey from Varina Farms. He nervously allowed Cecelia to adjust his collar before they arrived in Jamestown.

Pocahontas arrived from one side, Rolfe from the other, accepting Pocahontas from her father, Powhatan, and proceeding to the Reverend, who smiled, nodding gently. Though Puritans rejected music in services, some Anglican children sang a simple hymn to introduce the couple as they approached the make-shift altar near the center of the settlement under a sprawling, shady, oak tree, where Reverend Burke received them. A pleasant quiet came over the crowd as Burke started the service.

Dale, watching the ceremony, had an idea. To what extent, he considered, could he capitalize on this union of white man and native woman? Could he present the couple to the king, thereby representing Jamestown as the colony of the future where peace reigned among different people? The publicity would increase investments and maybe attract new colonists. Dale's thoughts were interrupted when a cheer rose from all assembled after they were pronounced married. Happiness, hope, and peace had finally come to Jamestown after the bitterness and suffering of the starving times.

The coupe waved to the crowd as they began accepting congratulations. Food and ale and dancing to native music livened the gathering even more as the first interracial North American coupe mingled with their guests.

*****

John Smith sailed to England on one vessel in May, 1614, leaving Captain Thomas Hunt as superior over the second ship. Smith decided to return with a load of eleven thousand excellent furs, cod fish, and samples of natural resources from the New England region. Hunt's assignment was to continue fishing and sail to Malaga, Spain, where a thriving market for salted fish would result in great profit.

Two weeks after Smith departed, Hunt decided to sail to the coast where the Pawtuxet tribes dwelled. Once there, Hunt told his men they would increase their money by taking some Pawtuxet natives with them, selling them as slaves in Spain. Luring about twenty Pawtuxet onboard with the promise of trading, Hunt signaled that the ship sail as soon as the native men were on aboard. The natives were stored below decks for the trip to Spain. One of the men was Tisquantum, or Squanto, of the Pawtuxet.

*****

In Leiden, Holland, multiple couples of the former Scrooby group of Separatists began having children, and this natural progression initiated unforeseen social issues, particularly for many of the mothers of their new children. Initially, each mother was aware of her perplexing feelings and attitudes she harbored daily. Together, however, mothers in gatherings began to speak openly about their private concerns of living in Holland while attempting to raise their children as English children.

Two mothers, Elaine Marshall and Mary Fauseth, along with Ann Plover, currently with child, discussed their discontent with life in Holland, agreeing one afternoon to take the discussion home. Elaine Marshall, mother to young Israel, raised the issue with her husband, Andrew, upon his return home from his trade as a fustian, a maker of cotton and linen fabrics. Other mothers vowed to do the same. Work had come easily to the men upon arriving in Holland, and the work was plentiful, fulfilling, and helped provide for newly growing families. Though the newcomers settled into the landscape of people in Leiden, growing concerns circled around the manner of raising English sons and daughters in foreign customs and traditions.

Elaine waited at the door for Andrew's return, two-year-old Israel perched happily on her left hip. She had already prepared tea consisting of a large wooden platter containing cold meats, several flavorful cheeses, freshly baked bread, sliced apples and pears, and a hefty tankard of ale since Andrew thoroughly enjoyed Dutch ale. When they sat, they spoke of Andrew's day and the fabric business, and Elaine raised her concerns.

"Andrew, I've come to realize something very important."

"Aye, have you?" he responded, breaking bread from the hot bread, vapor scaping when he split it open.

"Yes, I have, and quite a few wives have been discussing the same issue together." Andrew rolled his eyes.

"Aye, this sounds like big trouble," he said, laughing slightly, but sensing the issue wouldn't be funny at all.

"Now, now, Andrew Marshall, don't be disagreeable. This is important," Elaine said, picking Israel up from the floor, placing him on her knee, offering him bread with delicious Dutch butter.

"Alright, then, Elaine, out with it," her husband implored, eating a pear slice.

"It's very basic, really, Andrew, and it focuses on all our children." Father eyed son. "You see, Holland is beautiful, and the people are so gracious and friendly, but we prefer that our

354

children be raised with English customs and habits before they grow too old to know them at all." Andrew stopped chewing briefly, as his wife's unanticipated statement caught him off-balance. He drank some ale, sensing trouble ahead.

"So, are you saying you seek to return to England and religious persecution by King James?" he asked as Israel ate some apple, smiling at his father.

"Of course not, husband."

"What of here, Holland? There are other English families here in our congregation. There are the Bradfords, the Fauseths, the Plovers, and many others." Andrew worked with William Bradford, also a fustian.

"You are correct, husband, but the foreign influences among us are very strong now. The congregation has grown to more than two hundred, and the social customs and influences are so different from our proper English customs. We wish that our children be brought-up in the manner of English ways, else they never know them." Andrew sat chewing on his food, looking at their son, whom he thought wouldn't miss customs he never knew.

"Is that such a bad thing, really, Elaine? What would our son miss if he never knew them?" Elaine's face grew tense.

"That's just it, really. If he never knows English ways, how will he properly grow?" Andrew laughed.

"So, living as Dutch will stunt his growth?" Elaine didn't laugh.

"You know what I mean, husband," Elaine responded with some agitation. "I want our son raised with an English background. Is that so wrong?" Andrew worked to subdue his own increasing frustration.

"And I want to be a wealthy man in God's world." Elaine studied her husband.

"Perhaps, Andrew, you expect too much."

"And, perhaps, Elaine, you demand too much."

"The other mothers feel the same. We all do." Andrew shook his head.

"They are not my wives; you are. I am not concerned with their feelings. Let their husbands be saddled with them. I have my own issues to deal with." Elaine took offense.

"Ah, so I am a burden?"

"Nay, you miss my point all together, wife. I only – "Elaine stood, indignant.

"So be it, but Israel will be raised as an English boy," she declared with firm finality. Andrew was completely frustrated, having no control over society's graces, manners, or customs. They lived in a country that welcomed them openly and fully, offered total religious freedom, social liberation from religious persecution, and provided good jobs for reasonable pay.

"Well, it seems Israel is being taught the English way right now with a lesson in being recalcitrant."

"Well!" Elaine exclaimed, taking their son, retreating to the other room, closing the door.

Andrew sighed deeply. What would ever please these women? Coming home had always been a pleasure after a day of work. Homesickness, he thought, pushing away the remainder of his tea. He decided to talk with Reverend Robinson, calculating this was only the start of a rift brought-on by a group of chatty women.

*****

The Virginia Company at London directors agreed by vote, electing Sir Thomas Smythe as Governor of Somers Island, also called Bermuda, named after the late George Somers, former Company Admiral who died on the island four years earlier. Bermuda was claimed by England as a second new colony in the New World, the claim extending back to 1609 when Sea Venture shipwrecked there for ten months.

In accepting his newest position, Smythe assured investors he planned to govern Somers Island in close conjunction with Jamestown, due to their close geographical locations, as well as their promising commercial viability for trade between two English colonies. Smythe also called for increased investments in the Company as new colonies began to emerge in North America, the West Indies, and India. The receptive Puritan business crowd applauded its support for Smythe and his visionary ideas.

*****

Captain John Smith set sail for the maine coast in mid-August after finally obtaining funds for a replacement vessel after his previous ship was destroyed in a storm a year earlier. But now, he knew, Squanto and the others could be anywhere, unlocatable, perhaps dead.

On this 1615 voyage, Smith was not beset by a storm, but pirates. French pirates took control of his vessel and crew off the coast of the Azores, located off the coast of Portugal. Smith and his men were taken as prisoners of the French pirates.

*****

Susanna Hutchinson was born to William and Ann Hutchinson on 14 September 1614 at their home in Alford. The second child to the couple was healthy, and he happy parents praised God for her safe delivery.

*****

Thomas Pepsironemeh Rolfe was born healthy and hungry on 30 January 1615 to Pocahontas and John Rolfe at their Varina Farms estate. Pacing in a large sitting room on the first floor, Rolfe and a Powhatan brave, who would take the news back to the village, waited for word from the midwife's assistant, who suddenly called from the top of the stairs. Rolfe bounded up the stairs, followed by the brave.

"It is a male child, Mr. Rolfe," she announced. "All is ready, and all are well." Pleased, the men entered the room. Inside, Pocahontas lay back with the infant boy next to her. Congratulating Rolfe, the midwife continued cleaning after the successful delivery. The two men stood watching the baby sleep. His skin was tan, like an English child's after being in the sun in the Virginia summer.

"Seven pounds, six ounces, and quite healthy, Mr. Rolfe," the midwife told him, while Pocahontas relayed the information to the brave, whom she knew well. The most significant aspect of Thomas was his full head of black hair.

"Don't worry, Mr. Rolfe, that will fade. It's the most I've seen in a time, though, I'll say," the midwife said, chuckling. The brave, seeing what he needed, congratulated the couple, and made his way to inform Powhatan and the village of the good news.

Thomas was named for Governor Thomas Dale. Rolfe, after spending time with his wife and their son, wanted to tell Dale and Richard and Cecelia. Rolfe knew Richard was preparing the newest largest harvest for shipment to London. Rolfe and Plascomb had become the wealthiest men in the colony, and their business was the most important event in the colony's short, sometimes scandalous history. Rolfe decided to hire the same tutor for Thomas as was hired by Richard and Cecelia for Christian. Riding to Dale's home across the river in Henricus, Rolfe laughed, thinking about how Thomas would grow like Christian, now almost fourteen! Time was moving too quickly he thought. On the way, Rolfe saw Reverend Burke, sharing his good news. Burke offered a quick prayer of thanks and Rolfe continued on his way, where he was welcomed into the Governor's home.

*****

John Winthrop sought to advance his ideas of God's Kingdom on earth through every avenue he thought possible. His entry into law in London rapidly expanded his widening sphere of contacts connected to law, business, and society. After establishing himself with the proper connections, Winthrop was appointed to the County Commission of the Peace. The position allowed Winthrop county-wide decisions involving infrastructure, including road and bridge upkeep, issuing various licenses, and increased personal and professional visibility to other lawmakers, land owners, and other influential men holding positions as judges for minor local issues, including offenses. Winthrop's judicial powers were limited to those on his estate at Groton Manor, and those estate responsibilities were nearly as varied and demanding as those of his legal profession. Management of finances, staff, economy, supplies, provisions, livestock, gardens, and agricultural activities continued year-round. Mary had birthed a son, John, 1604, and a daughter, Mary, in 1612. They returned to Groton Manor the next year. While two children survived, two infant daughters died shortly after birth.

Currently, in the final week of June 1615, Winthrop sat at his desk at Groton Manor calculating animal feed costs while Dr. Willows was upstairs tending to Mary in her sixth birth. Dr. Willows mentioned Mary's increasing problems with each birth, yet his patient continued to, as she replied to him, "perform her wifely duties to her husband's will." A servant called for Winthrop to see the doctor, who'd already been at the manor house several hours. Upstairs, Dr. Willows informed Winthrop that Mary had not survived the delivery. Worse, the daughter, named Ann, died three days later. Both were buried together at Groton Manor.

At the graveside, the Minister performed his duties, offering Winthrop his condolences, adding, "they are in God's hands now, John." Winthrop nodded.

"Mary never did share my enthusiasm for God's place in our lives. "She was truly religious and industrious therein."" Winthrop turned from the grave, as there was work to be done at the manor.

*****

William Barlow, First Bishop of Lincoln, had criticized those who chose John Cotton as their vicar, though Cotton had become immensely popular with his parishioners. Barlow's disdain grew in relation to Cotton's slow continued movement away from required Anglican practices to an increasingly non-conformist position. St. Botolph's Church, Boston, was located in the eastern-central section of England, in Lincolnshire, on the Witham River, and close to The Wash, from where the Scrooby group secretly sailed to Holland. Barlow decided to pay a visit to Cotton at the parish church.

Initially, A Sunday sermon and a Thursday afternoon lecture were the extent of Cotton's sermons. But, within less than three years at his position, the demand to hear him sermonize and speak grew to include a sermon on Sunday, Wednesday, and Thursday afternoons. Cotton's annual salary quickly increased to £100, a significant income for a vicar, particularly a new one. Cotton, unaware of the visit, was also not privy to its purpose as he admitted the Bishop to his vicarage and his study, where tea was served.

Barlow, a burly, ruddy-faced, middle-aged man was not one to, as he called it, "waste God's valuable time." He accepted tea.

"Vicar Cotton," he began directly, "what is your manner of teaching to the faithful here at St. Botolph's?" Cotton sipped his tea, glancing briefly through the window to the garden.

"Your Grace, I must say that my position is that I truly believe a holy commonwealth can be established on earth. The Bible cannot save by merely being read. Everything begins with conversion, the pricking of the hardened heart to the calamity and blessed word of God." Barlow nodded.

"Esteemed thoughts, granted, Vicar, but your practices are edging from the Anglican mainstream. This I cannot, shall not allow." Barlow sipped, observed the garden. "You must reign-in the bridle of desire to preach," he said with finality, placing his cup and saucer on the table, standing.

"I shall continue this discussion upon my return from London in a fortnight. I bid you a good afternoon, *Vicar* Cotton."

Outside, the Bishop climbed into his garnet-colored carriage, and Cotton contemplated his words. It was these very trips to London the Bishop was forced to take that allowed Cotton the freedom he needed to preach in the manner he desired. Casting a perfunctory wave as the carriage departed, Cotton retreated to his study to prepare his Sunday sermon.

*****

Governor Dale and Samuel Argall joined at the Dale's office.

"The Council of Jamestown desires you broaden your scope of destroying French settlements below the Forty-sixth parallel. Your next mission is in the Acadia region north of the maine coast." Dale informed Argall of his newest assignment to rid any French settlements he discovered. Argall sat back, relishing the opportunity.

"Summer holds excellent opportunity for ridding us of French settlements. Good weather allows safe sailing," Argall said, stroking his greying beard with his left hand. Dale continued.

"The Port Royal area has been reported to be falling increasingly under French influences. Company fishing rights, as well as territorial rights, are being belligerently usurped. It is obvious that the French do not think we are maintaining what is legitimately ours." Argall snorted.

"They have not experienced my attendance at one of their settlements," Argall said scornfully. Dale nodded.

"Of that I am sure," he replied, assuring his military enforcer. "Gather your men. I shall provide munitions and plenty of provisions. Company directors have assured me they are sending enough of the same to maintain our ability to safeguard our interests on all matters." Argall stood.

"Thank you, Governor. I have also forwarded my report to London. If we both remain vigilant, we will be able to enforce Company directives." He walked to the door, turning back to Dale. "What of the other business we discussed?" Dale looked up.

"Do you mean the reality of the Rolfe half-breed and taking the family to meet the king?"

"That very subject," Argall replied, waiting for an answer, where Dale met him at the door.

"I'm working on it. I've offered the idea to Sir Smythe and Sir Sandys, requesting overtures be made to the Crown, but I'm waiting for a confirmed invitation before saying anything to Rolfe."

"Good idea. Take the baby, too?"

"Absolutely!" Dale exclaimed forthrightly. "And, we can toss-in several additional natives, living heathens, building-up a suspense, frighten everyone, even if just a bit."

"It may help increase migration here," Argall noted, opening the door. "I can't understand why migration has fallen-off so much recently and so severely, Governor. It's not good for long-term success." Dale agreed.

"I know. We haven't had any new settlers since De La Warr arrived with the group from Somers Island five years ago." Dale shrugged. "I suspect it will work-out somehow. Taking the Rolfe's to meet the king would truly spur interest in Jamestown."

"Agreed, Governor. Well, at the very least, our French problem is virtually nil."

"Yes, go sack Port Royal," Dale intoned. "Bring back their goods, destroy the buildings. Burn it to the ground."

"You have the right man for the job." Dale agreed.

"Of that I am positive. It is God's will," Dale asserted firmly. "God almighty so has disposed of the condition of mankind, as in all times, that some will be wealthy, others poor, while still others will be high, eminent, and others shall be mean and in subjugation." Argall prepared to depart.

"Our Puritan God has indeed spoken," he said, taking leave, while Dale returned to his desk.

*****

Captain John Smith set sail for the maine coast in mid-July after learning of Captain Hunt's taking native hostages to be sold as slaves in the Straits. Smith wanted to assure his native friends the men would be found if possible and returned. Smith, along with Sir Ferdinand Georges, were also worried that Hunt's blatant foolish actions, all made for personal gain, might start a new round of wars between settlers and natives. Word had also made it London stating that Hunt had problems selling his human cargo, and that Jesuit priests took the natives after they heard they were to be sold into slavery. Smith was also grieved to learn that Squanto was among the men taken as hostages.

Smith was only four days out of Gravesend when a violent storm arose, destroying Smith's vessel. He and his crew were forced to return to London on the second vessel, barely escaping death in the storm.

*****

Death traveled freely on the summer wind from the maine coast southward to Jamestown. This time; however, colonists were immune to the decimating winds. Natives, though, were not, and they began dying at an alarming rate.

When the first settlers arrived in Jamestown in 1607, there were over one-hundred-thousand natives of multiple tribes along the entire eastern coastline and interior woodlands, ranging from Port Royal and south to Virginia. The summer of 1615 carried bacteria and viruses no native had experienced. Sagacious medicine men, well-schooled and practiced in their healing and seeing, became, at first, dismayed by the failure of proven methods of the old ways to heal. Dismay turned to frustration, and frustration to alarm as native women, men, and children began dying in numbers never experienced in all their time of being.

Unaware of the causes, they could only mourn and bury. They had no immunity to European illnesses. Smallpox, yellow fever, and assorted viruses inflicted and infected, killing thousands every day across the span of summer.

*****

The Leiden group in Holland welcomed the newest addition to the Separatist family. Edward Plover was born to Ian and Anne Plover on 15 October 1615. Mother rested while her baby fed hungrily. This, her midwife, Mrs. Krebs, assured her patient, was a good sign of health and vitality.

"He takes after his father," Ann joked wearily, enjoying the bit of laughter her joke provoked between the two women. Edward's father also laughed, but his laugh sounded happy and prideful.

*****

In late October, John Cotton had identified the most 'select' members of his congregation as a segment of the larger Puritan congregations. By doing this, he held 'special' services where Puritanism, in all its manifestations, including hellfire sermons and teachings excoriating men for sin, could be privately practiced. Other church members, excluded from the special services, as well as not being chosen as 'elect' members, became indignant after word of the special services spread. Indignance was followed by envy, then anger, and grievances were logged with the Bishop's Court, in Lincoln, the county seat.

Vicar John Cotton quickly found himself suspended.

Just as quickly as his suspension was announced, one of Cotton's aldermen, Thomas Leverett, proposed a negotiation to win Cotton back to his pulpit. Over the course of a month, Cotton quickly endeared himself to the overarching political gamesmanship he first rejected soon after his initial arrival at St. Boltoph's. By late November, Cotton's official reinstatement was secured. Cotton realized he was not only a vicar, bur he also had to be a politician, a combination he detested. He had to find his way.

*****

John Winthrop, now twenty-eight, required someone to care for his children. He married his second wife, Thomasine Clopton, thirty-three, and daughter of a known Puritan family. The wedding took place at Groton Manor, Suffolk, on 6 December 1615.

Thomasine immediately proved to be more religiously pious than Winthrop's first wife, Mary. Since Puritans did not celebrate Christmas, the wedding was a holy ceremony celebrated with Puritan prayer.

*****

Two days later, on 8 December 1615 at Alford, Anne and William Hutchinson welcomed their third child to the world. Richard Hutchinson was born strong and healthy. Soon after the midwife departed Ann and William began talking about their next child.

*****

In Jamestown, Puritan Minister Alexander Whitaker wrote to his like-minded Puritan cousin in London as the year 1615 drew to a close. His last sentence before signing-off read,

"But I much more muse, that so few of our English ministers, that were so hot against the surplice and subscription, come hither where neither is spoken of."

Signing-off as 'the Apostle of Virginia', Whitaker told his cousin that the Puritan cause, where every man will be up working before the sun, and doing it all the day, will find a firm foundation for growth in the New World, particularly in Virginia.

*****

John Smith made his escape from the French pirates in late December, and began bargaining his way back to England aboard merchant vessels willing to accept his assistance for passage.

Part One, Chapter Twenty-Six

January 1616 – April 1616

Human history is the recording of events that take us to the future despite our worst intentions. The harsh Puritan regime of Governor Dale, supported by the militaristic Argall, weighed heavily on the inhabitants of Jamestown. Offenders against 'Dale's Code', as the laws became known, had their heads and feet were bound regularly, sometimes for a month. Public whippings became a spectacle, and no one of any gender or age was spared. No less than eight men and boys, the youngest thirteen years, were sentenced for minor infractions to one year working in a galley aboard a convict ship that aimlessly roamed the seas. "There," Dale asserted, "they shall feel the wrath of God's justice." Fathers of punished youths were also punished themselves for failing, as Dale claimed, to secure proper government of the family and home.

Dale's Puritan stance held that the fundamental problem with children originated with poor family governing. To Dale, it was, "obvious the husband had no control over the wife, who was absent of any and all maternal control of the offspring of her loins." Thus, Dale considered that the father should also be subjugated to the irregularities of his children if they violated the Code for failing to properly govern his marriage and household. Children seven years and older were held to the rules equally as adults because Puritan belief held that they could properly reason.

Jamestown's Puritans understood this approach to family control and social behavior, so they readily accepted it. Anglican families, unused to such brutal methods of governing and pubic shaming in the name of law, quietly remained disgusted by such harsh rules.

"It's really the application of martial law, Richard," Rolfe told Plascomb as they cured the last of the largest crop yet. Standing in a curing barn, Richard agreed, reading a copy of Dale's Code handed him by Rolfe. It read:

Lawes Divine, Morall and Martiall, etc

Every man and woman shall attend church services twice a day on each work day upon hearing the tolling of the bell. Non attendance will result in losing his or her day's rations for the first offense, being whipped for the second offense and being condemned to the gallies [probably refers to some type of coastal sea service] for six months for the third offense.

Every man and woman shall attend church service on Sunday morning and afternoon. Non attendance will result in loss of provisions and allowance for a whole week on the first offense. For the second offense, he or she shall lose their allowance and be whipped. For the third offense, he or she shall suffer death.

Anyone who takes an oath untruthfully or gives false testimony about another person shall be punished with death.

No one shall criticize, tell lies about, disobey or resist the orders of the Lord Governor and Captain General, Lieutenant General, Marshall, Council or any authorized Captain or public officer. For doing so the first time, one will be whipped three times and must, upon his knees, ask forgiveness on Sunday before the church congregation. For a second offense, one will be condemned to the gally for three years. For a third offense, one will be punished with death.

No man shall say or do anything to disgrace another person in the colony. For doing so, one will have his head and feet tied together every night for one month and be publicly disgraced himself. He will forever after be unable to possess any place or hold any office.

No man, unless appointed by a lawful authority, shall barter or trade with the Indians, upon pain of death.

No man shall take away anything by force from any Indian coming to trade or in any other situation, on pain of death.

No man shall take, lose, or willfully break a spade, shovel, hatchet, axe, or other tool, upon pain of whipping.

Every tradesman shall work at his trade dutifully each day or lose meals for one month for the first offense, three months for the second offense, and one year for the third offense. If he continues to be negligent in his work, he will be condemned to the gally for 3 years.

No man or woman shall run away from the colony to the Indians, upon pain of death.

Anyone who robs a garden, public or private, or a vineyard, or who steals ears of corn shall be punished with death.

No member of the colony will sell or give any commodity of this country to a captain, mariner, master or sailor to transport out of the colony, for his own private uses, upon pain of death.

"It's ghastly, John. I've not seen the Code before this day. I've only heard about it," Plascomb replied, handing Rolfe's copy back to him. "We Anglicans disagree with the treatment of people in such brutal ways."

"Aye, Richard, but the Puritan way of thinking is being instilled here, and I hold it shall carry forth a long time in the future if this colony succeeds." Folding the paper into his pocket, Rolfe added, "And, you know, Richard, we escape all of it solely because we have a strong impact on the economy." Plascomb gave his friend a surprised look.

"Have you considered that, Richard? We've never done all the church attending like others." Richard laughed.

"That's because we're always working, John!" Rolfe laughed too as they returned to their curing activities.

Between the pair of growers, they produced over three thousand acres of tobacco at their two farms. Croplands had increased in size to over eight thousand acres of fertile land, and Plascomb was continually rotating plots of land with a schedule that also allowed for growing beans, squash, pumpkins, and corn from seeds originally given by the Powhatan. Plascomb also allowed for fallow fields for soil nutrient replenishment. Now entering their fourth year of tobacco growing, Rolfe and Plascomb achieved financial success neither expected.

In the last week of a cold January, 1616 the pair released the latest cart load to be sent to the docks for shipment to the London Market. In the warmth of the curing barns, small controlled fires burned in pits dug around the barn floor. Smoke rose to the ceiling, floating lazily around the hanging tobacco leaves suspended form poles, or bars, running lengthwise from the barn's front-to-rear. Upwards of seventy bars hung in each barn, curing in the smoky environment from fifty-to-sixty days. When they entered the next barn, Rolfe scanned the full set of bars and sighed.

"With the shipping season almost at a close, Richard, we'll not be able to ship all this tobacco," he announced, surprising Richard, who scratched his head, surveying the full barn. "This is barn forty-nine," Rolfe continued. "We yet have eleven more after this one." Richard agreed.

"What can we do?" Rolfe suggested building a super-sized curing barn.

"You mean like a warehouse?" Richard asked. Rolfe nodded. Richard's face registered an idea.

"I know! We can build a warehouse-sized curing barn, cure product longer time, and call it 'aged' or more mature." Rolfe caught-on instantly.

"Right! And for a premium price!" he added energetically.

"Exactly!" Richard countered.

"But where?" Rolfe asked, thinking. "Say, why not the docks?" Richard thought it a brilliant idea.

We can cure longer, ship faster, and directly from the warehouse to the ships!"

In agreement, the men started collecting product from barn forty-nine, ideas being traded quickly between them, including a visit to the wharf to select a site for the new curing warehouse.

*****

Rolfe and Plascomb met with Governor Dale to sign a deed for land they purchased along the wharf on the James River to erect a curing warehouse. The site included enough land to build a thirty-thousand-square-foot structure, thirty feet high.

Wooden floorboards would be pegged to permit fire smoke to rise to the uppermost floors to cure the newly-named 'special mellow' tobacco, the newest idea the pair devised to describe their slow-cured, aged tobacco.

Dale, fully supporting the idea, understood the enterprise was giving the colony an even more stabilized economy. It gave men and boys a livelihood. It offered the Puritan structure of hard work all day. With documents signed and a significant down-payment made in product because there was no currency in Jamestown, the men were free to start planning the building. Dale also took the opportunity to speak privately to Rolfe. Excusing themselves, Richard said he'd walk around the property. Dale and Rolfe walked along the cold wind-swept wharf.

Though small by London standards, the Jamestown wharf had grown significantly in the six years since De La Warr's surprising arrival in 1610, forcing everyone back to the colony after it was officially abandoned. Looking out across the river, Dale removed an envelope from his pocket.

"I have an invitation for you, Mr. Rolfe," he said, handing Rolfe the large, white, sealed envelope. Rolfe was stunned when he saw the red wax seal bearing the insignia of the lion and saber.

"This is the royal seal," Rolfe said, somewhat disbelievingly.

"Open it," Dale directed. "I've already read mine."

"Yours?" Dale nodded, telling Rolfe he'd understand when he read it. Rolfe gingerly broke the seal with care and respect, eyeing it with a thrill he couldn't describe.

28 December 1615

Hampton Hall, London

Dear Mr. and Mrs. Rolfe,
   His Royal Majesty, King James VI of Scotland and I of England and Ireland, and Queen Anne, do hereby request the pleasure of your company as a family for a grand tour of England as special gusts of the King and Queen at Court at Hampton Hall, Oatlands, and additional royal residences to be visited. The Royal Couple and the people of England open our hearts to you. Therein we do hope you shall afford yourselves the pleasure of accepting this royal, gentle, and generous invitation to visit with us in England. Governor Dale shall detail the particulars for you.
Sincerely,
King James I and Queen Anne
London, England at Hampton Hall

   Rolfe looked incredulously at Dale, who nodded.

"John, this is an opportunity of a lifetime for you and Lady Rebecca. Your marriage has sparked a real interest in the New World as nothing else has yet, or could have, for that matter since its discovery. I do hope you accept." Rolfe said he was at a loss for words." For once, Rolfe actually heard Dale laugh with human genuineness.

"A 'yes' will be all that is needed, John" he coaxed. "It is not every day a man is invited to meet with the king."

"Of course I shall accept, Governor! I only seek to speak with Pocahontas about it. I know she will readily accept such a gracious invitation."

"Very well, John. You and the Lady Rebecca shall be introduced at Court. Let us work and plan, and I shall relay the most basic set of plans. I will say there is a plan to sail in August this year."

The men returned from their discussion, Dale telling Rolfe he would maintain communication with him as plans became known. Seeing Richard, Rolfe waved him over, relaying his thrilling news to his surprised supportive friend.

*****

George Calvert braved late February winds to meet with the king in a surprised announcement made by George Villiers, the king's closest advisor, replacing Robert Carr, who was ousted after he and the king had a falling-out the previous year. Calvert had no idea what the disagreement was about, but decided to remain aloof of the entire affair since he had his own secrets he kept hidden from public knowledge. He figured everyone did for one reason or another.

The murder of Thomas Overby occurred in the same year of the king's and Carr's fall-out, and the recent guilty plea by Carr's wife, Frances in that murder spelled doom for anyone associated with the case. Calvert wondered if Carr himself would be implicated in Overby's murder. Calvert also heard that Villiers was rising rapidly through the peerage ranks, being named Gentleman of the Bedchamber in 1615, and now, recently, King's Master of Horse, named as Baron Whaddon, Viscount Villiers, and made a Knight of the Garter.

All those considerations vanished when Calvert was admitted to the king's apartments, where the king and Villiers sat laughing over something it appeared Villiers said. King James smiled at Calvert in a way he'd not done before. Calvert bowed.

"Calvert, this is your beginning," the king said in an almost sing-song manner, inviting Calvert to join them at the table, where Villiers held-out a set of keys to Calvert as he sat.

"These are yours, Calvert," the king said merrily, enjoying the curious look on Calvert's face. "For your superb and unwavering service to the Crown, you are endowed ownership of the Manor of Danby Wicke in Yorkshire." Calvert was dumbstruck. The Manor of Danby Wicke was said to be thousands of acres with an excellent Elizabethan Manor House and superb country grounds.

"Majesty," Calvert said hoarsely accepting the keys from the king's favorite, who winked at Calvert.

"And there is more," the king said, stroking Villiers hair. Tell him, George." Villiers nodded, turning to Calvert.

"You are to be knighted in the coming year, Mr. Calvert." If Calvert was stunned before, he was truly befuddled now. He took a deep breath, realizing how very different his life would be from this point. Here he was, thirty-six, a member of the privy council and Member of Parliament, and soon to be knighted.

*****

There are times when opportunity is surprisingly presented to individuals when they believe they are at their lowest point in life. Walter Raleigh, once Queen Elizabeth's favorite, a very wealthy land owner, Member of Parliament, military leader, poet, and world explorer, was presented with an opportunity.

Raleigh and his family remained living in a spacious set of apartments in the Tower of London continuously since 1603, a total of sixteen years. Walter, his second son, was now twenty-three years, while Carew, born in the Tower, and living there since birth, was almost twelve.

Raleigh's 'History of the World' was published in 1614 to great fanfare and a wide audience. initially written at the request of the late Prince Henry, it proved to be another success for Raleigh. In March, 1616 the doors to the Tower apartments were flung open and the Raleigh family was freed to establish a London residence following an audience with the king.

The opportunity, in addition to his family's freedom, came in the form of Raleigh's leading an expedition to the Orinoco River in South America to find El Dorado. The news was delivered by Villiers, who stated the purpose was to explore for colonization and return with Spanish gold rumored to be stored in Spanish colonies in the area. Villiers talked with Raleigh while the family hastily packed.

"Count Gondomar, the Spanish Ambassador, has, of course, protested our presence in the area, but our mere presence does not bode ill will or negative actions since the oceans and rivers are available to all." Raleigh agreed, calculating his position in this political chess match. Raleigh's tenuous position was made more dubious when Villiers continued his explanation.

"Because of the ambassador's stern protests, *no* acts of villainy, including taking control of territory or looting Spanish treasure, other than gold, of course, will be undertaken by you or your crew. Any such actions will be met with execution." Villiers was firm when he spoke the words. This gave Raleigh pause for thought. He was sixty-two years, passed the typical age of strenuous ocean travel. But he was determined to maintain his freedom. Death on the seas was better than the Tower! Raleigh willfully accepted the king's offer channeled through his chief advisor and favorite. When he signed the document agreeing to

378

terms, Villiers told him he'd set the audience with the king. Raleigh started packing.

Two hours later, Raleigh sat with the king and Villiers in the royal meeting room.

"Majesty, it is most difficult for a man who has always had something expected of him to awaken one morning and realize nothing is expected of him." King James nodded.

"Well, Mr. Raleigh, today is a new day. I cannot recall why you were sent to the Tower, but, as of this day, a great deal is expected of you once again."

"Thank you, Your Majesty."

"You are most welcome, Raleigh. Remember, history is made, not guessed at." Villiers handed Raleigh a set of documents and funds for a home in London. He departed as strongly as he had arrived, older, wiser, and finally feeling stronger than before. Opportunity offers more than a chance; it breathes life into a being.

*****

Thirty-seven-year-old Thomas Morton continued his countryside travels as a lawyer representing the down-trodden and penniless, claiming it was his responsibility to represent and legally save those, "whose economic straits filled growing tent cities, furnished prisons and the gallows, and pushed men to the Bristol sea-trades." Morton's adventurous anti-establishment views were instilled in him as a boy.

Born in the County of Devon in southwest England near the River Exe in 1579, Morton's wealthy family was rooted in the deeply gentrified Anglican religion, steadfastly adhering to the Elizabethan rejection of any and all attempts at reformation.

Protestants themselves even referred to Devon as the 'dark corner' of the realm for that reason. Simultaneously, though, Morton's father retained a local folk tradition so strongly connected to the mystical magic of the winter solstice that it was said, at least by Puritans, to border on paganism.

Together, the meeting of the two polar ends of the religious spectrum met within young Thomas Morton, who held to the ethereal magic of the unknowable universe, planets, and stars, mingling and blending those eerie qualities with the special emotional spectacle of the Church of England. The combination of the two worlds was often referred to as 'Olde England', harkening back to the mysteries of Stonehenge and the Druids. It was in the midst of these worlds where Thomas Morton found his own path in life, shaping him as an independent and irreverent free-thinker who chose, as he said it, "to give and not take."

By the late 1590's, Morton was, ironically, studying law, perhaps the most focused-based trade possible for a libertine free-thinker. A creative mind is not limited by a finite profession. Through his industrious studies at London's Clifford Inn, Morton cemented many influential contacts and made similar friendships, some lasting his entire life. As he grew and matured, Thomas remained an ardent Royalist, yet his studies and his reputation as a ribald bawdy jokester slowly pushed his support for the growing common law against the strengthening, direct, legal power of the Crown and the Star Chamber, an English court of civil and criminal jurisdiction that developed in the late 15th century, trying especially those cases affecting the direct interests of the Crown, and noted for its arbitrary oppressive judgments.

During his county travels, Morton met Sir Ferdinand Georges, now the Governor of the City of Plymouth, on the coast in southwest England. Georges quickly realized Morton was especially intelligent, highly versed in law, and quickly came to respect his astute mind, unaffected by his easy affable personality. Georges also understood Morton could bring a light-hearted approach to potentially difficult legal situations, and that was the reason Georges hired him in a legal capacity. Morton's assignments kept him moving between Plymouth and London. Presently returning to Plymouth from London, Morton, who enjoyed the travel because it kept boredom at bay, would not forget the poor and forgotten of English society.

*****

Captain Thomas Hunt refused to surrender Squanto to the priests who took-in the others unsold as slaves in the Straits. Instead, Squanto lived as a slave at Hunt's estate home in High Wycombe, west of London for nearly eighteen months. Now about thirty-one, Squanto learned geography, English, and numbers. He was reunited with John Smith on the previous Christmas at the estate. Offering Squanto his address, Smith told him, "if I can ever help you or steal you from Hunt, come call upon me." He also informed his friend that he had twice attempted to return to the maine coast, explaining the failures, including his own capture by French pirates, from whom he escaped.

Squanto wrote notes in the evenings to recall what happened from day-to-day. He also wrote names, dates, directions, and locations he visited to help having not to memorize everything. In April, Hunt announced an ocean voyage to Spain was being planned, and Squanto was to prepare for the voyage. They would be departing in a fortnight. He missed his people, his home, and he wanted to return. Squanto started to plan his escape.

*****

In London, the directors of the Virginia Company opened their spring meeting in early April with the news that John Rolfe and Lady Rebecca had accepted the royal invitation to visit England. Directors were asked to plan events at their estates for the visiting couple, informed by Sir Edwin Sandys that the lead time was five months.

In addition to the news of the exciting visit, Sandys asked his fellow directors, mostly Puritans, to consider ways they could make Jamestown a more appealing destination for new colonists.

"Equity on member investments remains only marginal," Sandys told the gathering, adding that, "new settlers are needed to bolster investment and expand the population in the slowly growing colony, and that tobacco is having a firm, positive, and stabilizing force."

Sir Thomas Smythe added that, "new growth is required to strategically increase trade and demand for English goods abroad, and we need people to buy those goods. We have no idea why new settlers were not emigrating to the colony."

With agreement on these pressing issues, one sociopolitical, the other of economic imperative, Sandys concluded his opening statements, and opened the meeting to new business.

*****

The Dutch continued their unabashed explorations of the northeast North American coast through the Dutch East India Company for several years after Adrien Block explored for Holland. He and Captain Cornelius Henderson, recently returned to Amsterdam from a new expedition of the area called Manna-hatta, originally joined together in 1613 for an exploration of the northeast coastline.

Unknown to Hendrickson, who sailed up an unnamed river in the Chesapeake Bay area, would have landed at Jamestown if he sailed further south along the coast, entering the James River. His findings and reports determined that the area around Manna-hatta would be excellent for new Dutch settlements. He produced a highly detailed map of the area, including the coastline, declaring it could become a New Amsterdam to Company directors. The Dutch had already opened a trading post and warehouse in Nassau in 1615, and Block remained there acting as director. As a result, Company directors began planning the newest expedition for Dutch colonization around Manna-hatta.

*****

Activities at Croplands and Varina Farms increased as the new growing season began. Ove one hundred men and older boys worked the fields and curing barns, or in new construction of the wharf warehouse. With no currency or banks, workers were paid with tobacco or produce. Tobacco suddenly became a local currency, with people trading it for goods and services. This led Richard to tell Rolfe that they should ask for a higher price because their product was an economic power.

Rolfe agreed, and together they wrote a letter to their London Market representative detailing their ideas, requesting also if there was a way to consolidate their efforts into a single business entity to ease record-keeping, accounts management, and communication. They also described their plans for an 'aged, mellowed, special' tobacco, developed with an extended curing period, asking if there would be a market for it. The letter was sent in mid-April, and the pair returned their attention to the business of growing tobacco and constructing their new warehouse, which was nearly complete, and would be ready by harvest for the first new special tobacco. Christian, now fifteen, was regularly included in all business dealings and discussions.

Governor Dale received a letter from Sir Edwin Sandys in early June. He opened it, sitting at his desk on a splendid late spring afternoon.

19 April 1616
Virginia Company at London
London, England

Dear Governor Dale,
The realization that a Puritan God is on our side in all our endeavors causes me to find faith in the belief that this letter finds you in Holy grace, robust, and healthful. The news that the former heathen native has transformed herself into an acceptable Christian woman, a true lady, her English husband, and their half-breed offspring have accepted the royal invitation has truly stirred the peoples' imaginations here. Though natives have been kidnapped and brought here for theatrical purposes in the past, no one of them has ever had an audience with the Royal Family at Court. Desire to be on the receiving line at Court grows every day. Grand estate gatherings are being planned in multiple counties from Essex to Cornwall in honor of the visit. Your idea to use this visit as a propaganda campaign to increase migration to Jamestown is a stroke of political astuteness and business opportunism at their best. Company directors fully support your initiatives in this masterful marketing campaign aiming to increase investments, population, and return on investor equity.

Lastly, there is word that Rolfe and his business partner, a Richard Plascomb, are being advised to consolidate their two businesses into a single company much like the Company. This inside information comes from their representative at the

Market, Mr. Ramplay. I inform you of this in order that you may consider investing now to reap a potentially large return in the near future. Their tobacco is considered the industry standard to which all others are measured. Interest in their joint venture is quite keen here.

I look forward to discussing additional business with you personally after your arrival in London later this year. Safe travel and God speed.

Sincerely,
Sir Edin Sandys

Dale considered the letter's contents, placing it on his desk. He would have to discuss the new joint venture between Rolfe and Plascomb because a lucrative return on an investment would be a lucrative opportunity because Puritan beliefs held that some men would be rich, others poor. As a chosen one, Dale was to be wealthy. Sitting back, Dale handed the letter to Captain Argall, sitting across from him.

"You shall enjoy reading that letter," Dale told his military representative. "There's money to be made."

*****

Captain Hunt, his entourage, and crew traveled through Spain from their stating point in Bilbao, in the northern tip of the country, to Madrid, in the central region. From Madrid, the party ventured southeastward to Murcia, on the southeast coast, then Malaga, with intentions of ending the trip in Gibraltar.

Squanto, given proper clothing for the journey, served Hunt and the party for the entire trip. He was as exotic as the language, the richly spiced foods, and the beautiful Spanish residents, whose dark skin was much darker than Hunt or his people. Oddly, though, Squanto thought, many Spaniards had skin tones equal to his own. Their hair, shiny, long, and black, was much similar to his own, yet he also saw many blonds in Spain, and this surprised him.

What surprised Squanto more was that he was readily accepted by the local people, who seemed to take an interest in him and his obvious position with the white men. He was dark-skinned, handsome, and not English. Squanto planned, sensing his escape was near.

*****

Opening the anticipated letter from Mr. Ramplay at the London Market, John Rolfe also discovered documents for signing by himself and Plascomb. In his letter, Ramplay wrote about the family's upcoming visit, and his plan to meet Rolfe in London, and asked if the Plascombs were also traveling with the party? Rife slowly walked to the hearth room at Varina Farms, reading as he walked.

Ramplay explained that investment in the joint company was difficult to contain because large amounts of investments were ready to be made when the company started. He directed Rolfe and Plascomb to act diligently and quickly to reap the business investment benefit. Buyers were already seeking the new special tobacco. He ended by telling Rolfe that he and Plascomb were at the right place at the right time. Location is everything, he wrote.

Entering the hearth room, Rolfe found Pocahontas holding Thomas. Kissing her lovingly, he told her he loved her deeply.

"I've been wondering what I am to say to the king of England," she told him as he stroked Thomas' soft hair, which had changed from black to the color of deep honey, growing with a slight curl. Rolfe was amazed at how much his son's appearance had changed in the fourteen months since his birth. His skin was a glowing, coffee-cream tone. His eyes were large and round, and he was quick to smile. He was as happy with his native grandfather as he was with his parents. Rolfe chuckled.

"What to say?" he asked, smiling. "You are a princess, and your father is a king." It was Pocahontas who laughed now.

"My father is a chief, John, a sachem, not a king." John shrugged.

"He's a leader who heads a land of people who obey his word."

"You have a point, John. I'm nervous all the same."

"It shall be grand; worry not, my wife," he said confidently. "I'm off to Croplands with business to discuss. I'll take the boat, and I shall return before sundown."

"My regards to Cecelia if you see her." Agreeing, Rolfe kissed his wife and son and departed.

*****

On 28 April, 1616, Master John Hope, Captain of the Treasurer, and his crew, welcomed Sir Thomas Dale, John Rolfe and his wife, Pocahotas, and their son, Thomas aboard the vessel for the journey to England. Also in the company were Pocahontas's sister, Matachanna, and her husband, Uttmatomakkin, also known as Tomococo, a religious leader of the tribe. There were also another dozen selected Powhatan braves traveling as Dale's guests. To everyone's surprise, Rolfe

387

asked Richard and Cecelia to take Christian on the voyage. Following some initial hesitation, Cecelia decided the trip would be more beneficial than frightening. Christian was going to meet the king of England! Sir Dale agreed to take the young man.

With all aboard, the call to sail went out to the crew. As her sails dropped to catch the wind, they turned to wave to those on the dock who had come to wave goodbye. Cecelia, crying, and Richard, proud for his son, and Christian, now fifteen, taller than his mother, with dark brown hair and a deep voice, waved to each other. All waved to their friends as the Treasurer made-way along the James River, heading to the Atlantic Ocean. Rolfe carried the documents establishing his and Plascomb's joint company to be called Varicrop Farms. He also stored several hundred pounds of additional tobacco aboard to offer to Mr. Ramplay when he met him in London.

Samuel Argall replaced Dale as Governor, fully prepared to rule with authoritarian Puritan control through Dale's Code.

Part One, Chapter Twenty-Seven

May 1616 – August 1617

By the time Squanto reached Malaga, he'd become quite accustomed to the smells, sounds, and customs of the Spanish and English. Enabled by his English language mastery, he realized he only needed the opportunity to escape. The remainder would fall into place when he freed himself. The needed opportunity came when Hunt and his entourage returned one evening after a boisterous afternoon of eating and drinking Sangria at a local taverna. None of the company were hungry, but they decided a siesta would be appropriate before the night's revelry began.

Following his duties to assist some drunken men to their rooms, Squanto waited until everyone, including Hunt, were sleeping soundly. With some money he saved, and some he took from various guests when helping them to their rooms, Squanto walked calmly out the front door, heading to the port, only a few blocks away. Once there, he found a French merchant vessel preparing to sail to Acadia, north of his own home. Speaking broken, yet acceptable French, Squanto was hired by the captain to work in the galley aboard the vessel. Within an hour, Squanto sailed from Spain a free man. He was getting closer to home.

*****

A sizeable crowd had formed at the wharf in Plymouth, England as the four-masted Treasurer docked on the twelfth of June, 1616. A cheering crowd waved and called when Pocahontas appeared on the gangway leading to the dock. Christian was amazed by the Plymouth harbor, his first view of England, from where his family had started many years earlier. Onlookers tossed flowers to the dock as the special couple passed along the wharf, smiling and waving to the waving cheering crowd as the travelers moved to waiting coaches.

"So many people!" Pocahontas commented to Dale, who agreed.

"This is only the start, Lady Rebecca," he told her in reply.

*****

On 8 December 1616 John Winthrop waited for news of his wife, Thomasine, who remained ill following the delivery of the couple's daughter on 30 November. Unfortunately, the infant died two days later, and her mother remained bed-ridden.

Winthrop waited in the downstairs study for news. His three living children, brothers John the Younger, Henry, and Forth, sat waiting on a sofa, each quietly reading their Bibles. A fire warmed the great room while the family waited for the doctor's news. Minutes passed like hours, and four heads turned in unison when a gentle knock sounded on the door. Winthrop opened it to find Dr. Willows wearing a grim expression. Winthrop knew.

"I'm sorry, John, she could not survive it, he said quietly, leading Winthrop upstairs.

Thomasine Clopton-Winthrop was buried with her daughter at Groton Manor the following day.

*****

"I miss Christian, Richard," Cecelia told her husband two nights before Christmas as they sat before the great hearth that opened to several new rooms, one for dining, the other for sitting and reading. Tall, thick, tallow candles increased available light, and the fire warmed them as they sipped sherry. Wealth allowed them luxuries they never anticipated possessing or experiencing.

"I'm sure he's doing well and behaving properly, Cecelia. We've raised him correctly. John and Pocahontas will also look-out for him."

"I can't believe our son will meet the king of England!" Cecelia exclaimed, smiling at Richard.

"Agreed," he said, nodding. "This shall be a journey he shall not forget." The following day, a letter from Rolfe arrived at Croplands. Richard read it aloud.

27 October 1616

Oatlands Palace
Surrey, Southeast England

Dear Cecelia and Richard,
We all bid you the best of health from England. We are currently at Oatlands Palace in southeast England. Our visit has been a continuous series of dinner engagements, society galas, theatre attendances, parties, and greetings since our arrival in June. We are exhausted every evening, and ready for rest. You should know you son, Christian, is a supreme gentleman, and was praised by the Royal Family at one of our

engagements with them two weeks ago. You would have thought him a prince if you did not know him.

The entire Court is absolutely infatuated with Pocahontas and her sister, and Thomas as well. I am merely a prop in this great spectacle. London is smitten with my wife, son, and your son, believing him to be ours. They are also in awe of the Powhatan braves traveling with us. Queen Anne held Thomas and kissed Christian's cheek. He blushed for an hour after that. All the newspapers carry stories of our every move from place to place. We shall return to London tomorrow.

We did take time to visit my family at Heacham to introduce my wife to my mother and her second husband, Dr. Robert Redmayne. You recall, Richard, my father died when I was aged nine. We had a wonderful visit with my mother, Dorothy, and my brothers. We visited for ten days before returning to London. Pocahontas prefers the air at Heacham to London's air, which she says is foul and dirty. She thinks it will make her ill.

We have spent time at Hampton Court, Oatlands, and Nonesuch, all royal residences. We are back at Oatlands for a weekend of riding and hunting, favorite activities of the Royal family. You should be glad you taught Christian to ride, as he and Prince Charles have become quite good mates! The prince is but only three months older than Christian. They are everywhere together, and they absolutely compete in riding.

We are scheduled to ride and picnic along the River Thames on a royal barge as a troupe plays madrigals. We are hoping the good, clear, crisp weather holds-out another week, when we return to London. At the same time, we have been assigned a governess for Thomas to allow Pocahontas ease of travel and socializing. Even Christian has a servant tending to him. The fact he comes from a strong Anglican family has not escaped the king's graces — believe me! This has truly increased Christian's standing at Court, particularly with King James. There is a particularly hostile environment between Anglicans and Puritans here. Puritans seek to 'purify' the Church of England by reforming it by banning all ceremonies, vestments, and ridding themselves of the Book of Common Prayer. Contrarily, Anglicans claim that the reform of the church has had enough effect on the church already, and the king is adamant that no further reforms will occur.

He is determined to root-out Puritans and squelch their practices. We, however, merely listen to what the king says. We never dare offer our opinions as guests. At one point, Christian was about to say something, and I purposely tipped his wine glass to prevent him from saying anything. The incident was treated an innocent accident. Later, I explained how and why we must refrain from offering opinions, especially about religion and politics. He listened acutely, assuring me he understood. I have no idea what he talks about with Prince Charles. But there is increasing sentiment here that the Crown is particularly harsh towards Puritans. That said, I am told many have departed to other countries to escape religious persecution.

We send our best for a Happy Christmas; a holiday Puritans do not celebrate. I suspect you shall receive this letter sometime in December. Our last subject — business.

I met Mr. Ramplay at the London Market. I must say, Richard, our present status has helped him rush our new company formation through all the legal and business hoops. Varicrop Farms is open for business, and big investments are coming quickly. Public chares will soon be available to all investors on 1 November 1616. Be ready to make some real money, Richard! I must go. Christian is reminding me that we are expected at dinner at eight o'clock. It is now half-seven. I must get ready.

All the best for a Happy Christmas and a festive New Year.
Sincerely,
Your friend & Christian's Uncle,
John Rolfe

Cecelia cried for joy, and Richard pulled her into his shoulder before the fire.

"It's alright, Cecelia. Our boy is doing well. A Happy Christmas we shall have."

*****

The New Year 1617 heralded increased troubles among the Leiden group in Holland over rising clamor over loss of English traditions. A fever-pitch of emotions arose when most of the group's children began speaking Dutch at home with their siblings, but not their parents. Some parents of younger children thought it 'cute', but parents of older children feared they were the subjects of teenage discussions, and were actually being balk-talked in a language they did not fully understand as easily as their children. Pressure at many Leiden homes was also increased by what many started calling the area where they lived 'stink alley'.

The men began complaining that they were being blocked from higher-paying work because they were not Dutch. Low-paying work was all they could find. With more children being born to families, money could not stretch as it had when they first arrived. For many, the pursuit of religious freedom was perceived as being gained at a significantly more financial price.

"Heaven may be wonderful," one man said forthrightly, adding, "but, 'tis bread that counts here, and my family cannot eat blessings." With the chorus of multiple problems becoming increasingly sharp to the ears of the responsible leaders, something had to be done.

In a meeting held to determine some movement in one direction or another, Brewster, Robinson, Bradford, John Carver, Miles Standish, and Robert Cushman met at the

Brewster residence in the area now being referred to as 'stink alley', particularly by the wives and mothers of the group.

Word of the New World being slowly developed on the North American Continent reached Holland and the Leiden congregation. Increasingly, the word 'Virginia' was on the praying lips of many in the group. Desire for solid English customs and traditions, the English language only, better work opportunities, and a sense of 'home', as opposed to being foreigners, had firmly settled on many in the group. Robinson shuffled a stack of documents on the table.

"It is apparent this congregation is set upon relocating to the colony of Virginia," he stated firmly, looking around at his peers.

"It is large enough," Bradford, now twenty-seven, replied, adding, "it extends all the way north to the forty-six-latitude. There is also news that the settlement at Jamestown grows successfully." John Carver folded his hands glumly.

"The desire is strong, but the finances are weak." Robinson agreed.

"We are nearly three hundred strong. The costs of moving such a large number of people is beyond all our abilities. Perhaps we require an underwriting to assist us in our endeavor." Robert Cushman nodded his agreement.

"I agree completely. I know of a group in London called the Merchant Adventurers. They're a group of financial backers who may be able to front us the funds needed to move to Virginia." Following additional discussion, the congregation's leaders assigned both Carver and Cushman the task of contacting the London backers, working with them to secure funds to include vessels, provisions, crews, and enough currency to purchase tools for building lodging and set gardens for food.

"We also require weapons," Standish, the military representative asserted. "There are wild killing natives to contend with, I assure you." The men quietly considered, perhaps thinking of the potential hazards they overlooked due to their unfamiliarity with wild uncivilized lands and people. William Brewster broke the contemplative silence.

"Alright, gentlemen, begin the discussions for backing. I contend they shall not require very much time, maybe six months at most. Any financial group would surely strive to support a religious family man to achieve his goals." With their assigned tasks accepted, the meeting ended. On his way home, William Bradford was stopped by John Willing, a group member, whose wife had just returned from Bradford's home, and who informed Bradford that his wife, Dorothy, had just given birth to their first child.

Increasing his pace, Bradford hurried to meet the midwife, Mrs. Krebs, who was remaining until he arrived home on the outskirts of 'stink alley'. The child, a healthy boy, was named John.

*****

Richard Plascomb greatly missed the presence of his business partner, John Rolfe. He missed his son even more. Their absences were made sharper by the knowledge they would be coming home, but no one knew precisely when. Standing in the new warehouse on the top floor, Richard allowed his mind to wander to his two deceased children, Ellen and Edmund, now dead longer than they had lived. He sighed deeply, recalling them. Their abrupt memory caused Richard to stop working momentarily to consider them.

Staring blankly at row upon row of the first hanging crop of specially aged tobacco, all enveloped in a hazy gauze of scented fire smoke wafting-up from the ground floor, Plascomb allowed his memories of his lost children to run unchecked through his mind in the spirit of recollection of a time that felt strangely distant, lost in a haze of emotional fogginess. Richard returned to work, continuing his inspections. The special aged tobacco, harvested the previous October, had been aging in the warehouse almost four months. It was mid-February, and the tobacco would remain here two additional months before collection, wrapping, and shipment to London, where Mr. Ramplay eagerly awaited its arrival.

Upon returning to Croplands, Richard was surprised to learn a letter from Rolfe arrived. Cecelia opened it eagerly, handing it to Richard to read for both of them. Cecelia poured wine.

27 December 1616

Windsor Castle
London

Our Dear Friends Cecelia and Richard,
    Have you forgotten us by now? We think not. I do believe that Christian has grown at least two inches since we arrived in June, eight months ago! Prince Charles is planning a festive birthday gathering for Christian in February 1617 (Here, Cecelia broke into crying, realizing the date was 14 February, Christian's 16th birthday).

    We spent Christmas at Richmond Castle. The countryside is so beautiful in winter. We are all plump as partridges from the unending festivities, including

banquets, balls, fetes in our honor. Guess who dined
with us at Christmas? None other than John Smith! He
was thrilled to meet Christian, and sends his sincere
greetings to both of you. We returned to Windsor Castle
two days after Christmas, where I am sitting in a
superbly decorated royal room at the castle's east end.
Christian keeps busy with the prince by riding and
hunting, which is where they are presently. It seems
very quiet without that energetic pair running about!
We are spending New Year's here, and we will return to
London for a theatrical presentation. I think Pocahontas
is growing weary of all the attention, and we both are
enjoying these few days of solitude at Windsor Castle.
We are dining with the king and queen this evening
after he returns from the hunt with the boys, who
usually play chess before a roaring fire.

I can tell you we are planning a return to Virginia on
the 17th March 1617. Sir Dale has informed me our
journey will depart Gravesend, taking about eight weeks
to cross back to your side of the pond, as is said here.
Dale will remain in England for the foreseeable future. I
take it Argall has complete control over the settlement
at this time. We shall sail aboard the George.

I must sign-off at this time, as my wife is reminding
me of our walk through the winter garden. Lastly, we
are attending a celebratory Mass at Westminster at

*week's end to give thanks for our wonderful visit. We all
are well, and we look forward to returning home.
All the best,
Your friend,
John Rolfe*

Cecelia buried her maternal tears in her apron while Richard placed additional logs on the warming fire.

"We shall need a servant for our son upon his royal return home," Richard joked, sitting next to his wife.

*****

The French Merchant ship, Recolte, meaning harvest, docked at Port Royal, near Acadia. Squanto was invited to remain aboard as gally leader, but he gently declined the offer. Shaking hands with the captain, he disembarked, and began heading south to his people. He was almost home after almost two years.

*****

Walter Raleigh was a man with a title once more, captaining a ship headed for the distant Orinoco River in far-away South America. Presently, Raleigh steered his vessel along Spain's northwestern coast, passing Porto, then Lisbon, and onward on the currents of the African countries of Morocco, Western Sahara, and ultimately, Mauritania. He already knew that when he passed the Canary Islands, he would change course, crossing the Tropic of Cancer. Another eight weeks would find him in the mouth of the Orinoco River. Among the crew on this journey was his son, Walter, now twenty-three years. Standing at the ship's prow, the younger Walter waved to his father at the helm as he adjusted his sextant.

*****

The five, remaining, mutinous crewmen of the ill-fated Discovery under the leadership of Henry Hudson, went to trial for murder in March 1617. As the trial began, the men were charged with murder, a decrease in charges of mutiny as the result of influential business interests claiming their knowledge of the region would help exploration and settlement initiatives. As such, death sentences would afford no one a victory. Prosecutors capitulated after the court agreed.

A major portion of the defense lay in the notebooks kept by Robert Bylot and Henry Greene, deceased, killed by Eskimos. The journal, along with spoken testimony, would provide the major portion of testimony and material fact. The crowded courtroom became immersed in an energetic quiet as the judge took his seat and proceedings began nearly six years after the fact.

*****

On 18 March 1617, the line of carriages carrying the Rolfes, Christian Plascomb, and the company of natives to their return vessel the George, arrived at an inn at Gravesend, where a final celebratory dinner was to be held before the morning departure to Virginia.

Rolfe and Pocahontas entered their room, where Rolfe noticed his wife's agonizing suffering. She said her lungs hurt. Both Rolfes thought her with child, but the loss of pallor in her face frightened Rolfe, who recalled there was a doctor among the almost seventy guests at the inn. He called on Christian to

401

quickly fetch the doctor. When he returned, the doctor was accompanied by Henry Rolfe, John's brother.

"what is wrong, John?" Henry asked with true concern. Rolfe explained as the doctor's wife entered to assist him. Dale entered, a look of sincere worry on his face. Rolfe was explaining, when the servant girl holding Thomas cried out.

"He's burning up as well!" she cried, beginning to cry herself.

"Separate mother and child!" the doctor ordered. "I need water. Put the boy in the parlor." Additional orders were briskly delivered. After forty minutes of chaotic shuttling between two rooms for two patients, Dr. Waters sat with a tall whiskey with John, Henry, Christian, and Matachanna, Pocahontas' sister.

"Mother and son," Waters said speculatively, looking at the assembled in the room. "Everyone here is well, no problems, and..." his voice trailed-off.

"And what, Doctor?" Rolfe asked nervously. Waters shook his head.

"Everyone here is English, except for Matachanna. It appears to me that Pocahontas has been afflicted by something to which she has no immunity. Thomas may have a small immunity to whatever it is because of you, John." Doctor Waters shook his head again, sipping. "It is to be a very long night."

*****

George Calvert, now thirty-nine years and affirm supporter of King James, accepted his new status as Sir George Calvert following a knighthood bestowed by King James. Known as the 'king's mouthpiece' for ardently pursuing the Crown's political and diplomatic policies to an increasingly recalcitrant

Parliament hostile to continued religious persecution and a growing coziness with its long-time enemy, Spain, Calvert towed the political line, ever aloof to questions of religion. His particular desire was to secure silence of his own Catholicism, for its knowledge would cast him out of all wealth and status, including his place as a Member of Parliament.

Simultaneously, this festering pressure within himself began, strangely enough, to manifest a desire to, "have it all out" of himself, like casting out a demon that possessed him. But on this regal day of his knighthood, Calvert permitted himself to bask in the royal gratitude shown by the king. Calvert felt an unquestionable rush of powerful, enveloping emotion seize his entire being as the same royal sword that was used to knight Lord Burghley, Robert Devereaux, Edwin Sandys, Thomas Smythe, Thomas Dale, and Walter Raleigh touched his left shoulder, then his right. Calvert felt renewed, transformed, spiritually and consciously. His shoulders shook in his effort to contain his welling emotion as the king chanted, the choir sang, and the organ music reached its crescendo in his head.

*****

The defense for the Discovery crew established testimony detailing the terrible storm that claimed the lives of Captain Hudson, his son, John, called Jack, and the other seven men lost at sea when they were swept overboard by a wave. Robert Bylot offered details of the terrible night the storm set-upon Discovery and her crew, and the, "hellish confusion" after the men were swept out to sea. All the remaining crewmen gave similar accounts in their testimonies as furtive glances among the five were traded secretly. When the defense declared itself finished, the prosecution took over.

*****

403

John Winthrop widened his sphere of associates through his law work, but moreso on the County Peace Commission. During one of the quarterly Commission meetings, Winthrop caught site of a woman who, he discovered, was Margaret Tyndale, the thirty-year-old daughter of the Tyndale Family of Great Malpstead, one of the greatest land-holding families in the county. Garnering assistance to be introduced to her since someone had to care for the children, Winthrop planned to contact her father at Great Malpstead.

*****

Pocahontas died sometime in the early hours of the twentieth of March, 1617. Her fever would not break, and her breathing became so labored and raspy. Doctor Waters also noted formation of some small pustules as he prepared to give Rolfe the sad news. In a small room, he informed a gathering of Rolfe, Dale, Matachanna and her husband, Tomococo, and Christian Plascomb. The news was devastating for all.

A requiem Mass was officiated the following day, and Lady Rebecca was laid to rest in the chancel of the Church of St. George, in Gravesend. Rolfe had little time to grieve, for he had to care for Thomas, who was recovering, but still sickly, and only just over two years in age. In a solemn discussion with his brother, Henry, and the vicar, John decided to leave Thomas in his brother's care, where he would have medical care and a superior English education. His father would send for him at the proper time. Henry agreed, promising to raise Thomas as his own. In an emotional daze, Rolfe dejectedly boarded the George, which had been held-up for three days, returning wifeless and childless to Virginia. Christian joined him in boarding, also deeply affected by his aunt's sudden death.

In his estate home, Sir Thomas Dale pondered Lady Rebecca's death, trying to understand why God would do what He had done. What had Lady Rebecca done to anger Him? He also considered the seven-month promotion of Jamestown would take a loss over this sad ending to an otherwise sterling story.

The weather, yet cold, but sunny, was at least agreeable as the George entered open water and Gravesend shrank as a memory in the distance.

*****

Prosecutors pressed every Discovery crewman about storms, men washed overboard, losses at sea, entries, arrival dates, geography, dates of storms, desperate to pierce the defense's iron-clad presentation. Following three additional days of contentious cross-examination, the judge ordered the jury to decide. They were to recall that the charges were murder. Affirmed they understood, the jury retreated to deliberate.

*****

Walter Raleigh surveyed the many tributaries of the Orinoco River while hugging the Venezuelan coast near Trinidad and Tobago. Sailing to the largest of the tributaries near the Guyana border, Raleigh figured he could travel almost fifty miles upriver to seek the Spanish gold that surely awaited him. Once there, the crew could rest and plan.

*****

As late spring continued to approaching summer in North America, native illnesses and deaths mounted rapidly after starting the previous summer. No tribal medicines worked on the mysterious illnesses, and appeals to the Great Father in the Sky fell silent. Native federations along the entire North American coast, from the maine coast to Virginia were reeling from deaths. Inter-tribal talks were started in an attempt to understand what was happening to the native population.

*****

Supportive cheers and screams by the welcoming crowd in Jamestown turned quickly to shock and grief as the terrible news quickly spread through the settlement after the George docked in late May 1617. Cecelia was overwhelmed with emotion by the combined return of her son, coupled with the disturbing news of Pocahontas. Grabbing Christian, Cecelia fainted, as other women did upon hearing the news. Many were moved to tears, but not all were so moved.

A group of men on the periphery gathered to jeer the 'half-breed' marriage, remaining mostly silent, satisfied that their Puritan God had found a way to put the matter asunder.

"A white man is born to marry a white woman," one said bitterly. Another spit on the ground.

"I guess that'll put Rolfe in his place," he said with a sneer.

*****

Roughly three months later, in August 1617, Anne and William Hutchinson announced the successful birth of their fourth child, a girl they named Faith, partly to symbolize their strong faith in God. The family from Alford had grown again by one. Edward, the oldest at five years, looked curiously at the newest mouth feeding at his mother's breast.

*****

"Not guilty on all counts," announced the lead jurist, much to the outrage of the Hudson family sitting in the stands. Katherine Hudson fell to tears, realizing her husband's and son's lives meant nothing but Company profits. Contrarily, defendant's families were elated. It was over for everyone. Five men could live their lives, while the others would be claimed by history as its own.

Part 1, Chapter Twenty-Eight

August 1617 – December 1617

John Rolfe threw himself onto his tobacco business and work upon his return to Virginia, imploring Richard to keep him busy with crops to help him cope with what he called his double loss.

Richard had almost single-handedly exported half of the first special aged tobacco crop in May. Sampling some, Rolfe agreed it had a distinctly different flavor than the regular crop. He laughed, declaring they'd better plan to double the load next season. The remaining half of the special aged crop remained stacked and stored in the warehouse, away from the curing load. The second half was prepared for shipment following Ramplay's demand for shipment. Taking a chance, they shipped it early, guessing Ramplay would want it. The shipment departed on a merchant vessel in the last week of August 1617.

Harvest started, keeping everyone busy from shortly before sun-up until early evening. Rolf departed shortly after noon, sailing upriver to Varina Farms, which lay lonely day after day. He preferred working the fields with his men as opposed to sitting alone in his stately home.

*****

Harvest rolled strongly into November, and Rolfe and Plascomb worked with a renewed vigor to be ready for their usual January shipment of regular tobacco. Special aged product remained curing in the warehouse. In early December, a letter from Ramplay arrived. Rolfe explained Ramplay as being, "friendly, but with one ear always on business." He offered his condolences to Rolfe, blending them with business.

Ramplay explained that Varicrop Farms was one of the fastest growing businesses in the London Market. The company currently held investments approaching £50,000, and profits of £580,000. Both men were stunned. They were the wealthiest men in the New World! If that news wasn't enough to take calmly, the special aged tobacco was a rave, and more must be shipped rapidly.

"I'm glad we sent it already," Richard expressed, and John agreed, saying their decision would save time.

Ramplay wrote that the received shipment of special aged product sold-out in thirty minutes. They yet had work to do. With Christmas approaching in several weeks, the work load increased as curing continued.

*****

The Plascomb Family was sitting to dinner one cold December evening a few days before Christmas, when Christian plainly stated, "we need servants." The attention-grabbing pronouncement by the sixteen-year-old spilled nonchalantly from his mouth without a second thought. Both parents shared silent stares across the table while their son continued eating and expanding his idea.

"If I was in England at this moment, Prince Charles and I would be returning from riding or hunting. Servants would take our horses, caps, and riding crops. We would retire for a hot bath, then play chess before the fire until dinner was announced," he declared, looking from mother to father. "We're rich. We should have servants," he said, shrugging. "It's how the wealthy live, just saying." A second shrug followed. Father decided to prod.

"Who says we're rich, Christian?" he asked, glancing to his wife across the table before looking back to Christian, who seemed to have grown almost five more inches since his return six months earlier, and his voice had dropped even lower. There was also the scant hint of a mustache. When did the little boy suddenly grow so quickly? Youth knows no filters. Thoughts form, shaping words that absolutely tumble from their mouths. Youth holds the keys to the future, while adults only understand the past.

Christian's dining habits had assumed a manner his parents never saw. Holding a fork with his left hand, Christian sliced the mutton with his knife in his right hand. Then, he placed the knife on his plate, changed the fork to his right hand, piercing the meat, and then eating it. Father wanted to inquire about this ritual as well, but he'd wait for the answer to his first question. Youth holds the future keys, but they don't always know how to properly use them.

"It's the talk wherever I go," the self-assuming prince said plainly, dabbing his mouth with a large piece of square-shaped fabric.

"People take no account of me," he continued. "They see me only for whom I am, a field worker. I, in turn, take no account of them except to keep working with my mouth closed and my eyes and ears ever-open to all about me. The men say we're the richest people in the colony, besides Uncle John, of course, and they say we're friends of the king of England himself. I nearly had a row with Eli James when he was impudent enough to challenge me when I told him of riding and hunting with Prince Charles.

"They're jealous, all of them. They disdain the fact that someone has something they don't -and can't- have, whether it be wealthy, good looks, or a friendship with a royal." Mother explored her growing son's mind.

"You seem angered by it, Christian." The teen shook his head.

"No, mother, not angry," he said, softly dabbing his mouth again. "I just don't like the fact we don't live the way we should. The wealthy in England have servants who do what you do. They clean. They wash dishes. They cook and clean the house and tend gardens." He laughed. "We don't even have a garden, unless you count the vegetables and tobacco." Richard sensed a definite haughtiness in his son that he didn't like, deciding to put the situation into some perspective.

"Christian, tobacco put us in this grand home. The vegetables we grow used to feed the people during the worst times in this colony. Now we sell them and use them for payment for work. We are here only as long as the tobacco crop is successful and sells in England. If you want a servant, you must pay for him from your funds when, one day, all this becomes yours. You can fill the house with servants, but they cost money and resources. They can also be an intrusive force in the home if you're not careful. But the way, when did you learn to eat in that foreign manner?" The boy-man shrugged again.

"Prince Charles and the Royals. We always eat in that style.

"Did they explain why?" his mother asked sincerely.

"Of course they did, mother," came the reply hinting at sarcasm not lost on both parents, but parents needed more information. "You see, we eat in leisure, as opposed to the hurried style of the lower classes who must eat and return to work. Therefore, we slice, change hands, pierce, and eat what we wish." Christian smiled glowingly at his mother, as if he had imparted the world's greatest lesson.

"Who is 'we', Christian?" his father asked, looking again to his wife.

"The Royal family always speak as 'we', father, even when Prince Charles and I were fishing, hunting, riding, or swimming. He referred to himself as 'we'.

"Like you've been doing since you returned home," his mother said with some humor. The boy-man nodded affirmatively.

"When any of the royals speak, they refer to themselves as 'we' because, as Prince Charles explained to me, whatever they say, they do so for God and themselves. Hence, 'we'." Privately and separately, both parents decided to speak with the other about increased liberties and responsibilities for their growing, insightful, and worldly son.

*****

As December came to a close, Walter Raleigh decided to divide into two groups to go searching for Spanish gold. To help his son, Walter, mature without being at his father's side, he placed him in the cadre of his good friend, Lawrence Kemys, whom Raleigh knew for several decades, also having traveled to Guyana with Raleigh in 1598. After the scouting parties were set, the teams planned to begin their scouting in early January. Presently, some of the men went in search for wild boar to roast for New Year's dinner.